Praise

'Sales is no longer an art; it is a professio
newcomers who are entering the profession to gain the knowledge
needed to be not only a professional salesperson but a successful one.
Experienced salespeople will refresh their understanding of what
they need to continue their success. The book is the cornerstone for
those who are taking part in the degree apprenticeships programme
for sales. It will ensure everyone in sales has the knowledge, skills and
behaviours to have a successful career in selling. The Association of
Professional Sales has championed the value of having professionally
qualified and professionally developed salespeople, having blazed
the trail for sales apprenticeship in the UK and globally with our
premier sales qualifications. Beth Rogers and Jeremy Noad have
used their expertise to create this book to support sales professionals
undertaking these qualifications and apprenticeships. We know this
book will help all those looking to improve their sales ability.'
— Andrew Hough, CEO, Association of Professional Sales

'Where do you get the knowledge you need to be successful in today's
highly competitive world? You could do it the hard way, as I did, by
reading books and articles, by going to sales conferences and working
with top professionals. Or you could learn it from this book.'
— Professor Neil Rackham, author of global best sellers *SPIN
Selling* and *Rethinking the Salesforce*

'The APS has shown its ongoing commitment to the sales
profession with the creation of this thorough guide for aspiring sales
professionals and those studying apprenticeships and qualifications.
Drawn from best practice and robust research, it meets educational
needs, but is also an excellent read for many sales training and
development activities. Beth Rogers is one of our most gifted and
experienced authors. You will learn a lot from her wisdom.'
— Professor Malcolm McDonald MA (Oxon) MSc PhD
DLitt DSc, Emeritus Professor, Cranfield University

Selling
Professionally

A guide to becoming a world-class sales executive

Dr Beth Rogers FaPS PFHEA
with **Dr Jeremy Noad** FaPS FRSA

R^ethink

First published in Great Britain in 2020 by Rethink Press
(www.rethinkpress.com)

Contents

Introduction

There is a common misconception that selling is an art. It isn't. It is a professional service that helps customers get what they need or want. Becoming a sales professional requires you to understand what to do, how to do it, and how to do it well. This book will equip early career professionals with the knowledge, skills and behaviours needed to succeed in their sales careers.

This book is divided into four parts, laid out in a logical sequence so you can gain the knowledge of what to do and then understand more about the skills required to sell successfully and finally adopt the behaviours to make these skills second nature when working with your organisation and your customers.

This book focuses on supporting early career salespeople, and it can also be used by professionals from other disciplines transferring into sales. Additionally, it can serve as a useful reference tool for an experienced sales professional who needs to refresh their knowledge, skills and behaviour to continually reach their goals. Applying the knowledge gained from the book with your real-life experiences as a professional salesperson will help you improve your own performance and the support you provide to your customers.

Gaining the knowledge required to be a professional salesperson will give you a foundation for successful selling. This knowledge building starts in Part 1, which focuses on knowledge of the organisation where you work, its purpose and the role you play in achieving its goals. Part 2 focuses on the skills required when preparing to sell, and Part 3 describes the actual sales process. Part 4 looks at professional behaviours and values to ensure sustained success.

Good luck with your studies.

Dr Jeremy Noad, FaPS, FRSA, and Dr Beth Rogers, FaPS, PFHEA

PART 1

THE KNOWLEDGE BASE OF A WORLD-CLASS SALES EXECUTIVE

1

Organisational Knowledge

Introduction

Organisation is inherent in the human condition. It took organisation to work together to hunt woolly mammoths and to protect a tribe from sabre-toothed tigers. Over time, fulfilling the needs of customers has led to the development of ever more complex organisations. Before Henry Ford envisaged mass production, cars were built in small, craft-based factories. Bringing equipment and people together to produce something that others want to buy is expensive and requires a great amount of thought. Before the development of banking and a legal framework for companies, it was difficult to fund any large non-governmental project. Now we take it for granted that companies go to shareholders and banks to invest in making profits. We are confident that anyone can start and grow a company if they have a compelling idea to meet a customer need.

Most of us work within organisations and are grateful to do so. The organisation provides a formal infrastructure that makes our lives easier. We have the equipment to do the job, development opportunities to help us do it better, and we get paid regularly. In return, the organisation requires us to be good corporate citizens – to buy into the aims of the organisation and to help to fulfil them. You may hear colleagues say that good knowledge about where power lies in the company, and working with that power, is important in career progression. This is not a matter of cynicism; it is common sense. You need to understand what makes the organisation tick; this is the informal organisational structure. As a salesperson, you also need to understand what makes your customer's organisation tick. Your sales will not come from an individual's decision but from a decision made in an organisational context, with objective-based analyses and several signoffs.

Some organisations do become dysfunctional and seem to spout worthy objectives while operating in a questionable culture. A company called Enron frequently tops lists of corporate scandals. Far from its alleged vision and values published on its website, the company was engaged in defrauding investors, including employees, proving that organisations, like individuals, can go off the rails. Could you be observant enough to spot warning signs in an employer or a customer? If in an employer, you probably need to change your job. If in a customer, you may need to work with finance to change their terms of credit or design an exit plan.

The good news is that most organisations are functional and ethical, full of people who get some meaning from their roles and from helping their customers or service-users to succeed. Understanding how that all comes together is an important foundation for successful selling.

What is a company?

The company as a legal entity

A company has a legal status. Shareholders apply to a government body (such as Companies House) for the right to set up a legal organisation which focuses on pursuing objectives, which are usually commercial (ie involving making profits). A company has legal obligations and legal rights. A company can sue and be sued, like an individual. There are different types of companies – corporations, partnerships, associations and industrial societies – each with different characteristics. In the UK, we usually see 'Plc' (public limited company) or 'Ltd' (private limited company) after company names. Not all organisations that have a sales force are purely commercial. You may work for a not-for-profit organisation such as a government agency or a 'mutual' (owned by members) society such as a building society or co-operative. The terms to identify the different types of companies are often abbreviated. The most common abbreviations are:

- Ltd – a private limited company, often a small or medium-sized company which may be owned by a few individuals such as family members. Shares are not traded on a stock exchange.

- Plc – a public limited company, usually a large organisation with a large number of shares which are traded on a stock exchange. Large shareholders tend to be financial institutions, such as pension companies, who do not have an operational role in running the business.

Different countries have their own abbreviations for the two main types of companies. Table 1.1 shows the most common ones.

Table 1.1: International company type abbreviations

Country	Plc	Ltd
USA	Inc	LLC
France	SA	SARL
Germany	AG	Gmbh
Australia	Ltd	Pty Ltd

Before incorporation became common in the nineteenth century, anyone who wanted to go into business bore personal liability for the failure of their enterprise, and it constrained the opportunity for people with good ideas to bring them to market. Limiting this liability has been considered a good way to encourage enterprise, although there is some potential for its misuse. Once a company has been incorporated, the owners (shareholders) are not personally liable for its debts.

A company has a certain standing in law. It owns things like land and machinery. As we will see when we discuss finance, these company possessions are called tangible or fixed assets. But it is often argued that the true value of a company lies in its intangible assets, which include intellectual property such as copyrights, the skills of employees and the value of relationships with customers. The practice of a company trying to develop its position in the minds of customers is called 'branding'.

The company as a brand

An early meaning of 'branding' is the practice of burning a symbol onto the hides of cattle to indicate who owned them. It was a deterrent to cattle thieves, who could not then sell the cattle as their own. In the modern meaning, brands are still used for differentiation. Companies will develop brand personalities so that customers can distinguish them from competitors. Sometimes, brands are so firmly established in our minds that we use them rather than a general term (eg 'Coke' rather than 'cola drink', 'hoovering' rather than 'vacuuming', 'googling' rather than 'Internet search engine use').

Organisations such as Interbrand, Brand Finance, *Forbes* magazine and the *Financial Times* produce league tables of brands every year. In the 2020s, technology companies dominate them. Apple, Google, Microsoft, Facebook and Amazon are usually in the top ten, with consumer favourites Coca-Cola, Disney and McDonald's also likely to rank highly. Car brands, fashion brands and retailers might make the top twenty. Like all league tables, there is change over time. In the year 2000, Nokia was in most top tens, before it collapsed and became part of

Microsoft. Coca-Cola was number one in most league tables, and some of the technology names who are now dominant were nowhere to be seen.

A brand has visual cues (brand identity) which the customer can use as a shortcut to identify a particular company or its products. Some of these are symbols, such as Apple's apple with a bite out of it, or styles, such as the handwriting which distinguishes Coca-Cola from its rivals. However, marketers must do more than choose a clever design to develop brands into meanings for customers.

Brand development

Attributes

Companies invest in advertising messages to associate their brand with attributes such as 'quality', 'affordability' or 'sustainability'. This is also the case with business brands. IBM has a long history of encouraging customers to associate the brand with reassurance (ie IBM as the 'safe' choice).

Benefits

Customers need to experience benefits from a product or service so that they can trust it in the future. These benefits are not always as tangible as taste tests and price-perception surveys demonstrate. However, if customers feel that brand X tastes better than brand Y, and brand W is better value than brand Z, then the benefit means something to them.

Values

One of the challenges of branding is that when customers come to respect a brand, the risk of damage to the brand reputation increases. Associating values with a brand takes a lot more investment than mere advertising. For example, employees must understand that working for a particular brand means that they must always be friendly, or that their company uniform must always be immaculate. Brand values have to be demonstrated at every touchpoint with the customer. As a salesperson, you are expected to be a brand ambassador, so you have to understand brand values in detail.

Personality

Attributing human characteristics – such as 'exciting', 'sincere' and 'sophisticated' – to brands can help in consumer markets, but one can also apply it in business markets. You have probably seen 'celebrity endorsement' advertising, and this is an easy shortcut allowing consumers to associate the personality of the celebrity with the personality of the company's brand (Keller and Kotler, 2016).

Entrepreneur James Dyson is alleged to have said that the word 'brand' is banned in his company, but a company will have a position in the minds of its customers even if it does not have a budget specifically dedicated to 'brand development' (Beverland, 2009). In Dyson's case, the personality of the owner himself was the subject of media interest as the company was established and grew to take significant market share. Arguably, his personality is the Dyson brand personality. Google searches on 'Dyson' suggest that it is often associated with innovation, which is a brand attribute. As far as marketing commentators are concerned, Dyson has a brand, whether it likes it or not. And just as one person reaches out to another by saying and doing things which indicate their personality and who they are likely to socialise with easily, companies have to find ways of communicating with stakeholders that quickly establish mutually beneficial interconnections.

Who needs a company?

Who has a stake in a company? It is often argued that companies have to be customer-focused to succeed – management guru Peter Drucker made this point in the 1950s

(Drucker, 1955), when he explained that the purpose of a business is to create a customer. However, the media is never short of examples of companies treating customers badly. We also know that shareholders (stockholders in the US) expect a return from investing their money in a company. As a company grows, the number of people who are affected by its success or failure increases. These are people who can be said to have a 'stake' in the company. The word 'stake' is associated with gambling, and people do take the risk of allowing a company some control over their well-being. For example, an employee takes a risk in choosing to work for Company A rather than Company B.

Types of stakeholders

Shareholders

It is said that shareholders are primarily interested in the company's profits because the higher the profits, the higher the dividend they receive. However, not all shareholders take a short-term view of profit. They may prefer to see a company investing profits in future ventures to ensure its long-term sustainability. They may be concerned about the reputation of the company as well. In smaller companies, the shareholders may be family members who see the company as a part of the family identity.

Customers

Companies need customers, and customers need companies to provide them with the products and services that enhance their own businesses or lifestyles. Customers purchasing a company's products and services are the primary driver of cash to sustain the company's operations.

Employees

People who rely on the company for their household incomes are heavily dependent on its success, and of course they are expected to give their all to help the company to succeed and to sustain their employment. Some employees do not feel this sense of affinity for the company, but many companies have generated family-style cultures where employees feel a common purpose with the employer brand.

Suppliers

In business markets, when a customer decides to switch suppliers it can have a devastating effect on the supplier who is dropped. Retained suppliers can grow with a customer or suffer when it loses its market position.

Local communities

Wherever a company chooses to locate itself, it will find that it affects the people who live around it. A town may be shaken when the branch of a popular retailer closes, or residents may be enraged when a local company pollutes the water supply or the air near a school playground.

Legislators

Although generally associated with protecting community interests, politicians and civil servants are also interested in seeing companies succeed, such as eg by bringing jobs to certain areas or increasing exports.

Lenders

Significant company financing comes from loans from banks or investment companies. They want the company to succeed so that they can get interest on the loan and the capital repayment.

A company has many stakeholders to please. Senior decision-makers have to coordinate a wide variety of resources and sources of value creation to make the company successful. These include operations, supply chain, human resource management, finance and marketing.

How companies define their purpose: vision, missions and values

Organisations need to be recognised and understood. This need is both for their external stakeholders, such as customers, shareholders and other organisations, and, internally, to provide a reference as to their purpose and how they wish to operate.

This is usually expressed through three elements: the company's mission, its vision and its values. Larger companies typically document these things on their website. Publicly traded companies include them in their annual reports. A company's mission, vision and values are different from their brand slogan. However, this can also act as a key summary – usually a few words that encapsulate an organisation's purpose. 'Let's do it' may convey many things, but for Nike, it links to the company's sports equipment and sportswear market, sending messages of action, effort and achievement.

Can an entity that is not a sentient being, like a company, have a vision and hold values? Of course. A company only exists because people run it, so vision and values are often a way for the most powerful stakeholders to create a blueprint for how the company should feel. This is like leaders creating a culture for a club or association that people might want to join or support. The idea of a company having a vision and values can be controversial, especially to shareholders who likely feel that the primary purpose of a company is to make profits. However, it is now widely recognised that profitability is interwoven with other factors, which make the company sustainable in the long term. These days, many companies use the triple bottom line (TBL) reporting technique in their annual reports. 'Triple' refers to the impacts on people, profit and planet.

Vision

A company's vision outlines where the company will be and what it will be doing in the imagined future. Its purpose is to guide the company's mission and the strategies it implements so that it has a sense of direction and purpose.

A clear vision helps an organisation prioritise its activities and decisions in their journey to becoming a better company. When JF Kennedy said he wanted to put a man on the Moon within the decade (Kennedy, 1962), he was setting out a vision for the United States; as was the renowned civil rights leader Martin Luther King Jr when he described his vision for equality in his famous 'I have a dream' speech (King, 1963). An organisational vision does not have to be as potent as these examples, but there are examples of visions which appear to have had a genuinely motivating effect on companies. In the 1980s Bill Gates, Microsoft's founder, set out a vision to put a computer on every desk and in every home. Microsoft could reasonably claim to have been a vital driver of this social revolution, which was realised during the early twenty-first century. So what happens once a company has achieved its mission? Maybe the mission needs to broaden, as Microsoft's did, to accommodate more product and service possibilities: 'Our mission is to empower every person and every organization on the planet to achieve more' (Microsoft, 2018).

Microsoft's new vision is broad, and it is not even specific to the technology. Time will tell whether it is too broad, or if it enables them to diversify successfully into new sectors. Visions need to be re-evaluated every few years to ensure continued success and growth.

The company's vision needs to resonate with all stakeholders, providing a sense of optimism and purpose. Working for a company that has no vision, or even a questionable vision, is unlikely to lead to a career that is sustainable in the long term.

A vision without action or mission is just a wish that is unlikely to come true. A company's vision will often include multiple elements:

- People – how the company inspires and supports their employees

- Products – what the company offers to the world

- Community – how the company engages with its community, whether local or global

- Benefits – how the company contributes (generally by making a profit but also non-financial activities such as environmental or social actions)

Mission

Where the vision sets out the 'why' of the organisation and where it wants to go over the next few years, the mission is how the organisation will get to its desired destination. Mission statements have suffered from bad press in the past, predominantly because they are often full of corporate jargon and are not explicit. Successful companies need to make their mission comprehensible to all – their employees, their customers, their stakeholders. This transparency and clarity create the environment where the company's annual plan, quarterly goals, weekly objectives and daily tasks can have meaning and build a sense of value for the work that it does.

A mission describes what, where and how an organisation will conduct business. To understand more, this example from fictional popular culture can be explored to show how a mission statement can be used: 'Space: the final frontier. These are the voyages of the Starship Enterprise. Its continuing mission: to explore strange new worlds, to seek out new life and new civilizations, to boldly go where no one has gone before' (Abrams, 2009). If we break down this mission statement, then we can identify where the activity is taking place (space), who is doing it (the crew of the Starship Enterprise), what they are doing (exploring new worlds/seeking new life and civilizations), and how they will do it (boldly).

A mission statement does not cover all the strategies, tactics and activities that an employee or organisation will use. It does provide the overall direction and intent. While it may not always be clear where your precise contribution as an employee fits in, it is always good to be familiar with your company's mission. This acts as a self-check to help you decide if you are working on the right thing at the right time.

The Coca-Cola company identifies its mission as: 'To refresh the world... To inspire moments of optimism and happiness... To create value and make a difference' (Coca-Cola, n.d.). Coca-Cola is a vigorous competitor in a product category (sweet, fizzy drinks) that nutritionists may perceive as harmful. Some readers of the Coca-Cola website might be sceptical about the altruism expressed in this mission. However, a lot of people like Coke and associate it with fun. We must also remember that mission statements are future-oriented. The company uses its distribution network to help charities deliver medicines to remote villages in Africa. It supports 'get active' campaigns in the UK. It has diversified into smoothies and juices through its dominant stake in the Innocent brand. As the soda category contracts, Coca Cola's mission will help it to diversify into new categories and possibly new roles.

Values

The values of an organisation are there to guide its employees and processes to work ethically. Company values serve as a beacon to attract the right individuals to join the team. They outline the desired behaviours for the whole organisation. To make progress in the corporate world, not only do you have to achieve your targets and goals, you must display and be an ambassador for the company's values. If the company's values do not resonate with your own, you will experience a disconnect that may impede your career progress within the company. It is always important to be clear about the values of a prospective employer to ensure that the company is the right employer for you.

Many organisations have similar values, especially in mature westernised economies. When you think of the role of the sales professional, then many of these will be familiar:

- **Leadership**. In your role, you may not have to manage or lead a team but you will always have to lead yourself.

- **Collaboration** is also a universal value. You will always achieve more as part of the team, even if, as a salesperson, you have individual responsibilities and objectives. You cannot be successful without working with your team and as a crucial part of the broader organisation.

- **Integrity** is critical. Your work will often be unsupervised. As a salesperson, you are a trusted adviser to your customers and therefore any lack of integrity impacts on you, your organisation and your customers. A simple explanation of integrity is doing the right thing even if no one is watching.

- **Accountability** comes in many forms. It is linked to integrity and the work you do. You have a clear responsibility to work ethically and with integrity but also to be accountable for the sales you achieve and the customers you serve.

Many corporate organisations have further values. These are sometimes detailed and reaffirm what the company looks for in their people; these can include values around focus, curiosity, efficiency, and a desire to continually learn and develop.

These three elements of vision, mission and values help orientate the organisation to do what it needs to do, and they help employees understand the value of their work. They also signal to potential employees what the organisation would be like to work for and, of greater importance, communicates to customers, external stakeholders and other interested parties how the organisation contributes to the well-being and success of the community, whether local or global.

Company resources and capabilities

We have discussed what a company is and how it creates meaning around itself, but it has to deliver competitive products and services in order to win business and sustain itself for the benefit of its stakeholders. The resource-based view (RBV), developed by Danish economist Birger Wernerfelt in 1984, states that a company has to acquire, develop and manage unique combinations of resources and capabilities to achieve a sustainable competitive advantage.

Table 1.2 gives definitions for the different types of resources and capabilities identified by Wernerfelt (1984).

Table 1.2: Definitions of resources and capabilities

Resource/capability	Description
Tangible resources	These are assets that have a physical form – things you can see and touch, including machinery, buildings, stocks of products or raw materials.
Intangible resources	Assets you cannot see or touch; they have no physical form. These include trademarks, methodologies, company reputation and company culture.
Operational capabilities	Combinations of the company's skills, processes and technologies, which determine how the company does what it does to serve its customers.
Dynamic capabilities	The ability to change, switching operational capabilities to adapt to different market conditions. A company could have excellent operational capabilities, but if they cannot adjust as the market changes, they will fail.

Every company will have a different mix of resources and capabilities – and therefore different strengths and weaknesses – compared to competitors. These are usually documented and analysed before companies move on to set objectives in their business plans.

Company objectives and strategies

Objectives are **what** companies aim to achieve. They are future goals, but they may be informed by the company's past. What is the company's history of achieving objectives? How did it get to its current position in its sector? In light of that, how can it move forward? The trends in the sector are also relevant to objective setting. Has the company been behind the trends or ahead of them? If a company grows at 5% when the sector is growing at 10%, that is not a good story to tell shareholders.

Objectives should be measurable. They should also be specific rather than general and have a deadline. 'To achieve an increase in our share of the convenience retail market from 10% to 15% within three years' is a meaningful objective. You know the starting point and endpoint, and the time factor. Expressions such as 'maximise', 'minimise' and 'improve' are not specific enough. If the future is like a road map, quantifiable objectives show the company's destination. From here to there has to be mapped, with 'milestones', so the company knows it is going in the right direction.

Once the company's destination has been determined, the next question is **how** to get there. Strategies are 'how' statements. Tactics are also 'how' statements, but there is an important distinction. We can use a military analogy borrowed from Prussian General Carl von Clausewitz, who explained that strategy governs the conduct of the war and tactics are used to win each battle (Bungay, 2010). Many business plans are short-term and tactical. Strategies should be relatively high-level but clear about what activities they involve.

Business strategies

At the highest level, many companies refer to the three categories of strategy that Harvard strategist and management guru Michael Porter identified (Porter, 1984). These were:

Cost leadership

Achieving profitability through being the best in an industry sector at low-cost production and operations. There can only be one cost leader in a sector, and it is usually going to be a big player that has the scope of operations to be ultra-efficient and have access to the biggest discounts from suppliers. Cost leadership is not the same thing as price leadership, but cost leaders are usually the only players in a sector who can afford to be price leaders.

Differentiation

Differentiation is popular because it has more variation, and the differentiation chosen can be communicated to customers in brand positioning. A company can be differentiated by offering customers the highest quality, the best in innovation, the friendliest service, etc. An underlying assumption is that if a company is differentiated, it is appealing to a particular segment of customers who like their brand positioning and are prepared to pay a premium for it.

Focus/niche

A niche can be geographic (such as Japanese fast food), lifestyle-based (such as retro clothing) or technology-based. In consumer societies hungry for choice, there are multiple niches, and it is ideal for small companies to find a growing niche and serve it. But the concept of a niche market can also be limiting. Companies that outgrow one niche might decide to expand into complementary niches.

Most companies in developed economies identify themselves as differentiated in some way, even if that differentiation is 'best value', which implies a good balance of price and quality. So, what is the next level of business strategy? Many companies need to demonstrate growth to shareholders. In the Ansoff matrix, which was first published in the *Harvard Business Review* in 1957, Igor Ansoff identified four categories of strategic activity associated with growth (Ansoff, 1957). These can be described thus:

Market penetration – selling current products to current customers. Most companies would devote considerable resources to this strategy. In sales, we would recognise the terms 'upselling' and 'cross-selling' – selling more to current customers – as a relatively low-risk activity with good prospects of success.

Product development – developing new products for current customers. Not all companies want to be innovators, but even 'fast followers' have to keep up with trends in their sectors and make customers feel that they have a choice of new products and services. However, it can take time to build this strategy.

> 'Never assume that [customers] will automatically embrace your new ideas. We have seen many key account plans which have assumed that as soon as new technology rolls into production, customers will adopt it. They do not. New products can cause disruption and change, which are not welcome. For example, new packaging formats will not be adopted if they do not fit in with massive sunk investments in warehouse design and supermarket shelving.' (McDonald and Rogers, 2017)

Market extension – selling current products to new customers. New markets can be geographical or new customer segments. Companies need considerable marketing and sales investment to enter new markets where the customers may be happy with the suppliers they have got.

Diversification – selling new products to new customers. This is widely regarded as the most high-risk growth strategy, but it does happen. Companies often diversify via the acquisition of companies in the product-market category they want to enter. Even this can erode shareholder value if there is a lack of synergy in the relationship between the acquiring and acquired companies.

Not all companies are interested in growth. For those focused on cost leadership and profitability, *productivity* may be an overriding strategy leading to a focus on tactical efficiency, process by process.

As you read company reports, you will spot the strategies described above, but there are other ways that companies describe their corporate strategies. These are high-level strategies, and you will need to understand your employer's business strategies. In particular, you will be interested in how the high-level business plan affects marketing and sales plans.

How marketing and sales plans fit into business plans

There are many levels to a business plan. At the highest level there is the corporate plan, which states how the company intends to execute its mission and provides goals and strategic direction. Each functional team will use the overall plan to develop their own goals and strategies that will contribute to the achievement of the corporate plan. These plans become more specific as each sub-team creates their plan. Figure 1.1 shows the sub-plans of the marketing and sales plan.

Corporate plan								
Marketing plan								Other functional plans
Key account management overview			Major accounts plan	Plan for mid-tier		Consolidated segment plan		
Key account 1	Key account 2	Key account 3		Mid-tier sector 1	Mid-tier sector 2	Small customers segment 1	Small customers segment 2	
				Sales plan per territory	Sales plan per territory	Sales plan per territory	Sales plan per territory	

Figure 1.1: Marketing and sales plans (adapted from McDonald and Rogers, 1998)

The corporate plans have to drive all other plans, per function (such as operations, R&D and, of course, sales), per business area (if the company is involved in more than one product segment) and per geographical area. Strategists debate to what degree corporate plans should be bottom-up or top-down. Information about customers and from customers should inform a corporate plan, and salespeople are often asked to make that happen. Equally, experts in Human Resource Management and Finance would want to make sure that the latest best practice in their fields informs the corporate plan.

However, bottom-up plans have a reputation for being over-cautious. Most senior managers are willing to listen when drawing up the plan, but they also have to listen to experts such as investment analysts. They will also want to make sure that targets are realistic enough to be motivating. So, there tends to be several rounds of discussions about the plan. If a company works in volatile markets, it will also need contingency plans. This is because not all strategy can be planned; sometimes, strategies must respond to external shocks, and these are called emergent strategies.

The plan that usually sits between the sales plan and the corporate plan is the marketing plan. Marketing plans are not just about advertising and short-term campaigns. They should include rigorous analysis, such as identifying how company capabilities match customers' needs. From that, they can map out how to deliver and communicate value.

The marketing plan determines marketing objectives and tactics at the levels of product/service activity, promotional campaigns, channels to market and pricing. These are often called the Four Ps.

The Four Ps

1. **Product**: product launches, product withdrawals, which products in which market segments

2. **Price:** price positioning consistent with branding, policies on discounts and other types of price promotion

3. **Promotion:** brand development; which messages through which media, including advertising, public relations and digital marketing

4. **Place:** retail locations, or choice of channel partners such as distributors and resellers

There is often rivalry between marketing and sales. Indeed, marketers often claim ownership of all customer-facing strategy and dismiss sales as an operational function, although this is less likely in business-to-business (B2B) sectors, where some powerful customers can expect their sales contacts to have strategic input. Marketing and sales should work together in strategic planning. Successful sales planning relies on robust marketing plans, and successful marketing plans rely on robust sales plans and account plans (development plans for large or important individual customers). Of course, marketing and sales should also co-operate in tactics and operations. For example, an advertising campaign can underpin a telesales campaign, and marketing information online should be designed to drive incoming sales enquiries.

Senior marketing and sales managers will discuss which revenue objectives are to come from which product/market segments and major accounts. For each product/market segment, they will derive individual sales targets, possibly by geographical territory. Sales managers will consult data in the customer relationship management system, which shows sales trends, sales activity and the progress of sales leads. There may be a gap between a sales forecast based on the statistics in the system and a forecast based on the analysis feeding into a future-focused marketing plan. Ultimately, judgements must be made about what high-level figures to provide to shareholders. Stock markets do not like poor forecasting; neither do colleagues in operations, who use the sales forecast to determine how many products to make, or accountants, who use it to negotiate cashflow with banks and other lenders.

Ultimately, marketing and sales share responsibility for revenue generation, and they have a big role to play in customer satisfaction. You should feel confident as a sales professional that your target is based on sound market analysis. Equally, marketers rely on sales professionals to understand the 'bigger picture', reinforce marketing messages and be good brand ambassadors. In addition to your sales target, you may have objectives for customer satisfaction and accuracy in your reporting (as it feeds into the sales forecast).

Summary

In this chapter, we have looked at what a company is and how it plans to sustain itself. The sales function plays a critical role in the company's prosperity; without making sales, all other functions will soon stop. A large amount of information and insight goes into generating plans for the company, which are divided up into targets for individual salespeople. You carry a lot of responsibility for achieving the plans' objectives, and, of course, nobody wants to miss their targets.

2

Product, Service And Sector Knowledge

Introduction

This chapter is about how business sectors operate and how products and services meet needs in the various sectors. In a textbook, we can only talk about sectors and products in general and give examples. You will have to go to separate books, articles and Internet sources to research your own sector and products. You will also have to research the sector and industry in which your customer operates. This may sound like a lot to ask, but customers value sector/industry and product knowledge highly, so every effort you make will pay off. Before we get to the dynamics of sectors, you need to be aware of the business environment's effects on your company's and your customer's current situations and how they are going to have to change. Figure 2.1 shows the company surrounded by its sector and the sector surrounded by the business environment. Companies are like planets orbiting within solar systems which are orbiting within galaxies – they are dependent on these systems for survival, and if they cannot adapt they may go out of business.

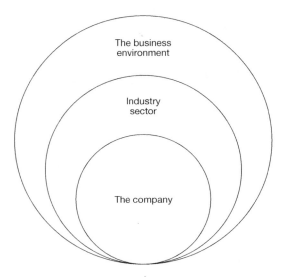

Figure 2.1: The company in the business environment (adapted from McDonald and Rogers, 2017)

The following are some useful definitions related to business sectors:

- **Business environment** – The business environment consists of the external factors that influence the way a company can operate, now and in the future.

- **Sector** – Economic activity is broken down into a number of sectors. A sector is an area of economic activity, for example, agriculture, automotive, manufacturing, financial services. These are typically broad in scope and include a large number of companies.

- **Industry** – An industry is a more specific grouping of companies within a sector. Agriculture, for example, could be broken down into meat production, cereal production, forestry, etc. Most countries have classification systems for sectors and industries.

- **Product** – A product is an article or substance that is manufactured or processed for sale.

- **Service** – A service is an act of doing work that helps someone who does not have the time or capability to do the act themselves. Services range from small tasks, such as maintenance/repairs and fast-food services, to the provision of major utilities, such as electricity.

The factors that drive change in sectors and markets

The opportunities and threats that drive business change come from the business environment, which drives changes in sectors and industries, which in turn drives change in individual businesses. Opportunities and threats cannot be managed, but they must be monitored and drive strategic thinking in the organisation.

Exploring the opportunities and threats facing a business usually starts with the business environment. It includes the following categories of factors, each of which may have several sub-factors.

Politics – This encompasses legislation already passed, a government policy which may result in future legislation, and the potential for a change of government or even political system change. Non-governmental political movements should also be considered. The 2016 Brexit campaign, largely driven by a party without MPs, was extremely successful but has caused great uncertainty for a lot of businesses.

Economics – The state of the world's financial systems greatly affects the health of businesses. Some suffer more than others. In shipbuilding, for example, there were over 6,000 ships built in 2007, but after the global crash in 2008 completions in 2009 were minimal (Grant and Rogers, 2010).

Social – This incorporates easily measured population changes (such as the ageing of the 'baby boomers' who were born between 1947 and 1961) and the subtler trends in consumers' lifestyle choices and attitudes.

Technology – New technology can wipe out whole industry sectors. It normally happens quite slowly. Consider, for example, the devastating effect of the growth of car ownership on companies who made harnesses for horses. If you are on the wrong side of technology, consider diversification, as the risks of diversification are overshadowed by the risk of extinction.

This collection of factors has an acronym: PEST. You may also see it called STEP. PESTLE and STEEPLE, in which 'environment' and 'legislation' are listed separately from 'politics', also feature in some textbooks. For sectors influenced by the weather, such as agriculture and fashion retail, the separation of 'environment' may be justified; in sectors which are heavily regulated, such as utilities, the separation of 'legislation' may be relevant. Bear in mind that these factors interact. Social change may lead to changes in government policy; technology may drive social change; government policy affects the economy, etc.

Of course, you could list many factors in the business environment, but the search is for ones which are relevant to your business (or the customer's business, if you are researching them). We should not constrain our thinking too much in the early stages of the plan; otherwise, we may miss some interesting factors. Be creative, to begin with, and then subject the possibilities you have listed to a reality check (see Table 2.1).

It is not always clear whether a PEST factor is a threat or an opportunity. For many businesses, all change is threatening, and all change requires actions which may have knock-on effects. Is it a matter of attitude? The ageing of baby boomers may be a great opportunity if you can plan to deliver products and services that they will like, but it's a great threat if you are a government agency trying to find funds to care for them.

Table 2.1: Business environment reality check for a food retailer

Factors	Relevance to food consumption	Relevance to this company	Level of impact in the next three years	Opportunity or threat?
Political				
Measures to address supply chain fraud in the food industry	Consumer confidence in packaged food, eg lamb really is lamb	Need control and visibility of the supply chain	High	Threat
Change in approach to planning law to protect town centres and local markets	Facilitates direct access to local food providers	More competition for top-up shops	Medium	Threat
Economic				
Possible change from food deflation to inflation	Food prices rise, requiring a change in spending habits	May need to change assortment and price promotions	High	Opportunity
Social				
Higher proportion of single elderly people in the population	Growing segment needing easy packaging and small pack size	Work with suppliers for new ranges	High	Opportunity
Increase in special dietary requirements	Growing micro-segments for gluten-free, lactose-free, vegan, etc.	Work with suppliers for new ranges	Medium	Opportunity
Technological				
Sensors for stock control – in logistics, warehouse and on shelves	Technology-savvy customers expect special offers at the food shelf	Technology arms-race with competitors to maximise supply chain efficiency and customer responsiveness	High	Opportunity
Increased use of technology anytime, anywhere	Customers are able to shop for anything from home or mobile device	Technology arms-race plus the need for time-specific 'click and collect' and home delivery	High	Threat

Sector and industry forces

The Harvard strategist Michael Porter designed a technique for assessing competitive pressures (and therefore the potential profitability) in industries. As shown in Figure 2.2, it is called the Five Forces (Porter, 1979).

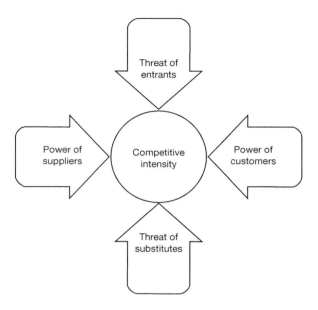

Figure 2.2: Porter's Five Forces (adapted from Porter, 1979)

Power of suppliers

This is the degree to which companies supplying the industry can affect its profitability. For example, in the case of car retail, the actions of car manufacturers can influence the profitability of the whole industry. Depending on where you sit in a supply chain, you may need to look further than immediate suppliers. For example, if you are in retail, your immediate suppliers may be wholesalers, who are supplied by manufacturers, who are supplied by people who grow or mine raw materials.

Some supply chains can be very complex. Even a simplified view of the journey of a humble green bean from the ground to the plate (see Figure 2.3) has many branches. If you are working for a wholesaler, additional considerations include:

- Who supplies the farmer? Can they upset the supply chain?

- What happens if the manufacturer has beans but there is a shortage of tins to put them in?
- If there is a bad harvest, which players in the supply chain will be prioritised?

Note that supply chains are also called 'value chains', as value is added to the product as it gets closer to the consumer. They are also called 'demand chains', under the assumption that the end-consumer drives demand from their own needs (eg hunger for beans) through the chain to raw material extraction. Another expression you might come across is 'market map'. A market map is likely to show much more detail about sales channels and what percentage of output from each industry in the map goes to different industry types at the next level.

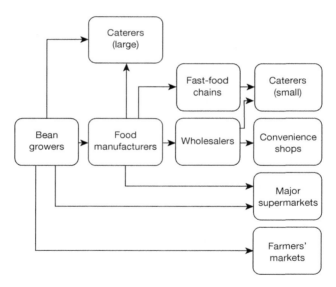

Figure 2.3: Supply chain of green beans

Power of customers

Most industries have powerful customers, but some are more powerful than others. For cars, the powerful brands in the industry are often the ones telling the manufacturers of gearboxes, clutches and car radio aerials what they have to do to retain their custom.

Threat of entrants

Even when industries have matured and appear to have no discernible room for more competition, new players emerge. Grocery retail in the UK has always been highly competitive, but new entrants Aldi and Lidl have been able to make an impact with their combination of everyday low prices and non-food offers.

Threat of substitutes

Typically, a substitute is an obvious like-for-like product in a category; in hot drinks, for example, do I have a cup of tea or a cup of coffee? Be careful and think deeply when you list your threat factors: what would your customers do if there were a shortage of your product? Even without a shortage, could they do without it? *'Do nothing' is a viable substitute* in industries like information technology (IT). Even in food retail, wage erosion is persuading consumers to buy less.

Competitive intensity

How many players are there in an industry and how ferociously do they compete? The strategic positioning of companies within an industry can sometimes mean that the dynamics of competition are stable. If there is a price leader, an innovation leader, a quality-of-service leader, an online-only and a collection of niche players focused on particular customer segments, there may be comfortable profits for everyone. However, that is an unlikely scenario in the twenty-first century. Many products and services are commoditised, and the profitability of all players is squeezed as each tries to grab extra market share.

Five Forces analysis

Table 2.2 shows a worked example of a Five Forces analysis:

Table 2.2: Five Forces analysis of the competitive environment in food retail

Factors	Relevance to this company?	Level of impact in the next three years	Opportunity or threat?
Suppliers			
Decline in preference for food brands	Suppliers competing for business	Medium	Opportunity
Could be the source of provenance/ hygiene scandal	Supplier selection	High	Threat
Entrants			
Discounters	Price deflation	High	Threat
Farmers' markets	Limited	Low	Opportunity
Substitutes			
Online models	Pressure to provide more online choice and delivery	High	Threat
Customers			
Increasing availability of information and power to choose	Pressure to provide more choice, flexibility and price competition	High	Threat
Intensity of competition			
Major players desperate for market share	Need to differentiate	High	Opportunity

Competitor analysis

From a sales point of view, you want to know a great deal more about your competitors than just their general positioning in the industry. You can learn a lot from industry analysts' reports and what the financial press thinks of them. What is most important is that you learn how the customers see the industry and the players in it. Companies such as Mintel and Keynote Research can provide in-depth market research reports on particular industries.

Make sure that you have accurate, recent, relevant and detailed information about competitors. Be sure that you understand the factors on which customers say that they base their buying decisions, how they are weighted and how customers rate the major players (including your own employer) against each factor.

In Table 2.3, the 'success factor' column shows the typical buying factors. Most of us, when we make any buying decision, consider price, perceived quality, availability (can I have it today?) and novelty, among other factors. The 'weight' column attempts to capture the trade-off between factors. In this example, the service level is more important than price, which is more important than innovation. Of course, each customer has a different trade-off pattern. In the case of a key account, you might be able to find out exactly how they weight buying factors. If you have a whole segment to consider, you might be able to estimate attitudes to price and quality using market reports.

The 'weight' and 'niche' columns represent the performance of four players in the industry. Each factor for each player is assigned scores out of ten and weighted scores out of 100, the latter of which are totalled to scores out of 1,000. These players' scores are similar at the total level, but we can see a major difference per buying factor.

Table 2.3: Success factor analysis for four competitors

Success factor	Weight	Major A		Major B		Niche X		Niche Y	
Low price	20%	3	60	5	100	5	100	8	160
Product quality	20%	8	160	7	140	9	180	6	120
Product range	10%	9	90	5	50	4	40	6	60
Service levels	30%	9	270	7	210	9	270	6	180
Stock availability	10%	9	90	8	80	7	70	5	50
Innovation	10%	4	40	7	70	9	90	2	20
Total	100%		710		650		750		590

Table 2.3 shows that Niche Y has the lowest price, Niche X has the highest product quality, Major A leads on the product range, and so on. Armed with such detailed competitor analysis, you can have a meaningful conversation with customers about their choices. They will not be impressed if you simply criticise the competition and suggest that they must be mad to consider buying from them. We will discuss conversations with the customer in more detail later in this book, but for now think about the following 'objection' from a prospective customer:

> PROSPECT: Why should I pay your prices when Niche Y is so much cheaper?
>
> SALESPERSON FOR MAJOR A: Yes, Niche Y offer low prices, and I can understand why you would want to consider them. They do have to reduce their quality, range, service and availability to do that. That means that you might not be able to get what you want when you want it, and if something went wrong you would not have the level of service back-up that you want. We focus on better quality and service to make sure that our customers have peace of mind when they buy from us. I can let you have some comparisons from Bloggs Market Research, or would you like to see some customer references for our after-sales service?

Of course, the prospect might still object to the large price difference, but at least you have moved the conversation on to other buying factors.

Understanding the customer's sector

You need to study the business environment and Five Forces of your own sector to understand the opportunities and threats facing your own organisation and how you compare to competitors in the same space. Everything we have just discussed regarding understanding the business environment and the Five Forces is relevant to customer analysis as well. A detailed understanding of your customers' opportunities and threats will enable you to make sales proposals that can help them to succeed.

We will explore customer analysis in more detail in a later chapter. For now, consider the examples in Table 2.4. In this scenario, you work for an IT solutions provider, and your customer is a car insurance specialist.

Table 2.4: From business environment change to sales opportunity (B2B)

Factors	Relevance to insurance	Relevance to this customer	Level of impact in the next three years	Opportunity (OPP) or threat?	Relevance to IT supplier
Political					
Tax breaks to encourage electric/ hybrid cars	Assessing insurance risk for electric vehicles	Consumers expect a specialist to offer cover for electric cars and expect premiums to be lower than for petrol	Med	OPP – get ahead of the trend	Ensure forms cover electric and hybrid as well as petrol and diesel; ensure connectivity to specialist underwriters
Economic					
Car insurance premiums rising above inflation due to the cost of fraud	Need for fraud prevention measures	Need for fraud prevention and detection technology	Med	Threat	Customer behaviour analytics to pick up unusual activity
Social					
Higher proportion of elderly people in the population	Elderly drivers can be high risk	Need to discern between careful elderly drivers and medically impaired ones	High	Threat – could turn into OPP	Optional technology in cars, as with younger drivers?
Technological					
Longer-term – driverless vehicles	Insuring technology rather than a driver	May need to diversify into new categories of insurance	Low	Threat	High-level planning with stakeholders to work out implications

Cont.

Table 2.4 *cont.*

Factors	Relevance to insurance	Relevance to this customer	Level of impact in the next three years	Opportunity (OPP) or threat?	Relevance to IT supplier
Power of suppliers					
Underwriters slow to respond to new technologies	Customers trade down, or price competition	Need to work with relevant experts	Low	Threat – but OPP to compete	N/A
Power of customers					
Shopping around for quotes	Discounts offered to new customers	Preference to retain customers, but must compete on price	High	Threat	Develop formulae for visibility of profitability per customer
Threat of entrants					
New types of insurance broker online	Need for marketing effectiveness online	Need to promote track record and specialist skills	Low	Threat	Make sure the website is easy to use and useful; search engine optimisation, etc.
Threat of substitutes					
Switch from owning to sharing or hiring cars	Possible new models for insurance when hiring cars	Too small to break the mould?	Med	Threat	Search for new IT models to support personal portable insurances
Competitive intensity					
Stagnant market; lots of players	Erosion of profitability	A niche player, but may need to become multi-niche	Med	Threat	Ensure IT platforms can enable rapid change

The principles of following business environment and industry trends can also be applied in business-to-consumer (B2C) markets, as in Table 2.5. In this scenario, you work for a car insurance specialist, and your market segment is recently retired persons (aged 58–68) on a private pension.

Table 2.5: From business environment change to sales opportunity (B2C)

Factors	Relevance to this product category (car insurance)	Relevance to this segment	Level of impact in the next three years	Opportunity (OPP) or threat?	Relevance to car insurance offer?
Political					
Tax breaks to encourage electric/hybrid cars	Assessing insurance risk for electric vehicles	Cheaper fuel costs are attractive; this segment expects a specialist to offer cover for electric cars and expects premiums to be lower than for petrol	Med	OPP – get ahead of the trend	Promote special offers for electric and hybrid cars; possible sponsorship links to environmental causes?
Economic					
Car insurance premiums rising above inflation due to the cost of fraud	Need for fraud prevention measures	This segment less likely to be involved in fraud	Med	Threat	Customer may ask to be reassured that this company prosecutes fraudsters
Social					
Higher proportion of elderly people in the population	Elderly drivers can be high risk	This segment is likely to see themselves as careful and still medically fit	High	OPP	Offer customers optional technology in cars, as with younger drivers?
Technological					
Longer-term – driverless vehicles	Insuring technology rather than a driver	Not likely to be interested	Low	Threat	N/A
Power of suppliers					
Underwriters slow to respond to new technologies	Customers trade down, or price competition	Usually loyal but will switch if provoked by high premiums	Low	Threat – but OPP to compete	Need to make sure choices are available at renewal/change of car
Power of customers					
Shopping around for quotes	Discounts offered to new customers	Usually loyal but will switch if provoked by high premiums	High	Threat	Need to make sure choices are available at renewal/change of car

Cont.

Table 2.5 *cont.*

Factors	Relevance to this product category (car insurance)	Relevance to this segment	Level of impact in the next three years	Opportunity (OPP) or threat?	Relevance to car insurance offer?
Threat of entrants					
New types of insurance broker online	Need for marketing effectiveness online	Expect good online presence, but more likely to use the phone	Low	Threat	Make sure the website and call centre are easy to use
Threat of substitutes					
Switch from owning to sharing or hiring cars	Possible new models for insurance when hiring cars	May trade down to smaller cars but will not give up car ownership just yet	Med	N/A	Need to make sure choices are available at renewal/ change of car
Competitive intensity					
Stagnant market; lots of players	Erosion of profitability	This segment may shop around but will appreciate personal service	Med	OPP	Be responsive; emphasise good ratings on claims handling, etc.

Whether your customer is a business decision-maker or a consumer making a high-ticket purchase, they will be impressed if you understand the external pressures on them and talk about how your product/service can solve problems for them. Their next question will be how well you know your product/service. They are bound to ask: 'Can your product do X for me? Does Y come as standard or do I have to pay extra? Does the service cover Z?' Never bluff when answering such questions; you will be found out, creating a problem for the customer, your employer and your career. Equally, there is a limit to the number of times you can say 'I'll have to check that' before you lose credibility. You will have to learn about your employer's products directly from the product managers and handbooks. The next section provides some general knowledge about products which can help you to explore them in more depth.

Understanding products and services

What makes up a 'product'?

There are many competing views on the constituent parts of a product. For your initial learning, this chapter explores the ideas of core product, service and experience. Sometimes these elements are cumulative; for example, a restaurant meal consists of food, service and the experience of eating out. The 'three levels of product' concept was originally developed by Philip Kotler (Kotler, 2019). In other cases, these concepts stand alone. A calculator could be bought without any expectation of service or experience, electricity supply is a commoditised service, and consumers largely judge the value of a football match based on their experience of the game.

The core of a product is what enables the main benefit that the customer wants. To judge how good a core product should be, consider the principles of David Garvin (1984):

Conformance – is the ability of a product to meet its design specifications, which are based on delivering what the customer needs. A product must do what it claims to do (eg a drill must make holes in things). In some sectors, there are clear industry standards for performance which products must meet. An example of this would be the BSI Kitemark, which was introduced in 1903. Originally called the British Standard Mark, it is used to show consumers that the product meets quality standards.

Aesthetics – A product should look and feel attractive to use, and a design can be protected from copying by competitors for longer than an invention. Aesthetics are important even for industrial products. As Yamamoto and Lambert (1994) suggest, 'Attention paid to product aesthetics may have a payoff in terms of sales performance.'

Reliability – A product should do what is asked of it every time for a reasonable period of time.

Serviceability – A product should be easy to maintain and repair. Simplicity and standardisation in design can ensure that the customer has minimal hassle when a product needs a new part.

Durability – Products should have reasonable lifespans. Ironically, it is widely acknowledged that because consumers demand cheaper appliances, build quality is affected, which can result in products having a short lifespan (Cooper, 2004). It can be argued that a cheap washing machine will not last as long as a more expensive high-quality one, but customers no longer seem to expect things to be as durable.

UK law is vague about the amount of use a buyer should get out of a product, but it seems that most consumers have a timeline of five to six years in their head when they buy a major household appliance (it should last as long as any extended guarantee they might be able to buy).

Performance – Does your product exceed expectations? Has it won any awards from industry associations or consumer associations? Being a 'best buy' rather than a 'don't buy' in consumer reviews clearly affects sales. In industrial markets, awards are also seen as reducing risks for the buyer, as the following quote from the Good Housekeeping Institute website shows (GHI, 2018): 'All products listed on this page have met the standards set out by the experts at the Good Housekeeping Institute. Whether products have been GHI Approved or GH Reader Recommended, you can trust the products will perform.'

Features – All products have features. Some could make a virtue out of having fewer (those products are simple, with less to go wrong), and others might make a virtue out of having more, which gives the buyer more choices.

Perceived quality – Although some might classify perceived quality as an intangible aspect of a product, the effect of branding can reach deep into the product core. Does the customer automatically associate this product with quality because the company has a longstanding reputation for producing good products?

Services

A core product is something that you can touch and test and store for re-use. Services are quite different. You may have some physical evidence of service level, such as the whiteness of the tablecloth in a restaurant, but spending money on a service involves a lot more risk for a buyer. This is particularly true of decision-makers buying services for their organisations (such as training), where outcomes may be variable. A service provider does not pass ownership to the customer; you cannot buy a manicure and use it again and again. You can go back to the same salon, but the service could be different every time. The difference may depend on your own input, from what nail varnish colour you choose to how much you want to chat with the staff.

A service is:

- Something you cannot touch

- Something that you cannot own

- Something that cannot be stored

- Potentially different every time

- Affected by the customer's involvement

For all these reasons, a service can be difficult to evaluate.

Services are used to enhance physical products. For example, companies that sell cars usually offer maintenance, repair and servicing as well. Services are also value offerings to customers in their own right in many industry sectors, such as catering and healthcare. The research on service quality applies whether you are offering a service as an enhancement to a product or a standalone service, such as a package holiday.

The dimensions of service quality identified by Berry et al (1990) are:

Reliability – Companies have to keep their service promises. No one wants to travel with a 'usually reliable' airline or deposit money with a 'usually reliable' bank. Of course, things go wrong when you are delivering services, so good service companies often include a compensation clause in their promises to customers, such as 'Satisfaction or your money back'.

Tangibles – There are some services that you can observe with your senses. In a hotel, you can feel if a bed is comfortable or not. You may prefer a restaurant with tablecloths to one without them. Clean floors, smartly dressed staff and a coffee machine say something about a car retail outlet. Whatever physical evidence is on offer for a service, it needs to be consistent with the brand positioning.

Responsiveness – Customer reviews of services often mention the helpfulness and timeliness of service. In the 1970s, consumers longed for reliable products. Now, consumers take product quality for granted and long for better post-purchase service as they wait on hold with call centres listening to tinny music and search websites in vain for information about how to get help from a supplier. We hope that all service will be as prompt, friendly and informative as it is at our favourite independent restaurant. However, few companies differentiate themselves on after-sales service. Salespeople may be asked by consumers (and will certainly be asked by professional buyers) to prove that their company's post-purchase service levels meet customer expectations.

Clarke (2015) found that 'Consumers are most frustrated with broadband and energy providers, who ranked the worst overall for their long waiting times, poor staff knowledge and lengthy phone menus'.

Assurance – As with products, customers can acquire confidence about a service from a brand, awards and independent reviews. Some are very interested in the degree to which customer service is part of the company's culture. Customers also need assurance at the individual level; they want to be confident about the knowledge and helpfulness of the personnel they are dealing with, as the following quote illustrates:

> "'Core ingredients of excellent customer service – employee competence, attitudes and behaviour – have become even more significant differentiators," said Ms Causon of the ICS [Chief Executive of the Institute of Customer Service] … "Mass marketing or a 'one size fits all' customer experience is delivering diminishing returns and diluting valuable customer relationships.'"
> (Davidson, 2016)

Empathy – When it comes to service, we would all like to be in a market segment of one. Service providers create a feeling of personal and corporate empathy by listening to customers as individuals and offering solutions relevant to their needs, although this might not be relevant to a cost leader. Some budget airlines are upfront about their lack of personal service, but their customers are willing to trade empathy for low prices. However, companies do need to consider their duty of care regarding consumer law and their reputations.

In the tough world of B2B services, expectations are high, and elements of quality are frequently perceived to be missing. Operational problems are often escalated to senior buying decision-makers if the users of a product are unhappy with service levels from the technical support engineers. Salespeople will receive service complaints, and you will spend time negotiating with colleagues to find solutions to the customer's concerns. It is not an enjoyable part of the job, but it is highly risky to ignore customer dissatisfaction. Acting as soon as possible can regain trust. Remember that the written content of a service level agreement is not what matters; it's the level of service that the customer *perceives* they should get. Familiarising yourself with the customer experience, perhaps by spending time with them on the factory floor or in the IT labs, will help you to understand the difference. Studies of customer index ratings vary between B2B and B2C companies, as McKinsey & Company (Maechler et al, 2016) have found: 'B2B customer-experience index ratings significantly lag behind those of retail customers. B2C companies typically score in the 65 to 85 per cent range, while B2B companies average less than 50 per cent.'

Experience

Experience factors enhance some products and services. Professional buyers frequently discuss 'value-in-use' – how much we get out of a product as we use it again and again. Do we have a good experience with this product, or does it cause us hassle? We are becoming a more impatient species, so products must deliver quickly and frequently to create any 'feel-good' effect. Some 'products' consist solely of how the customer feels about them, and the purchase of experiences is a growing trend in consumer markets. *The Guardian* reported in 2016 that: 'Average household weekly spending on clothes and food has fallen since 2010 while spending on recreation and culture has risen, according to the Office for National Statistics (ONS)' (Allen and Butler, 2016).

To deliver excellence in an experience is an even more abstract challenge than delivering excellent service. In some cases, customers will want a 'wow' factor; in others (such as a spa break), they might wish for an overwhelming sense of calm. In the case of a theatre company, planning to deliver an inspiring experience starts with a clear and strong artistic policy and is implemented through careful choice of scripts, casting, venue consultation and rehearsal – all to test the excitement levels each play generates. Sometimes, customers choose uncertainty in experiences, such as buying a ticket for a football match. Even more so than with services, customers make their own contribution to the experience they have bought. In the case of a football match, they will clap and cheer; to minimise a bad experience, they may sing ironic chants in the face of defeat for their favoured side.

How can experiences be sold? You can take care to research what your target customers enjoy and build that into your offer. Customers research holidays and look for testimonials from other tourists regarding a resort or hotel. It has been alleged that TripAdvisor affects the tourism industries of entire countries (Oxford Economics, 2017). You can only imagine what an experience is like from the descriptions of those who have had the experience before. Your marketing department might make a mini experience out of the promotions for the experience to help the customer try before they buy.

The role of events in brand marketing reflects the growing shift towards consumers wanting experiences. Events and experiential purchases have evolved, especially among millennials and Generation Z. Jo Coombs, CEO of OgilvyOne, doesn't think that these trends are a fad (Hibberd, 2018) – she sees them as the future of the industry: 'Consumer needs are changing, we're coming into an economy that's driven by doing things rather than buying things.'

In the case of trying to sell a genuinely new experience, there is a small minority of consumers who will love something just because it is new, and you have to find them (with the help of your marketing department) and reduce their risk in trying something untested. Products have life cycles, and you could segment the market for your products on customers' attitude to innovation.

The product life cycle

There are many life cycles in the business world, and one of the most frequently discussed is the product life cycle.[1]

---

1 The marketing approach to product life cycle management was originally explored by Theodore Levitt (1965).

Products require different investment levels in different stages of the cycle.

Consider, first, how much investment goes into a product before it is launched. Product ideas have to be generated, evaluated and tested. Development can be a long process with high risk levels. For example, it can take many years for a new drug to be approved for use in healthcare. The costs of launching a product are also eye-watering. Some companies do not invest in their own new products. They have a strategy of being 'fast followers' of technology trends, or they buy mature products and focus on extending their lives.

The stages of a product life cycle are straightforward:

- **Introduction** – In a product's introduction phase, it must be supported by large marketing and sales spend. New products are exciting, but they are difficult to sell because customers are aware of the risk of change, especially where technology is 'bleeding edge' new rather than 'leading edge' (which implies some proven results).

- **Growth** – As evidence of a new product's benefits becomes established, more customers are interested in its potential to fulfil their needs, leading to more sales.

- **Maturity** – Some customers will wait for a product to become mature before buying, especially if they perceive that a mature product will be stable and compatible with most other standards in the category. Many consumer goods can stay in this stage for a long time, such as chocolate bars and washing liquid. In fact, new formulae can be regarded with suspicion and rejected.

- **Decline** – Some companies withdraw products soon after their peak, but older products can be cash generators. There may be ways to extend the life cycle of some products; for example, they may have a niche as 'retro' models.

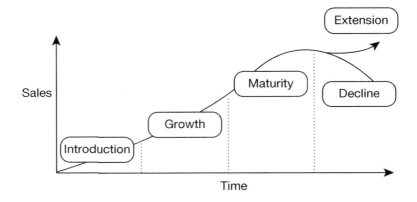

Figure 2.4: Product life cycle

How consumers react to innovation

Who likes new products and who prefers those in decline will depend, to some extent, on attitudes to risk. Some new products offer significant benefits and will be adopted very quickly. Business video conferencing has been dominated by a few players over the past twenty years, Skype being one of the earliest mainstream solutions. The global pandemic in 2020 resulted in customers and companies needing to communicate quickly and effectively, as offices around the world closed and employees worked from home. With a rapidly changing business environment and a lack of time to assess all the options, one video-calling service reached new heights: Zoom gained users at a rapid rate, moving from 10 million daily users in December to over 300 million by April (Turk, 2020). The ease of use of Zoom created a rapid growth along the product life cycle.

Not all new technologies and new products move swiftly from introduction to growth and maturity, though. In the 1960s, Everett Rogers identified that different attitudes to technology adoption existed, and there is an overlap with the product life cycle (Rogers, 1962). Innovators (a small proportion of customers, estimated by Rogers to be 2.5%)

are keen to try out new products; however, a new product will never succeed unless 'early adopters' (13.5%) believe that they can gain an advantage from it. Early adopters want to be ahead of their competition (or neighbours, in B2C), but they do not want to look foolish if a new product fails. Hence, there is a gap between innovators and early adopters, and many inventions fall into it. An electric vehicle called the Sinclair C5 (launched in 1985) was still topping polls of technology failures in 2013 (Holt, 2013), showing that sometimes people remember failures more than successes. It reinforces the belief that people can be slow to adopt new technologies due to the risk of failure, and some failures are simply overtaken by better technology.

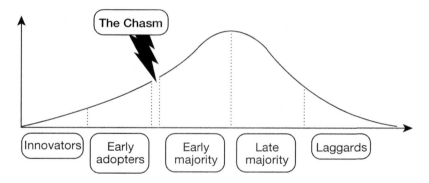

Figure 2.5: Diffusion of innovation curve (adapted from Rogers, 1962; Moore, 1991)[2]

Early adopters drive the growth phase of the product life cycle. Then comes an even bigger hurdle for innovative suppliers. In the 1990s, author Geoffrey Moore (1991) took a critical look at the IT sector and noted the number of technologies that had not become established as standard. He argued that in technology markets, there is a chasm between early adopters and early majority

2   The concept of the chasm was developed by Geoffrey Moore (see Moore, 2014). The concept of the diffusion of innovation was developed by Everett Rogers (see Rogers, 2003).

customers which is hard to cross. In their 'Hype Cycle' (Gartner, n.d.), IT industry analysts Gartner argue that as early adopters implement new technology, there is a 'peak of inflated expectations'. Unfortunately, this is followed by a 'trough of disillusionment', when some implementations fail and when the trade media is full of stories of the downsides of the new technology.

To a certain extent, early adopters are still visionaries for new products; they can imagine the benefits they can achieve from these products and they are willing to take risks to get them, perhaps by buying from a start-up company and replacing their previous product early. The early majority are very pragmatic. References from early adopters will still be met with scepticism because pragmatists see early adopters as risk-lovers. If you are trying to get a new product over that chasm, you must make a finely tuned effort to pinpoint the needs of conservative customers that are met better by the new product than old products; the cost or value benefit has to be verifiably large. This needs to be backed up by accreditations, compatibility with their current platforms, services to overcome perceived implementation risks, and a company or brand reputation to reassure them. If you are a start-up, you can often do this by working with bigger, more established partners.

Be aware that marketing and sales are sometimes blamed for good products failing. If your product meets a customer need better than the dominant incumbent brand, do not assume that it will sell itself. It takes a lot of hard work.

Late majorities are even more conservative and will purchase new technologies when they have become the norm. Laggards prefer products in decline (yesterday's 'norm' or even retro products).

Product management

Besides product life cycles and innovation curves, you are also likely to find product management colleagues using an analysis tool called the Boston Matrix. The terms used in this matrix have become part of business vocabulary.

The Boston Matrix is used for product portfolio analysis. It was developed by the Boston Consulting Group (Henderson, 1970), and it is still widely used in product and brand management, especially in fast-moving consumer goods. The axes of the matrix are market share and market growth. It is used to guide product management spend to optimise profit per product. An underlying assumption, based on sound research, is that a high market share results in higher profitability. The growth of the market or segment need which the product is positioned to fulfil is also assumed to be beneficial.

The other elements in the Boston Matrix (see Figure 2.6) have the following meanings:

- **Question marks** are products/brands with low market shares in fast-growing markets. Typically, they are new product introductions which may or may not cross the chasm.

- **Star** products have high market shares in fast-growing markets. They are typically products in their high-growth stage and likely to be profitable if product managers invest in promoting them.

- **Cash cows** have high market shares in markets where growth has slowed, so these are product success stories which are now mature. You may have heard people talking about 'milking cash cows' because it is assumed that the product can now deliver profit with relatively little marketing investment.

- **Dogs** are products with low market shares in slow markets, so we can draw parallels with products in decline. Sometimes they can still be profitable (cash dogs), but once they are not they may be withdrawn.

Like any portfolio, the product portfolio needs to be dynamic. Dogs need to be withdrawn, and new products need to appear in the question mark quadrant. Some question marks will not become stars, and some stars may not make it to the cash cow quadrant. Most companies need a balanced portfolio. Profitability will vary per product, but the portfolio can be managed for overall optimisation. Your product management colleagues will have good ideas about what sales promotions to offer for products in different quadrants. Work with them to understand your role and the messages that will help you to sell each product.

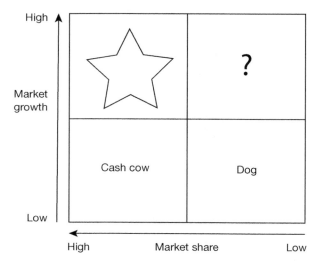

Figure 2.6: The Boston Matrix

Summary

In this chapter, we have looked at what you need to know about the business environment, both to understand your own company and to help analyse customer sales opportunities. We have also examined the product life cycle and how to analyse it, with a focus on how innovation may or may not be successful.

3

Market Knowledge

Introduction

World-class sales professionals have a passion for the world of business. They develop a deep understanding of the industry sector they work in and those they sell to. However, we can sometimes love our markets so much that we think that they will never change. By relying solely on experience in a sector, we can make errors of judgement about what might be happening in them today and what might happen in the future. Keep updating your knowledge and keep an open mind about what you might find, and do not be afraid to change sectors and learn about new markets during your career. The principles of professional selling apply across sectors, and cross-fertilising knowledge from one sector to another can re-invigorate companies.

'Selling to people who actually want to hear from you is more effective than interrupting strangers who don't.'
— Seth Godin, business author (1999)

An important starting point for learning about sectors and markets is thinking about what needs they fulfil. A market does not exist because a product or service has been invented; it exists because humans need products and services to survive and to thrive. A market exists when people are prepared to pay hard-earned money for something that they feel improves their life.

People develop preferences about how they fulfil their needs, especially when they can afford them. The grocery store of 1919 would have focused on staple foodstuffs and is unrecognisable from the grocery store of 2019, where consumers could be bewildered by too much choice. However, we must note the recent rise of discounters, who understand that real incomes are falling. They appeal to a broad range of consumers by offering lower prices for fewer product lines – they focus on fulfilling basic needs.

Markets, even B2B and business-to-government ones, are driven directly or indirectly by what consumers need. Even the commissioning of an aircraft carrier is a derived demand; it happens because a country's citizens want to feel safe and their government, therefore, invests in a well-equipped navy.

If we start with a need, we are less likely to make mistakes when technologies or consumer attitudes change. A successful economy is one where market needs are understood and companies compete to fulfil them now and spot new opportunities to fulfil them better. This chapter contains models for the needs-based analysis of markets which can get you closer to talking to the people who want to hear from you. It also explains how companies position themselves in markets through branding.

What is a market?

Traditionally, markets were physical places where the dynamics of demand and supply played out through direct communication between buyers and sellers. Most markets were defined by where they took place (the Marlow market or the Wigan market), but big cities would have specialist markets. In London, Billingsgate was the fish market, Smithfield was the meat market, and Covent Garden was the fruit and vegetable market. Shares were traded on the London Stock Exchange.

If you search for modern definitions of 'market', you may wonder if a market is the same thing as an industry or a product. You might find a Central London Office Space Market Report, or an Organic Milk Market Report, or a UK Festivals Market Report. The regulator OFCOM (2017) defines the communications market as the products which its consumers use: 'The report contains data and analysis on broadcast television and radio, fixed and mobile telephony, internet take-up and consumption and post.'

Marketers generally avoid defining markets as products because if a substitute comes along, it could put you out of business. Some textbooks refer to a market as the actual and potential buyers of a product, but how can you identify and count them? You need to know that they have a requirement which your products/services or capabilities can fulfil. If you define your market too widely, you may not develop specific competencies which enable you to position yourself in the market; if you define your market too narrowly, you will always be a niche player.

We take floorcoverings for granted every day. We need different surfaces beneath our feet in different parts of our houses and workplaces for different uses (see Table 3.1). The 'covering the floor' market is huge but can be broken down by specific need, such as 'something hard-wearing to cover the floor' or 'something comfortable to cover the floor'.

Table 3.1: Floorcovering markets

NEED: Something to put on floors	Consumers need coverings for floors in their houses	Businesses need coverings for floors in their offices and factories
DURABILITY	Hall and stair carpets	Flooring able to carry heavy machinery
WATERPROOF	Kitchens and bathrooms	Where water is used in a manufacturing process
COMFORT	Bedroom carpet	Customer 'meet and greet' area
EASY TO CLEAN	Children's play area	Catering areas

There are many ways to sub-divide the need for effective floorcoverings and many ways to meet those needs.

You may manufacture luxury floor tiles which are great for hallways, but the market you serve is not a luxury tile market. All the square metres of a floor which could be covered by your superior tiles could also be covered by carpet, vinyl or wood. Fashion may influence your success unless you can widen the customers' horizons about where to lay luxury tiles. You could also extend your capabilities to other floorcoverings and offer more choice.

How companies define the market(s) they serve drives strategy and operations. Each definition needs to be clear so that the company can understand its opportunities, focus on fulfilling needs in the market and identify relevant competitors.

For planning purposes, there also has to be some calculation of how much of the market your company can reasonably consider accessible. You are likely to have only a rough concept of the total size of a market, but it is worth knowing how big it is and thinking about it as your territory. For example, if you are producing durable floorcoverings, you might be able to calculate from government statistics how much office, factory and household floor space needs durable covering. How much of it is covered by your products?

Of course, floors do not need re-covering every year, so there needs to be a further calculation of how much of the market is 'addressable' in a given planning period. If people typically change their flooring every ten years, it is a tenth of the floor space. It is also the case that there is competition in the market, and therefore not all of the *addressable* market is *accessible* to you (see Figure 3.1). You may only be the favourite to fulfil the needs of some of the buyers in the market.

When setting company-level market share and revenue objectives, you need to make realistic calculations of achievable progress. To make targets more granular, it is necessary to segment the generic market need into smaller categories and to start to calculate which segments to target.

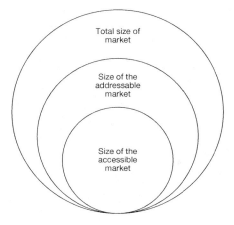

Figure 3.1: Accessible, addressable and total markets

Market segmentation

A market is a whole that companies divide into segments, just like an orange. These segments comprise of buyers with distinct profiles, which are based on variables which can be analysed and measured (see Table 3.2).

Table 3.2: B2C market segment variables

Segmentation variable	Sub-variables	Advantages	Disadvantages
Geographic	Region; town size; population density; climate	Can be aligned with retail outlets	Customer behaviour can vary dramatically within a geographic area
Demographic	Age/generation; family size; income/job type; education; cultural background	Popular and easy to measure	Risk of stereotyping
Psychographic	Social class; lifestyle; personality types	Reasonable predictor of attitudes to products	Difficult to size the segments and measure performance in them
Behavioural	Occasions; benefits sought; usage patterns; loyalty	Can be closely linked to product promotion and development	Difficult to size the segments and measure performance in them

Companies use market research and monitoring of consumer behaviour via loyalty cards or electronic-point-of-sale (EPOS) data to combine these variables. The comparison of multiple consumer characteristics and/or buying behaviour patterns to create addressable market segments using statistical techniques is called 'multivariate segmentation'. From the profiles that emerge from the data, marketers create 'characters' who represent the customer segments. These characters can help customer-facing staff to understand the needs and motivations of customers and prospects and help marketers and sales-people to make emotional and practical connections with customers' purchasing preferences. Table 3.3 shows a typical characterisation of retail grocery segments.

Table 3.3: Retail grocery segment character profiles

Character	Sheila	Zara	Joe	Zach	Jane
Demographic	Over-65	16–28	40+	16–39	29–64
Job and income type	Retired; state pension	Student or young professional	Skilled worker	Semi-skilled	Skilled or semi-skilled
Main buying criteria	Price; availability of basic foods	Convenience; price	Layout; parking	Speed of service	Store ambience; quality
Service expectations	High – may have eyesight or hearing problems	Low	Medium	Low	Medium
Values	Tradition	Fairtrade; novelty	Family	Fun	Healthy eating
Buying occasions	Newspaper plus	Social	List-based main shop	Food-to-go for work	Specific meals
Information sources	Newspaper/TV/ local posters	Social media	TV/Internet	Social media	TV/Internet/ leaflets

Each segment in a market needs a different offer from a supplier/retailer. Sheila needs everyday low prices and easy access to basic food ingredients. Zara needs to be able to find trendy foods and drinks and may want to know how products have been sourced. Joe wants convenient parking and a logical shop layout so that he can get everything on his list and bring it home quickly. Zach wants his bacon roll and coffee for breakfast and a sandwich for lunch; the rest of the shop is of no interest. Jane notices things like how clean the floor is and whether the fridge doors close properly; she wants to know where her food comes from and how long it will last.

Stereotyping customers is always risky. We live in an individualistic society where everyone would like to be a segment of one. However, to optimise marketing spend and inform operational decisions (such as store layout in retail), segmentation still has a role. Do try to make all characterisations positive; there have been war stories of companies identifying negative stereotypes. Some years ago, a bank was alleged to have characterised 'lemon' (less profitable) customers, and staff were encouraged to give them poor service. This was noticed and resulted in bad publicity. Segmentation also applies in B2B markets, as seen in Table 3.4.

Table 3.4: B2B market segment variables

Segmentation variable	Sub-variables	Advantages	Disadvantages
Geographic	Region; urban/rural; business culture	Can be aligned with sales territories	Customer behaviour can vary dramatically within a geographic area
Positioning in our portfolio	Key accounts; mid-tier; tactical	Easy to measure	Neglect of new opportunities
Firmographic	Firm size; firm age; industry type	Popular and easy to measure	Customer behaviour can vary dramatically within a firmographic
Behavioural	Benefits sought; usage patterns; loyalty	Can be closely linked to product promotion and development	Difficult to size the segments and measure performance in them
Situational	Purchasing processes; operational characteristics; attitudes of key decision-makers	Reasonable predictor of attitudes to suppliers	Difficult to size the segments and measure performance in them

As in consumer markets, multivariate segmentation is needed. Different customers need different approaches. B2B marketers also use characterisation to help to train salespeople to communicate with different decision-makers in customer firms. A salesperson with a geographic territory may need to adapt to various behavioural and situational aspects of segmentation.

Segmentation on its own does not necessarily help a company to succeed. It needs to make choices about which segments are most attractive and thus require more marketing and operational focus. The company must implement the right strategies to position it to serve those segments, and that positioning has to be reinforced by investment in branding. Bearing in mind the magnitude of that investment, it is essential to get segmentation right. Marketers have to apply several criteria to test whichever segmentation method they choose.

Criteria for segments

Measurable – It is pointless identifying a segment if you cannot check how well you are doing with it. If you cannot track sales performance per segment using sales data or market research, investment in promotion and branding may be wasted.

Accessible – Can you identify where you need to promote and sell your products in order to serve the segment? Do your target customers read a particular lifestyle magazine or meet in specific types of clubs? In the case of B2B, which tradeshows do your segments attend?

Substantial – Are your segments big enough to matter? Most grocery stores now have meat-free and gluten-free ranges for particular dietary needs, but the prices usually reflect the costs to serve a niche requirement. If segments are not big enough to matter, adjusting promotion and operations to serve them will be too costly. It is, however, possible to serve micro-niches online.

Differentiated – Will the segments respond differently to different marketing messages? If so, to what degree can you justify operational changes such as moving 'food-to-go' to the front of the store to help Zach? If such changes bring in more Zachs but put off Sheilas, is it worth doing?

One of the challenges of identifying segments is that you can immediately see that some segments have more potential for your company than others. Segmentation in isolation provides limited benefit, though. Companies need to move on to targeting particular segments and positioning to serve them.

Targeting

A company has to consider which market segments are most attractive to it. Marketers should list the market segments on a thermometer chart, with 'most attractive' at the top and 'least attractive' at the bottom. The most attractive segments will probably also be most attractive to your nearest competitors, who may have similar analyses; therefore targeting must be followed by positioning. Table 3.5 shows an example of a typical multi-criteria comparison of segment attractiveness.

Table 3.5: B2C segment attractiveness

Attractiveness factor	Weight	Sheila		Zara		Joe		Zach		Jane	
Growing	20%	8	160	5	100	5	100	5	100	6	120
Profitable	20%	3	60	7	140	7	140	9	180	7	140
High spend per visit	30%	3	90	5	150	7	210	4	120	7	210
Loyal	30%	8	240	3	90	6	180	3	90	6	180
Total	100%		550		480		630		490		650

Most segment attractiveness analyses will include growth and profitability; these are things which all companies want. Most retailers want customers to spend a lot at every visit and for customers to come back often; however, competitors may differ in their weighting of attractiveness factors. Several decision-makers should be involved in determining what segment attractiveness factors should be used and how they should be weighted, but different decision-makers will also have different priorities. An Operations Director may be more interested in high spend per visit than the Finance Director, who is focused on profitability. Exciting debates arise when deciding which weightings represent a strategic advantage to the company overall.

The scoring system should also be objective. For example, what is the maximum profitability you would expect from a segment? If it is 5%, then 5% is a score of 10, and all other possibilities are graded downwards from it. Of course, it is possible for a market segment to be unprofitable, so determine your bottom point (eg a score of 0). A customer portfolio may include minimally attractive segments, just as a product portfolio may consist of products which have not achieved their potential or whose potential has passed. As with Table 2.3 in the last chapter, scores are multiplied by the weights and aggregated to create scores out of 1,000.

We could criticise this model because only one factor is future-oriented (growth). Perhaps, since Zara and Zach are young and have decades of shopping choices to make, they are more attractive segments than are shown here. We could also criticise it because if Joe and Jane have such similar scores, are they separate segments or are we missing some discerning factor in the analysis?

Table 3.5 is a simple example, and some companies will have much better analytics. They may also offset segment attractiveness with the company's current success with each segment, as measured by the share of their spending. So, if Zach currently does 20% of his grocery shopping with us, while Sheila does 70%, that would affect the arguments for retaining Sheila or trying to win more of Zach's spending money.

Targeting is also important in business markets, where individual customers are sometimes big enough to be as powerful as an entire segment. For a company that makes gearboxes, BMW or Toyota could represent 10% or more of their turnover, but it is risky to have turnover concentrated in one or a few customers. Just as a healthy company has a balanced product portfolio, a balanced portfolio of customers or segments is desirable to investors. No targeting system can be perfect; they are a means to an end – making decisions about which segments are going to get the company's limited resources.

Positioning

Positioning is what a company does to occupy a place in the target customer's mind. Some companies make no effort to position themselves, but consumers will do the positioning for them. We are all busy people, bombarded with information about products and suppliers, and we need mental shortcuts. If a company does not say much about itself, what do people I follow on social media say about them?

The classic book about positioning is *Positioning: The battle for your mind*, which was written by advertising executives Al Ries and Jack Trout. They claim to have invented the term 'positioning' in 1969 (Trout, 1969), although it seems to have been practised by advertising agencies much earlier. As Ries and Trout (1981) stated: 'A product is something made in a factory. A brand is something made in the mind. To be successful today, you have to build brands, not products.'

A position is the perception that customers or prospects in a market segment have about a company or product in relation to its competitors. Sometimes, companies have an open conversation with consumers about their position. In 1962, car hire firm Avis, who were trailing Hertz in market share in the US, used the advertising slogan: 'When you're only Number 2, you try harder', and they kept the 'we try harder' slogan until 2012 (Ketchen, 2013). Figure 3.2 illustrates the marketing concept of 'positioning maps' with generic categories rather than brands, but you can substitute brands your-self, like Versace and Prada for designer brands, Florence and Fred (Tesco) for a supermarket brand, and Next for a high-street player. It shows how the gap between high-street brands and designer brands has been filled by outlet shopping, which has become a popular way for people to access last year's high fashion.

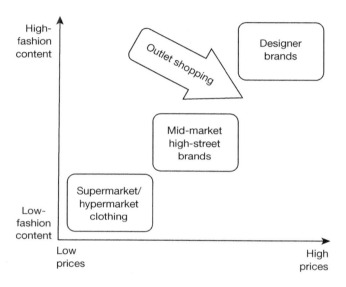

Figure 3.2: Positioning map for supermarket, high-street and designer brands

Positioning maps can only cope with two dimensions at a time, and you may need several to find gaps in mature markets. However, you must not only identify gaps but also understand where you sit with the customer segment and where you want to be.

Figure 3.3 shows a price/service map for the airline industry. You would think that each player is locked solidly into their slot in the minds of customers. People who use budget airlines know that they pay a low price and risk abysmal service. People who can afford to take a private jet expect high levels of service. The business-class service of major airlines probably sits in the middle of these extremes.

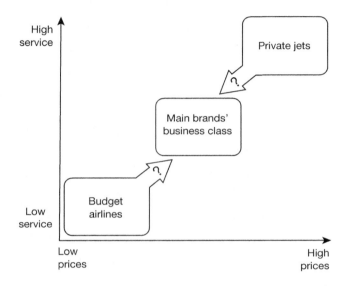

Figure 3.3: Airline industry price/service map

To maintain a position in a market, companies have to align all aspects of their marketing strategy and operational activity with their position. The positioning has to be evident in the product/service, the places where it is bought and communicated, and the people or skills delivering it. If you design and manufacture luxury fashion, you must be in luxury fashion retailers only, and you have to advertise in magazines read by people with a lot of money and who are passionate about fashion. If you position yourself as the highest-quality machine tool manufacturer in the world, you must invest in research, development and engineering, buy the best material and use the best processes, as well as appear at the right trade shows and buy advertorial space in trade publications where you can explain your latest technology.

Successful positions are:

- **Distinctive** – Even if you have close competitors, you must be able to demonstrate how you are different from them.

- **Superior** – Your distinction should be one of superiority on at least one factor that customers use in their buying decisions.

- **Relevant** – It would be a waste of money to take up a market position that customers do not find interesting or relevant.

- **Easy to explain** – Attention spans are short for a person surrounded by thousands of marketing messages. Your position must be instantly clear.

- **Aligned with company skills and resources** – If the positioning is not aligned with what the company can do, you cannot paper over the cracks indefinitely; the customers will spot the mismatch between message and reality.

- **Affordable** – Positioning is linked to brand development and involves communications campaigns which can be costly. This is especially relevant if a company is re-positioning or trying to de-position the opposition.

Re-positioning and de-positioning

Would it ever be possible for a company in a luxury position in a market to extend its market to middle-income consumers? The example of Burberry shows the risks of doing so. When Burberry became popular with soap actors and footballers' wives (in 2002 *EastEnders* actor Daniella Westbrook was famously photographed dressed head to toe in Burberry, with her daughter in a matching outfit) its core customers felt that its exclusivity had been compromised. It took several years to rebuild Burberry as a luxury fashion leader. During economic downturns, though, the luxury niche can feel very narrow. The breadth of range and sub-branding among car manufacturers shows appealing versatility in terms of multiple positions.

Would it ever be possible for a budget operator to win a share in the middle ground? Just as a middle-market player might decide to sub-brand a 'value' or 'basics' range to compete with discounters, it is possible for discounters to offer a 'premium' range: UK discount supermarket brands Aldi and Lidl, for example, have added premium own-label products such as steak, wine and baby food. These premium own-label brands have grown sales much more rapidly compared to other products they sell (Rodionova, 2016). It should be noted, however, that Aldi's and Lidl's sub-branded premium ranges are miles away from a re-positioning.

Most people in the UK today regard Skoda as a respectable sub-brand of Volkswagen. In the 1980s, Skoda was a joke brand. Quips such as 'How do you double the value of a Skoda? Fill it up with petrol' were common. In 2001, the company launched a multimillion-pound campaign of humorous advertisements which acknowledged the poor perception that viewers might have but challenging them to think again (Cozens, 2001). Sales improved and have continued to grow. Attitude studies suggested that the time lag between car buyers' willingness to believe that Skoda had improved its build quality and their willingness to buy a Skoda was long, so re-positioning is rarely an instant hit. In business markets, the re-positioning that many brands sought in the 1990s, from hardware suppliers to service companies, was tough to implement, and many customers felt that they were getting confused messages. Even the world's biggest IT brands took many years to occupy the service space in the customer's mind.

Re-positioning can be the riskiest strategy a marketer ever has to implement. In the 1990s, Yardley invested millions of pounds in a dramatic re-positioning from floral fragrances popular with the older generation to edgy aromas for young people, and it failed spectacularly (Victor,

1998). It was a classic case of bemusing new customers while offending core customers. The company, founded in 1770, went into receivership. We may wonder why such mistakes happen, but Yardley had used methods which had worked for a similar company in the US. Just a few contextual changes, such as Yardley having been regarded as a 'royal favourite' in the UK, led to a different outcome.

Re-positioning can be especially difficult if it involves de-positioning a competitor. If your competitor is the market leader, how can you persuade millions of consumers who think the market leader is OK to try something different? Ries and Trout used the successful example of painkiller Tylenol, which de-positioned aspirin by drawing attention to aspirin's side-effects (Ries and Trout, 1981), but it is certainly not an easy strategy to implement. Apple tried to de-position big players in the PC market in the 1980s by portraying them as 'Big Brother' dictatorships, but it was unsuccessful. Marketers are careful about de-positioning, although if they never attempted it, markets would not have their current dynamics. It is unprofessional and unethical to criticise competitors, and it can annoy customers, so de-positioning has to be fair and accurate.

Branding

A brand can be a reflection of a company's reputation. Brand development has a high-level function in establishing the company's corporate citizenship, but it is also a follow-on from positioning. It is undertaken to boost product sales by reinforcing messages about product positioning with target customers. Brand symbols such as the name and the logo should enable a customer to instantly recall the benefits being offered (best service, best price, most sustainable, etc). A strong brand can secure customer preference and loyalty – it provides a shortcut to the benefits that they want. Some are powerful global icons; the Nike logo, the McDonald's 'M' and the Coke bottle shape have fixed themselves in the minds of most people on the planet.

Such recognition can be worth more than the tangible assets of a company, such as factories and machinery, and there is debate about how brands can be valued. If Company X buys Company Y for £1m when Company Y's balance sheet assets are only worth £600,000, the difference (£400,000) could be equated with the value of Company X's brand. It will appear on the combined balance sheet as 'goodwill', but marketers will perceive that it is brand equity. Since companies are not being taken over every year, many companies commission research to get a brand valuation.

Summary

In this chapter, we have learned about markets and how they can be segmented. We have considered how to target particular segments and how to position a company and its products/services, and we have noted how accurate positioning is interdependent with successful branding.

4

Customer Knowledge

Introduction

The main source of cash flow is customers parting with their money in return for goods and services. A company with no cash flow has to borrow from banks, and banks are not going to lend unless they see that customers are going to be won in a reasonable timeframe. To win customers, you have to know them, and what they need to make their lives easier (eliminating the obstacles). They do not want to buy the features of a vacuum cleaner; they want a cleaner carpet in as short a time as possible. 'If you can stay focused on eliminating the obstacles along your customers' journeys, your company will turn out much more than all right' (Nelson, 2017). Without customers, there is no company. In the twenty-first century, customers are powerful.

After the Second World War, markets grew rapidly. It is easy to sell in growth markets because the customer's drive to buy is strong. The seventy years since have seen markets mature. The buying function in companies has become strategic and influential, and consumers have become more informed and sceptical.

The power of professional procurement is based on what purchasing savings can achieve for companies that are in competition to please shareholders (or taxpayers, in the public sector). If 40% of a company's cost base is incoming purchases (raw materials and process costs such as heat and light) and its profits are 5%, reducing the spend on purchases to 38% dramatically improves the bottom line to a 7% profit. Companies who lead in procurement gain measurable cost reductions that are twice those of average companies, according to AT Kearney's 2014 global Assessment of Excellence in Procurement Study (Kearney, 2014).

In the years since the financial crash of 2007–2008, many television programmes and websites have urged consumers to reduce their regular spending so that they can pay off debts. The pressure is the same for companies. When cost matters, companies and consumers will be much more discerning about what they buy. Suppliers have to convince them that the benefits they offer will deliver value. To do that, salespeople must know what makes customers tick.

Of all the knowledge a world-class sales executive needs to have, the understanding of their customers may be the most important. Employers correlate it with success, and customers prefer salespeople who understand them – and they express frustration with suppliers who fail to investigate their needs:

> 'When describing conditions that lead to a sales organization's proposal not being selected, buyers are vocal in terms of the seller not understanding their firm's most important needs… they displayed no desire to learn about [us] and never showed any interest to be involved, to educate us, or to provide new suggestions.' (Friend et al, 2014)

Investing time in understanding customers is important. First, you have to evaluate the relative importance of each customer in order to decide how much time you should invest in analysing them. You also have to bear in mind that some types of customers want to make decisions for themselves for many of their purchases. It does take time to learn about prospects and customers, and your time is limited, so the first section of this chapter explains how to develop your knowledge of customer portfolio management. Then we move on to general knowledge about consumer behaviour and organisational buying behaviour. Finally, we look at where customer needs come from. All customers are different, and you will also need to explore their needs using the techniques described in the Customer Needs Analysis chapter.

Customer portfolio management

In order to balance the risk for your company, it is important to have a balanced customer portfolio and focus resources only where investments in improving the strategic value of a customer are robustly justified. While some customers demand a detailed understanding of their business and reward suppliers who have it, others are oriented to buying 'at arm's length'. In other words, they want to drive the transaction and are not interested in a business relationship. It is as important to recognise the need for 'no intimacy' as much as the need for co-creation of value and long-term partnership. In a shop, you can start to assess that need by simply approaching the customer and offering help. Some will be grateful and start talking about what they are looking for; others will decline and be determined to find something for themselves, even if it takes longer.

Companies must make strategic judgements about how much resource to allocate to customers. In addition to those who do not want to engage with suppliers, there are other customers that you cannot afford to serve fully because their value to the business is limited. While you can do business with them using low-cost media, such as a web portal, you should not offer a personal sales meeting.

Figure 4.1 shows a portfolio designed for B2B sectors, where each customer would be mapped. In B2C sectors, you could have a similar map for customer segments. On the vertical axis, a formula will be applied to calculate a customer's strategic value to the company. There is no 'right' formula because each supplier will have different strategic objectives, although you might expect to see customer profitability or customer lifetime value (CLV) included in the formula. Many customer relationship management (CRM) systems focus on CLV.

CLV is the present value of the anticipated cash flow derived from a customer relationship over the lifetime of the relationship. The value of a customer relationship varies over time. For example, during and just after the acquisition of a customer, costs to serve are high, but the customer contributes greatly to the business when their service needs are minimal or if they provide references to new prospects. Therefore, it's best to have a long-term outlook in assessing the value of a customer. Formulae to calculate CLV can also vary, but you need to predict how much revenue a customer will generate and subtract the costs to serve that customer, phased over time. That cash flow then has to be discounted by a percentage which represents the changing value of money over time (net present value).

Sales volume is often considered an important factor in customer evaluation, but it would be more valuable to a process manufacturer who has to keep the factory running 24x7 than it would be to a professional services firm working on a project-by-project basis. Larger companies value volume more as they have to sustain the scope of their operations, whereas smaller companies must balance the desire to grow with having bigger customers and the cash flow risks they can cause.

On the horizontal axis, which in Figure 4.1 travels from right to left, we try to map our value as a supplier to the customer. Very often, that data may not be available, and assumptions have to be made based on what we know about our share of the customer's spend in the categories we serve.

If a customer sits in the 'strategic' box, there is mutual strategic value in the business relationship, which may be closely integrated to achieve supply chain efficiency and cost-effectiveness. If a customer sits in the 'prospective' box, they are a target for the supplying company, but the supplier is not necessarily of interest to the customer. Therefore, the supplier would have to take care before making investments to gain account share from competitors. If a customer sits in the 'tactical' box, that is not necessarily a bad thing for either party. It is quite possible to do good and profitable business on a one-off or arms-length basis (such as buying standardised products via a portal).

If a customer sits in the 'co-operative' box, their dependence on the supplier does not mean that the supplier perceives strategic value in the relationship. Perhaps this is a big company which drives a hard bargain on volume discounts, so the business is not so profitable for the supplier. The customer may be a former strategic account which has lost market position or a public body which has had its funding cut. Not all business relationships have to be strategically aligned. It is still possible to do business co-operatively, but there is potential for conflict which needs to be managed.

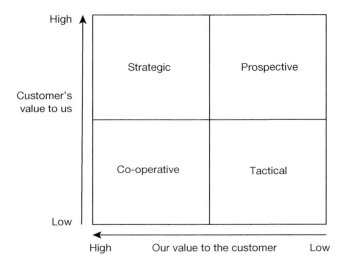

Figure 4.1: A simplified customer portfolio matrix (Rogers, 2007)

The purpose of a customer portfolio matrix or similar analysis tool is to:

- Map the relative strategic value of customers
- Map the relative competitiveness of the company's position with each customer
- Consider customer or segment-specific sales objectives and strategies

If you were going to do this analysis manually, you would need to:

- Select the accounts or segments to include (start with about ten)
- Agree on the formula for 'value to us' with internal stakeholders, such as sales, marketing, operations and finance
- Score the customers using the formula and locate their positions on the vertical axis

Table 4.1 provides a simple formula for 'customer value to us'.

Table 4.1: Customers' relative strategic values

Strategic value factors		Customer comparisons					
Factor	Weight	Customer 1		Customer 2		Customer 3	
Volume	20	6	120	9	180	4	80
CLV	40	9	360	3	120	6	240
Partnership approach	20	7	140	7	140	8	160
Growth rate	10	3	30	5	50	9	90
Approach to innovation	10	7	70	8	80	3	30
Total	100		720		570		600

Check your sales records for any feedback from the customer about how they judge you as a supplier versus your competitors. Note that each customer or segment will have different success factors and weightings for its supplier base.

In Table 4.2, you can see an example of a simple comparison of suppliers which gives an indication of competitive positioning. In B2B, customers may provide success factor analyses, or you may have to assume your position from the share of their spend in your product/ service category.

Table 4.2: Supplier comparison for competitive positioning (adapted from McDonald and Rogers, 1998; 2017)

Customer 1's critical success factors		Our score versus competitors					
Factor	Weight	Us		Competitor A		Competitor B	
Price	20	6	120	8	160	4	80
Delivery	40	9	360	3	120	6	240
Quality	20	7	140	7	140	8	160
Innovation	10	4	40	5	50	9	90
Range	10	7	70	8	80	3	30
Total	100		730		550		600

This example shows a relative advantage over the competition, enabling you to map this relationship as 'high' on the horizontal axis. If you have a high score but it is still lower than a competitor's, you should position your value to the customer as 'low'.

We can use Figure 4.1 to complete the analysis. First, we take the totals from Table 4.1 to identify the customer's strategic value to us and decide where we sit vertically in the matrix (low to high). Then, to show how important we are to the customer, we can use the totals from Table 4.2 to map where we sit horizontally in the matrix. By mapping the example data, we can see that for this customer we are in the top-left quadrant, because we have the highest scores in both tables. This would make our relationship with the customer strategic.

Consider the sales objectives and strategies relevant to each customer, depending on their position in the matrix, as in Table 4.3.

Table 4.3: Sales objectives and strategies for clients in various positions (adapted from McDonald and Rogers, 2017)

Account type	Potential objectives	Potential strategies	Other considerations
Strategic	Secure future development projects and invest. Sustain or incrementally grow volume/ revenue.	When business is already this good, the only way to grow is by helping the customer to grow. Shared strategic planning and opportunities to introduce new products or enter new markets can be considered.	Consider the risks inherent in this business. Does it represent a high proportion of your revenue? Should you invest more in other customers to diversify your portfolio?
Co-operative	Sustain volume, revenue and profitability.	These accounts should be defended from competitors, but not at any cost. Relationship development is still important.	Where there is a mismatch in supplier and customer intentions, it is not always a problem, but there is potential for conflict which needs to be managed carefully.
Prospective	Gain account share but be selective about investments in bids.	Knowing when to invest in a prospect is difficult. They are happy with another supplier. Taking small bits of business can help to build account share and may be more successful than a full-on assault on the competitor.	Keeping in contact with the customer while waiting for the incumbent supplier to make a major mistake is also a viable strategy.
Tactical	Minimise costs to serve. Maximise cash flow.	Standardise product offers and processes. Make it easy to do business by telephone or on websites.	The CRM analytics system needs to flag when a customer's purchasing activity is scaling up.

Since the 1990s, researchers have been keen to identify ways of developing customer relationships all the way from establishing the customer as a target to having a fully integrated business relationship. If you are focused on converting prospects into strategic customers, it is worth considering the stages you may have to work through (see Table 4.4).

Table 4.4: Business relationship stages (adapted from McDonald and Rogers, 2017)

Exploratory	The customer has been identified as potentially strategic, but they are happy with their current supplier, and you have a minimal share of their spend in your product category. The customer may not want to risk change. You need to encourage the customer to explore your capability. Work with marketing to build on reputational capital, such as customer references and professional acclaim and awards.
Basic	The relationship has moved on to some regular, small-scale transactions. It is easy for the customer to exit the relationship, but there is also the opportunity to grow the business by demonstrating reliability on their core purchasing criteria. A challenger can gain a reputation for being 'easy to do business with' (reducing hassle and risk).
Established	You are one of a few suppliers 'preferred' by the customer, so you have a middling share of spend. There are multiple contact points and information exchange between supplier personnel and customer personnel. This may be a comfortable level for many business relationships. Many customers do not invest all their spend with one supplier. However, there may be good opportunities to grow account share. There is convincing evidence that business relationships are at their best in the growth phase.
Interdependent	Both supplier and customer acknowledge their strategic importance to each other. The supplier may even be the sole supplier for a particular category of goods or services. There is open information sharing and evidence of cross-organisational trust. There will be joint strategic planning and excellent opportunities to grow both businesses. Such relationships are difficult to develop and will be few in number.
Decline	Business relationships may decline as mutual commercial interests between supplier and customer diverge, or they may be hit by crises – either external ones such as recessions or internal ones such as a major change in decision-makers. Many purchasing decision-makers are concerned about over-commitment to powerful suppliers. It is always prudent for both parties to agree on an exit plan for both decline and crisis scenarios.

Drawbacks of the portfolio management approach

Like many analysis tools, customer portfolio management is not perfect. It is a starting point for clear thinking about how to allocate resources to customers, and companies tend to adopt a 'continuous improvement' approach to their evaluation and selection process year-on-year. The following points are worth considering when you are reviewing the customer portfolio with your manager:

- Generally, we start planning with our current customer and prospect base, which may inhibit our ability to see where new business will come from in the future. Are there any rapidly growing small businesses we need to pick up?

- There may be political pressure within the company to over-value powerful customers and under-value emerging key accounts. Typically, customers whose lifetime value is in decline are still classified as strategic when they should be co-operative. Are there too many 'strategic' customers? If so, can you divide the 'strategic' quadrant of the portfolio to get more differentiation between customers?

- There may be over-optimism about the subjective element of evaluations. Try to stick to measurable factors where possible.

- Portfolio diagrams are snapshots, yet we want to use them for planning purposes, to change the positions of customer relationships as well as understanding where they are now. Resourcing decisions need to consider where the relationship with the customer is going or can be made to go, as well as where it is now.

- The dividing quadrant lines are absolute, but there will be many borderline cases, especially in the middle of the diagram, where customers might be bouncing between two or more quadrants.

When you start to discuss a customer's position in the portfolio, you realise you need to know why that relationship got to its present position and where it can go. The current portfolio position represents an accumulation of buying decisions made by the customer. Where did those buying decisions come from?

Consumer buying behaviour

Even if you work in B2B, bear in mind that movements in markets are driven by demand from the end-consumer of a product. You cannot sell aluminium to an aircraft manufacturer unless there are millions of consumers who want to travel by plane.

It has often been assumed that consumers buy on impulse. Companies have spent billions trying to make consumers think of them the way they think 'Coke' when they think 'fizzy drink' and 'Heinz' when they think 'baked beans'. Advertisers look to neuroscientists to help them get closer to a 'buy' button in the consumer's brain. To some degree, this is welcome to the consumer, because we need shortcuts when we are buying. A supermarket trip would be murder if we all examined every choice on every shelf before putting our preferred product in our baskets. However, as more and more information has become available to consumers, there is more professional buying behaviour in consumer markets. Even if we do not do our own research, we might consult specialist websites such as MoneySavingExpert for advice, especially for high-value purchases such as cars. Of course, digital intermediaries have a particular interest in this trend: 'Consumers spend, on average, nearly 11 hours choosing the exact vehicle that is right for them. This shift online has created a "digital forecourt", which allows consumers to make their car purchase decisions long before they set foot onto a physical forecourt' (Auto Trader Group, 2016). In light of this trend, it is prudent to update some of the more traditional models of consumer buying behaviour, as shown in Figure 4.2.

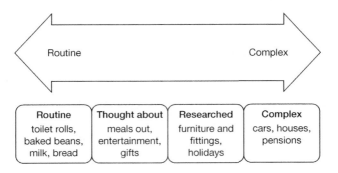

Figure 4.2: Consumer buying behaviour categories

The degree of effort that a consumer puts into buying something will usually depend on the cost and risk involved, although we may be concerned that houses are sometimes bought on impulse because of location and pensions are bought without a full understanding of the competitive offerings. Nevertheless, the trend is towards more purchases being researched, apart from the very routine items bought on the way home from work in a convenience store. Even in convenience stores, some shoppers will focus on own brand and special offers to keep their spending down. Convenience stores also know that they need to keep the prices of basics low so that consumers do not take a detour to a discount store. The savvy consumer holds all suppliers to account.

Buying decisions also take place in contexts. Supplier stimuli, such as advertisements, are just one source of information and preference. Consumers often supplement it by checking the performance of particular brands with consumer association reports or magazine and online reviews. We also take into account 'big picture' factors, such as the state of the economy. For example, there has been a significant switch to discount supermarkets since the economic crash of 2007–2008. Counterbalancing this rationality, we are also individuals formed by many years of social conditioning. We rarely buy things which do not fit in with our culture, class, or family values. We expect to be buying differently according to our age, education, and status.

If you work in fast-moving consumer goods or retail, your marketing department will have researched how consumer needs vary for your product/service category and provided you with information about consumer segments (see the 'Market segmentation' section in Chapter 3).

In the example below, we examine the profiles of three groups, using market segmentation to identify what customers may desire and who those customers might be:

CASE STUDY: PROFILING FOR HOME FURNISHINGS

Group A – preferring stylish designs for smaller rooms

Typical location: flats/small houses in regional city or capital city suburbs

Socioeconomic: young professionals

Group B – preferring practical items, for example, washable, fitting a variety of uses

Typical location: medium/large houses in suburbs/rural locations

Socioeconomic: medium income; young families

Group C – preferring luxurious, classical furnishings

Typical location: large houses in cities and rural areas

Socioeconomic: top 10% of earners; older families or empty nesters

Although there are drawbacks to stereotyping customers, it is useful to have segment profiles to help you to understand how particular customers might be managing all the factors affecting their buying decisions. Be aware that changes in these factors will affect buying preferences. For example: 'My company might be making redundancies soon, so I'm looking for a used car, not a new one' or 'I am a new father, so I need a less sporty model of car now'.

If you are selling in international or multicultural contexts, you will know that you need to be mindful of how culture affects consumer attitudes, but do not forget subcultures. The diversity of Britain will be familiar to you, so think how many subcultures there are in bigger countries such as the US, China and India. Even in a relatively small country such as Holland, there are a variety of long-established regional cultures together with cultural influences from recent immigration.

Many factors influence who we think we are as consumers and how we like to buy. Figure 4.3 shows the unfortunate consumer surrounded by the many stimuli that bombard them when making a purchase.

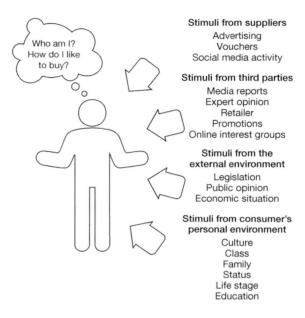

Figure 4.3: Consumer purchasing pressures

Few of us can say that personal factors and the general external environment do not play a part in how we buy. Equally, marketing messages (direct and indirect) are around us all the time and are likely to at least inform us, even if they do not influence us. In recent years, many of us have become particularly dependent on the views of strangers who post reviews online. For example, many consumers would not book a restaurant without checking TripAdvisor.

If you work in a B2C sector and are doing outbound calls, marketing will have given you profiles of people on your call list and advice about their possible needs and offerings that might be of interest. Your role is to check that the customer is interested and make the offer. Even with profiling help from marketing, you may not be able to guess the needs of a customer that phones in or comes into your store. In fact, even if you could guess, you need to check. You can only analyse customer needs when you have asked them some questions. There is detailed advice in later chapters on questioning tactics, but the following tips will give you an initial understanding of their needs:

- Introduce yourself and offer help. If the customer accepts, ask them what prompted them to phone/drop-in. Drill down from answers to find out which stimuli are on their radar today with questions such as: 'Have you looked at any Auto Trader reports?' or 'Are any other family members likely to be using the car?'

- If you are working in B2B, look at the consumer trends affecting your customer by finding relevant market reports. Even if your customer is fairly 'upstream' in the supply chain, such as an agricultural company or a mining company, they are affected by derived demand. If they are fairly close to the consumer (retailers and fast-moving consumer goods manufacturers), you will not be able to have a conversation with them without a deep understanding of the consumer trends affecting their categories and market position.

Business buying behaviour

Many textbooks give the impression that organisations buy in radically different ways from consumers. We have to ask: which organisations and which consumers? Some small family-owned companies may buy in ways which are similar to family decisions about cars and holidays. Some consumers may research certain buying decisions just as much as a company would. Nevertheless, there are some factors in the buying context which generally differ in scale (see Table 4.5).

Table 4.5: Consumer and business buying behaviours

Consumers	Businesses
Small-scale purchases	May be multimillion-pound deals
One person, or a few	Decision-making units (also known as buying centres), which can be complex
Based on limited research	Based on extensive research
No specialist knowledge of products or buying	Professional purchasing function (in large organisations); advice from purchasing consultants or banks (smaller businesses)
Not subject to scrutiny	May be challenged by auditors, government officials, or shareholders

If you are selling to businesses, your first challenge is researching who in the organisation is in the decision-making unit (DMU) or buying centre relevant to your product/service. The full DMU will probably only be engaged for major purchases or contract renewals. Routine re-buying usually only involves a user manager and purchasing. However, you need to be aware of the whole DMU. Table 4.6 outlines some of the roles in a DMU.[3]

Table 4.6: DMU roles

DMU role	Probable functional role	Contribution
Initiators	Line managers in the function that will be using the product/ service.	They may be your first point of contact, and they may have the need, but they could have very limited power in the DMU.
Specifiers	Technical support for the bid; engineers or other specialists who determine detailed needs.	They need to be convinced that your solution works.
Buyers	Purchasing/ procurement manager; they may have 'supply chain' or 'sourcing' in their title.	Drivers of the DMU. They are focused on the process of buying and establishing that the value for the purchase is worth the price.
Deciders	People who sign the cheque, typically the finance manager or even the chief executive officer.	Others will advise them in the DMU, but they may also want the supplier to present to them.
Users	The employees or contractors who come into contact with the office/ service and have to use it in their day-to-day jobs.	Never underestimate the importance of users. They may not have much power in the DMU, but they will scupper your product/ service post-purchase if they think that it is not useful and usable.

Cont.

---

3   The roles in the buying decision-making unit were first identified by Robinson, Faris and Wind in their book *Industrial Buying and Creative Marketing* (1967). The examples are the authors' own.

Table 4.6 *cont.*

DMU role	Probable functional role	Contribution
Influencers	Companies sometimes use consultants to advise on purchases or solving problems which create a need. Suppliers may be influencers (if the salesperson has done a super job of gaining credibility with the customer).	The role played by consultants is variable. Sometimes they do have considerable power and can keep suppliers away from the rest of the DMU.
Gatekeepers	Could have an official role, such as Health and Safety, internal lawyers or union officials; could be a particular personal assistant who is keen to keep suppliers away from their boss; could be an ad hoc member of the board who wants to block the purchase.	This needs some research. If a Health and Safety official asks for extra tests on our product, that is something logical that you can work with. If there is a gatekeeper who has high political standing in the company, it may be more difficult to understand where their objection is coming from. You do not want to waste time on a bid which is going to be blocked by an unknown detractor.

Each of these buying decision-makers will be in the middle of even more buying stimuli than the average consumer, as Figure 4.4 shows.

If your customer is a key account, you need to know how each member of the DMU responds to buying stimuli. This can take some time, but if they are on a business social media platform like LinkedIn you may get some idea from their profile.

You will also need to search company reports for organisation charts and board member statements. You can establish some external influencers where information is in the public domain. Auditors sign off accounts submitted to Companies House, and bankers and lawyers may also be listed in company reports.

In a sales process (or buying process, as the customer sees it) it is critical to get the right information to the right people at the right time. It may not be easy to gain access to everyone you want to engage with; be politely persistent in asking for introductions to the people involved in the DMU.

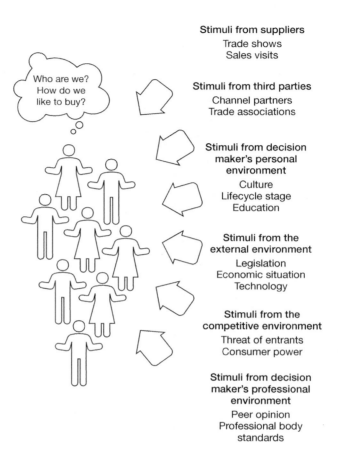

Figure 4.4: DMU purchasing pressures (adapted from Robinson et al, 1967)

It is often said that the DMU is two-thirds of the way through a buying process before purchasing engage with potential suppliers. At that point, they may be determined to negotiate price based on their own specification, without taking advice from suppliers about best-fit solutions.

To counter this assertion (largely heard from the purchasing community), there are many business relationships with regular dialogue between suppliers and customers. Suppliers are involved in new purchase specifications as a matter of course, and purchasing managers also insist on having suppliers bring them ideas, so it should be possible to observe the customer's needs and make a proposal without being promoted by the customer.

Purchasing departments conduct research every day about potential suppliers, and if a prospect contacts you it is likely that the purchasing manager knows a lot about your company already. In addition to public-domain online sources, they may have contacted fellow professionals in their network to see if they can reduce the risks inherent in the 'unknowns' of dealing with a new supplier. A key concept is the 'value-in-use' of your product/service: does it keep on delivering every day? And how easy is your company to deal with? What does it feel like to be one of your customers?

Most organisations, including public services, conduct research with customers which goes beyond assessing levels of satisfaction to ask whether or not the customers would recommend the company. It used to be assumed that if a supplier kept to contract, then a customer would be satisfied that they had done what they said they would. However, customers may perceive service differently. A supplier doing enough to avoid being sued for breach of contract may feel like poor service to the customer. It certainly would not warrant a recommendation. To create perceptions of value, a supplier needs to create a spirit of customer focus beyond the contract.

You need to be ahead of the game, supplying information and customer references to members of the DMU as and when they might need it. Table 4.7 could help you to make sure that you have all the angles covered.

Table 4.7: Purchase analysis (adapted from McDonald and Rogers, 2017)

Contact details for this contract: Sally Smith	Products/services being bought: Machine tools = Project Top Banana					
	Decision-making unit					
	Finance	Purchasing	End-user group	Operations	Health and Safety	External advisor
Buying process stage						
Identify needs				X		X
Qualify needs			X	X		
Detailed specification		X		X		X
Supplier search		X				
Supplier qualification	X	X		X	X	
Prepare tender documents		X				
Evaluate proposals	X	X	X	X	X	X
Negotiate terms	X	X				
Finalise contract with the chosen supplier		X				
Monitor implementation			X	X		
Decision considerations:						
Cost of ownership, payment terms, risk management, the reliability of machines, service, guarantees, skills, partners, company reputation, joint investment funds, customer references						
Notes:						

The purchaser's supplier portfolio

Just as sales departments like to analyse their customer portfolios, purchasing professionals also have analysis tools. One of the most widely used is the Kraljic Matrix (see Figure 4.5). Peter Kraljic was one of the first management thinkers who identified purchasing as a strategic sourcing role. The Kraljic Matrix (Kraljic, 1983) examines product/service categories. From the positioning of a product/service category, the purchaser decides how to manage the supplier.

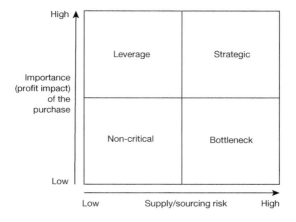

Figure 4.5: The Kraljic Matrix (adapted from Kraljic, 1983)

The vertical axis on Figure 4.5 measures the profit impact of a purchase category on the company, and the horizontal axis (which in this case travels from left to right) measures the risk in sourcing the product category. This means that if a raw material can only be sourced from a part of the world where earthquakes are common, there is a high supply risk. If the product is still under patent to a sole supplier, that is a high supply risk. Sourcing risk measures how easy it is to get the product. As with all analysis tools, the criteria that make a purchase more profitable or risky vary per company according to their sector, size and strategy.

In addition to economic and technical risks, be aware that purchasing professionals – and, indeed, all members of the DMU – have to manage professional and personal risk. No one wants to be the ex-employee who bought something that nearly bankrupted the company. Small business owners may have a larger appetite for risk, and they know that they need to take bold decisions if they want to grow. They also know that those bold decisions can ruin the company. When they decide to buy something, they can estimate the amount they can afford to lose. Purchasing professionals are working with their employers' money and tend to be risk-averse.

The purchasing system runs algorithms to determine the profit impact of purchases, with data drawn from the accounting system. The score for supply/sourcing risk is usually based on the judgement of the purchasing manager, although this may be backed up by data from external advisory sources. Each product/service category is then mapped on to the matrix. Table 4.8 shows what happens in each of these quadrants.

Table 4.8: Kraljic Matrix quadrant analysis

Quadrant in the Kraljic Matrix	How suppliers might be managed	How suppliers can respond
Strategic	Partnership is necessary if a product category has a high-profit impact on the business and supply risk is high. However, never assume that purchasing managers feel cosy with a supplier partnership. They are wary of being 'locked-in' to a single supplier who may misuse their power or become complacent. Even where they are aware of additional value from a supplier, purchasing managers sometimes use tactics to reduce the price (Hesping and Schiele, 2015).	Suppliers invest heavily in strategic customers. Usually, a key account manager will work with the customer to co-create new value through product development, process improvement and co-branding. They still must frequently provide evidence of value generated to avoid price challenges.
Leverage	If supply risk is low, the purchasing manager can play suppliers off each other. They probably need to secure a medium-term deal since profit impact is high, but they will encourage potential suppliers to compete on price and service. The purchasing manager must not over-push suppliers, as loss-making suppliers go out of business and leave the customer in a mess.	Suppliers usually bid where they feel that they can outpace the competition. They need to take care not to bid at a loss, so they must withdraw as soon as the 'zone of possible agreement'[4] is eroded. One option is to put standard products with standard terms and a standard price online.
Bottleneck	A low-impact item which a particular supplier can reliably source does not require much management attention. However, there must be regular monitoring for substitutes or new supply sources.	Suppliers need to make sure they have new technologies and alternatives when supply risk reduces.
Non-critical	Toilet rolls, stationery, and nuts and bolts should not take up much time. The supplier with the broadest catalogue range and most user-friendly web portal might be chosen, and all transactions will be driven online.	Suppliers need to partner to extend their ranges and provide the easiest buying experience.

---

4   The zone of possible agreement is the zone between buyer and supplier expectations of price where negotiation is possible. Outside of this zone, there is no deal.

As the salesperson, you need to know where your product/service category fits in the customer's Kraljic Matrix or equivalent. Ask them. Many purchasing managers will openly share this information. If they do not, you can make assumptions based on how much time they give you in meetings and the nature of the conversations. You have to see the world from their point of view before you have any chance of demonstrating the value that might improve their perception of you. 'The ability of the key account manager to see and understand the world from the customer's point of view, as well as their own, is central to being able to build a truly sustainable and value-creating relationship' (Darren Bayley, Sales Director, Straumann UK, quoted in McDonald and Rogers, 2017).

The buying process

Now that you know your customer segment and profile, or the DMU and the purchasing approach, you have to design a sales approach that matches the customer's buying process. When consumers and organisations make major purchases, they go through a buying process (see Figure 4.6). A need must be recognised. If the car is breaking down frequently, or the sofa is sagging in the middle, it is time for a new one. If the fixtures and fittings in the factory are scheduled for replacement this year, it is time to look at buying the latest equipment. Sometimes, the needs are not obvious. As explained in Chapter 2, changes in the environment of an individual or organisation can require them to make new purchases, but they may not be fully aware of possible improvements to their circumstances. It is the role of the salesperson to have conversations with customers about factors affecting their success and how new solutions might help them. This is discussed in more detail in Chapter 14.

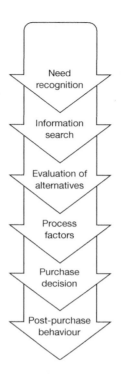

Figure 4.6: The buying process

Once a household or a business establishes a need, information must be gathered. A family member or a member
of the purchasing team might be asked to search the
Internet. Generally, salespeople have to rely on marketing to make sure that useful information and advertising
content is in the right media (both online and offline);
however, they can use their online profiles to invite information gatherers to make contact if there is something
specific they want to know.

The consumer or purchaser establishes their buying
criteria and starts to score potential suppliers. How are
they going to balance their desire for the highest quality
with the price that they can afford? How do they assess
their need for after-sales service? Organisations might

have several sub-steps in this process, such as formalising a specification and advertising for proposals from potential suppliers. Salespeople in established relationships with customers may be involved at this stage. If you are not, has the incumbent supplier made a strong case for themselves at this stage? Can you compete if the customer is happy with their 'value-in-use'? The evaluation will include negotiations.

Before a purchase decision is made, there may be some process considerations. A consumer might want to search for information, but do they want to buy from an online-only supplier? If they are in a shop and there is a long queue, will they wait, or will they try somewhere else or come back later? For an organisation, contract negotiation can be complex and legal advisors may insist on particular terms and conditions that the preferred supplier cannot fulfil. Perhaps the preferred supplier seems unnecessarily bureaucratic to deal with, and others are more flexible. The salesperson's role is to make it easier for the customers to buy from the company.

The purchase decision itself is a difficult moment for a customer. They have to part with money and hope that the new product or service will make their lives better. Immediately after the purchase, they will be particularly nervous and suffer 'buyer's remorse'. As it takes time to get used to their new car or new warehouse system, they may be irritable and impatient to realise benefits. It is during this period that wise salespeople take time to reassure the customer and make sure they have the necessary technical support.

Where does customer need come from?

You can read a company report, note that Company XYZ is expanding into the Middle East and deduce that, if you have successful subsidiaries in the Middle East, now is the time to explain to the customer how you can help with their expansion. But where does their desire to move into that region come from?

In Chapter 2, we looked at how companies analyse their external environment and competitive positioning to decide on their strategic direction. Your customer is doing that, too. Consumers also think from time to time about how changes in the economy or their business are affecting their life opportunities, and they make decisions aiming to enhance those opportunities.

In order to be the trusted advisor bringing new ideas to the customer, you need to do their strategic thinking for them. In Chapter 2, we explained how to use PEST and the Five Forces to analyse a company's environment. You should be able to list the opportunities and threats that your customer is facing. How are they going to respond to them? Having assessed who they are, you also need to think about how good they are at what they do. Some companies are quality leaders – how are they going to maintain that position successfully when there are cost pressures from consumers? The business is going to have to evolve with changing conditions, and sometimes companies have to make big changes when the business landscape changes.

The extended SWOT analysis in Table 4.9 shows how you can map opportunities and threats onto your customer's strengths and weaknesses to work out how they can achieve their objectives.[5] Remember that opportunities and threats are *external* to the business; the customer can do nothing about them. Strengths and weaknesses are *internal*; the customer can invest in changing (or acquiring) their capabilities:

- Where strength is aligned with an opportunity, they can move fast to make a quick win towards their objectives.

- Where strength is aligned with a threat, they can use strength to counteract the threat.

---

5   The extended SWOT was first described by Heinz Weihrich (1982).

- Where weakness is aligned with an opportunity, they must decide whether to invest in addressing the weakness and taking the opportunity.

- Where weakness is aligned with a threat, they need to take defensive measures to avoid losing out to competition.

You can address the changes that the customer needs to make to their business environment with a value-based proposal that you can include in your response.

Table 4.9: Extended SWOT analysis for a mid-ranking retailer

EXTENDED SWOT FOR MY CUSTOMER (Mid-ranking retailer)

Objectives	Strengths	Weaknesses
Increase market share to 10%	Food quality	Price
Maintain operating profitability at 5%	Store ambience	Range online
	Stock availability	Branding
Opportunities	QUICK WINS	INVEST
Emergence of micro-segments, such as gluten-free, vegan	Explore new specialist ranges with suppliers	Focus on growth with price-resistant micro-segments
Top 4 players undifferentiated	Invest in new CRM to	
New technology for CRM	focus marketing messages on quality position	
Threats	DIFFUSE	DEFEND
The consumer shift to online	Use quality in supplier	Align online ambience
Risk of supply chain scandal	selection policies to ensure quality in supply chain	with store ambience; use a partner for delivery

Having identified the customer's threats and opportunities, as a professional salesperson, you need to be the catalyst for change. Most people do not find change easy. Organisational culture, systems and processes have been established for decades and constrain change. Nobody likes to hear, even from a close friend, 'If I were you, I would…' You will have to diplomatically explain your suggestions for how the company can embrace the necessary changes. Always run through your suggestions with your coach or mentor first. As we discussed in the introduction to this textbook, purchasing decision-makers want suppliers to understand their needs and propose new ideas.

Preparation can help to start a conversation about strategic planning together.

Summary

In this chapter, we have looked at how suppliers analyse their customer portfolios, what drives consumer and organisational buying behaviour, and how you can discover the source of customer need.

5

Commercial And Financial Acumen

Introduction

Humans first traded through the bartering of goods – a pig for a goat or some shells for some grain. 'Tally sticks' have been found which suggest that in markets of the ancient world, traders kept account of what they had sold, what they received in exchange, and who owed them money or vice versa. However, the recording of trade became much easier with the development of coinage as a means of exchange. Coins were small and durable and had widely recognised value, usually with legal validity (the concept of 'legal tender').

'A mark, a yen, a buck or a pound
Is all that makes the world go round
That clinking clanking sound
Can make the world go round.'
— Fred Ebb, lyrics of 'Money', from the stage show
Cabaret (1966)[6]

For societies and economies to work, the recording of trade and tax, along with the concept of legal contracts,

---

6   Reproduced with the kind permission of the Fred Ebb Foundation.

was essential for governance. Perhaps its value to rulers was a driving force, but it also let traders be in control of their businesses, which allowed them to make a surplus to feed their families.

We may joke with our colleagues in finance about the value of 'bean counting' (excessive detail in monitoring expenditure), but, despite a growing trend for CEOs with technical backgrounds in recent years, there is a reason why 52% of the UK's top companies have chief executives from a finance background (Robert Half UK, 2019). Managing the finances of a company is critical to its survival. Income has to exceed expenditure, and the investments made to secure the sustainability of a company over time must show a return. Only by capturing the detail of day-to-day cash movements can the finance function develop a bigger picture of the company's financial health:

> 'One of the key roles of the modern finance professional is to understand, analyse and report back a holistic picture of organisational health... They weigh up the many risks and opportunities – both internal and external – that face the business and use this information coupled with their expertise and experience to plot a sensible route to sustainable growth.' (Weston, 2016)

If the finance function does such a good job, why do salespeople need any financial reporting knowledge? You need to know it because it is the language of business. Boards spend a lot of time monitoring and discussing financial statements.

Table 5.1 provides definitions of several financial terms which you will hear in meetings with colleagues and customers. (There are further details about some of these terms later in the chapter.) To be taken seriously as a professional, you need to join in such conversations. In this chapter, we explain what you need to know about accounting and finance at this stage in your career. As you become more senior, you will need to learn from financial analysis, especially if you aspire to be a chief executive.

Table 5.1: Definitions of key financial terms

Term	Definition	Notes
Asset	Something the company owns. These are divided into fixed assets, such as plant and machinery, which are bought for the long term and form an infrastructure for the company's operations, and current assets, such as stock, debtors and cash, whose value changes daily.	You may hear the term 'sweating the assets', which means making assets work as hard as possible to deliver returns.
Audit	Companies are required by law to have their financial statements examined by independent accountants called auditors. The process of examining the financial statements is called an audit.	Auditors are required to express their level of confidence in the accuracy of their client's financial reporting. The auditor's statement will be included in company reports.
Bottom line	Also known as 'operating profit'. This is the revenue minus all costs of operation.	Profitability is significant to shareholders because their dividends are paid out of profits; nevertheless, a company can have a positive operating profit and still go bust.
Cash flow	The movement of money into and out of the business over a set period.	Companies can fail due to a shortage of cash, so cash flow forecasts are essential. When cash is short, the company has to borrow from banks or sell more shares.
Creditor (accounts payable)	Money owed to suppliers (on a balance sheet). In general business conversations, creditors are the suppliers who have supplied goods but whom the company has not yet paid.	Typically, in business markets, goods and services are sold 'on credit', with the expectation of payment within 30 days, which is a legal requirement in the UK. The supplier can charge interest on late payment as the customer is borrowing from them; however, this is rarely enforced.
Debtor (accounts receivable)	Money owed by customers (on a balance sheet). In general business conversations, debtors are customers who have taken delivery of goods but have not yet paid for them.	In consumer companies which make cash sales, this is largely irrelevant; in business markets where customers typically have at least 30 days to pay for goods received, this balance sheet item has to be carefully managed. Although customers are called 'debtors' on the balance sheet, finance will talk about extending 'credit' to customers, and it is understood that the company is lending to the customer. A 'credit controller' should be involved in deciding how much a customer can owe.

Cont.

Table 5.1 *cont.*

Term	Definition	Notes
Depreciation/ amortisation	Although they are used for different types of assets, depreciation and amortisation are effectively the same thing. When one buys an asset that is expected to last several years, money must be put aside for its replacement. This is not a cash movement, but reserves need to be established for asset replacement. The asset is 'depreciated' at a given rate, say 10% per annum. The amount written off the asset is called depreciation.	If you are selling an asset to customers, they will need to consider the rate at which it depreciates in order to assess its value and plan their next purchase.
Earnings before interest, tax, depreciation and amortisation (EBITDA)	Revenue less expenses, adding back depreciation/ amortisation (which is a non-cash expense).	Senior managers closely monitor EBITDA figures as an indicator of the company's financial health.
Earnings per share (EPS)	Operating profit divided by the number of shares.	There are several variations on the calculation according to the type of shares which a company sells to shareholders.
Equity	Shareholders' funds. Typically, this is the share capital they own plus retained profits.	
Goodwill	This appears on balance sheets where a company has acquired another company and paid more than the book value of their assets. It is usually written off over time.	Goodwill is an indication of the value of the acquired brand.
In the black/ In the red	'In the black' means that a company is in profit or has positive cash flow; 'in the red' means that a company is in loss or has negative cash flow, or both.	These terms were invented when bank statements were printed in black or red, according to the health of the account.
Liability	Something the company owes. Liabilities are divided into long-term financing, such as shareholder's equity and long-term loans, and current liabilities, such as creditors.	A liability can be owed to suppliers, shareholders or banks.
Liquidator	A legal term for a firm appointed when a company ceases trading because it cannot pay its suppliers or employees. The liquidator sells off all the assets and pays the organisations that the company owes to the degree possible (30p per £ owed).	There have been some recent high-profile UK liquidations (Carillion). Companies monitor the financial health of customers and should cease trading with them if there is a risk of being exposed to their liquidation. However, since Carillion was a major contractor to the UK Government, its suppliers hoped it would survive.

Cont.

Table 5.1 *cont.*

Term	Definition	Notes
Liquidity	An indication of how quickly the company can turn assets into cash available for expenses or investments.	Cash in the bank is the most liquid asset, followed by money owed by customers. Salespeople are involved in negotiating when a customer pays their bills.
Margin	Usually 'gross margin' (GM) – the difference between revenue and the direct costs of making those sales. In a retailer, it would be revenue received less the cost of the stock sold. In large B2B sales, each sale will have a GM, also called a contribution.	Any price promotion or discount is also counted as a direct cost because it brings down the price at which a piece of stock is sold.
Overheads	Also known as indirect costs, overheads are expenditure which is used by multiple activities. Examples include insurance and utilities (power, water, telecoms).	At least part of your payment will be considered an overhead.
Triple Bottom Line (TBL)	The 'triple' refers to people, profit and the planet. TBL measures the positive impact of the company on its people (using human resource measurements) and the planet, as well as profit.	It is difficult and controversial to measure how a company might have a positive impact on the planet.
Top line	Sales or revenue – the money which comes into a business.	Marketing and sales are the functions responsible for generating the top line. The overall forecast for the top line is broken down into sales targets per salesperson.
Write down or write off	Something the company owns that cannot be recovered, and financial adjustments have to be made to clear it from the balance sheet. The business acknowledged that the loss could not be recovered and 'writes it off' the balance sheet as an asset.	You may be familiar with 'writing off' a car. A company may or may not have insurance to cover the loss of value from an asset, and the loss has to be absorbed by the business. When a customer owes money and goes bankrupt, their debt will have to be written down or written off. Where does the money come from to do that? Typically, a company accumulates a reserve account from previous profits to cover such losses.

The building blocks of financial reporting

How transactions are categorised

Money makes the world go round in little bits: a sale coming in here, a bill being paid there. Each 'bit' is a transaction. In accounting, there are categories of transactions which enable the transaction to be recorded for financial reporting purposes. Table 5.2 explains these categories, which you will find in company reports. There is some overlap with the terms discussed in Table 5.1. Some terms are repeated here in the context of their role in financial and company reports, rather than general conversations about financial matters.

Table 5.2: Transaction categories

Terms	Description	Notes for salespeople
Revenue	Money generated from the sales of goods and services. Revenue is the top line in profit and loss accounts.	Revenue *is* sales. We do what we do to generate this number.
Direct costs	Expenditure directly related to generating sales. These costs vary with sales activity.	In retail, direct costs refer to the costs of stock which is sold; for example, if a car was part-exchanged for £3,000, that is its direct cost. In manufacturing, it is costs directly associated with making the product, such as raw materials. Most companies treat discount and price promotions as direct costs, itemised separately from manufacturing costs.
Indirect costs	Expenditure which is used by multiple activities. It is difficult to assign all costs directly to goods and services sold. Items such as depreciation of assets, rent and administration expenses are treated as indirect costs. These costs are usually fixed and have to be paid regardless of sales activity.	The term 'SGA' (sales and general administration expenses) often appears in company accounts. Most companies aggregate the cost of running a sales department and paying salespeople and classify it as overhead. You may observe that commission is linked to sales activity; in more detailed financial planning documents (eg calculations of customer profitability), some sales costs are directly linked to customers.
Assets	Things that the company owns in order to produce and sell goods, such as property, equipment and shops.	In retail, the ambience of a shop is critical in attracting customers, so designing and fitting out shops well is vital to success. In manufacturing, customers can become closely involved in the specification of some assets.

Cont.

Table 5.2 *cont.*

Terms	Description	Notes for salespeople
Liabilities	A debt or obligation incurred during the making and selling of goods, such as debts to suppliers and bank overdrafts.	Customers are incurring a liability when they agree to buy from you. Will it have a substantial effect on their balance sheet? Will they be able to pay?
Equity	Shareholders' interest in the company, which is typically shown as a debt owed by the company to the shareholders. It rarely changes, but there are occasions when new shares are issued (to raise money for expansion). Retained profits are considered equity as they are technically owed to the shareholders.	Like every other function in the company, sales need to demonstrate that it contributes to shareholder value. Every profitable sale is a contribution to equity; every unprofitable sale is a risk to the business.

Profit and loss accounts

Profit and loss accounts (also called 'income statements') are presented for a given period. In company reports, we typically see the profit and loss account for a particular year, often compared with the previous year. In a board meeting, many directors review P&L accounts at least every month, compared with what was budgeted for that month and the past year's performance. They will look at trends on a monthly, year-to-date and rolling twelve-month basis. Most public companies make quarterly statements to the stock market about their financial performance; this can include your employer and your customers. There will be excitement about month-end. In some sectors, salespeople have monthly targets which are a subset of the revenue forecast promised to shareholders.

A profit and loss statement shows the money that came in and the expenditure that was incurred during the given period (Table 5.3 shows a simple example of this). Direct costs are deducted from sales to calculate the important gross margin (GM) figure. If you are making a sales presentation, you should comment on how much your product will impact the customer's GM by either increasing sales or reducing the direct cost of goods sold.

The P&L then has to report on the expenses incurred in running the business which cannot be attributed to particular sales. Deducting these expenses yields the operating profit. Of course, it might be a loss, hence the term 'profit and loss' account. Perhaps what you sell helps customers to reduce their operating expenses. Every reduction in an 'overhead' is a direct gain for the 'bottom line'.

Corporation tax is calculated on a company's operating profit. At the time of writing, corporation tax in the UK is 19%. There are many allowances which may be applicable, such as allowances on buying equipment or providing jobs in a particular region, to reduce the rate. You should also be aware that some international companies shift profit around their operations to pay tax in the countries where tax rates are lowest.

After tax is calculated, the remaining profit is available to distribute to shareholders in the form of dividends. Some profit will be retained to reinvest in the business and for contingency purposes. Even in a successful year, the directors may know that next year will be much tougher and retained profit from a previous year can be used to offset a loss and keep the company trading. Table 5.3 shows a simple profit and loss account.

Table 5.3: Sample profit and loss account

P&L account for Period 6 – ending 31 May 2020		Figures in £000s
Sales		**1,000**
Cost of goods sold	500	
Gross margin		500
Expenses		
Rent	50	
Wages and salaries	100	
Marketing expenses	50	
Administration and legal costs	50	
Depreciation	50	
Total operating expenses	**300**	
Operating income		200
Tax	30	
Profit available for distribution		170

You can see how the cost of running the company soon reduces healthy sales. Accountants frequently focus on cost reduction because it has a direct effect on the 'bottom line'. If you can reduce administration expenses by £10,000, that is £10,000 straight into profit. Perhaps administration costs could be reduced because IT has introduced efficiencies or some process redesign has eliminated unnecessary activity. Without investment behind the cut, there is always a risk of increasing costs if certain things no longer get done, and then customers start to complain about inefficiency, requiring more administrators to sort out the mess.

When you are selling to business customers, they will want to know what the effect of buying your product/service will be on improving their EBITDA. Are you going to help them increase sales or reduce an indirect cost? How long will that effect last? You need to make your calculations, in consultation with a finance colleague, and be confident in them.

Balance sheets

Whereas profit and loss accounts describe the activities of a company over a period of time, a balance sheet is a snapshot of the financial health of a company at a single point in time. Typically, a company report will include the profit and loss account for the year ending 31 December and the balance sheet at 31 December of that year. It explains the core accounting equation:

Assets = Liabilities + Owners' Equity

Sometimes this is shown side by side; other times, it's in a linear fashion. The simple example in Table 5.4 shows the balance sheet items that are usually in company reports. Assets are divided into 'fixed' assets, such as plant and property, which would take a long time to turn into cash, and 'current' assets, which should be convertible into cash within one year or less. Liabilities and equity are also itemised. As with the profit and loss account, the previous year's balance sheet may be included so that readers of the company report can spot any trends.

'Retained earnings' is an important item, as it is a bridge between the profit and loss account and the balance sheet. The profit after tax for this year is added to the 'retained earnings' from last year before deciding on the dividend distribution to shareholders. The remainder becomes the new 'retained earnings' amount. There are two important points to note: One is that dividends are not really an expense like interest paid to a bank for a loan. They are a distribution of profits to the owners of the business. The other is that 'retained earnings' do not just sit around in the bank account. Some may be used as a reserve, but more is likely to be re-invested to grow the business.

Table 5.4: Balance sheet at 31/12/2019 in £000s

ASSETS		LIABILITIES	
Fixed assets		Accounts payable	20,000
Land and property	200,000		
Plant and equipment	100,000		
Current assets		**Equity**	
Inventory (stock)	20,000	Shares	300,000
Account receivable	20,000	Retained earnings	30,000
Cash at bank	10,000		
Total assets	350,000		350,000

Double-entry bookkeeping

Most of us run our own finances on the basis of single-entry bookkeeping. We note money coming in and money going out. We take credit when we need to and pay it back according to the requirements of the bank or credit card company. We know that we own things which need to be replaced, and we try to save for holidays. In the case of major purchases, such as a house, we have to commit to a long-term mortgage and put a large proportion of our monthly income towards repaying it. The amount of detail we need when managing our cash flow depends on personal preference but may also depend on lifestyle stage. For example, when a new a baby comes along, financial management may have to be tighter than it was beforehand.

Companies in the UK are required to record their transactions according to Generally Accepted Accounting Practice (GAAP) – ie the accounting standards published by the UK's Financial Reporting Council (FRC). There is also an international set of standards for international companies: the International Financial Reporting Standards (IFRS). A fundamental principle in accounting standards is that double-entry bookkeeping must be used.

In double-entry bookkeeping, every debit has a credit. This concept is based on the core accounting equation:

Assets = Liabilities + Owners' Equity

Any transaction that the company undertakes is recorded in two accounts, according to the principle that a debit will increase an asset account and decrease a liability or equity account. A credit will decrease an asset account and increase a liability or equity account. In the case of the day-to-day operating activities that make up the profit and loss account, the principle is that revenues are credits (profit being a contribution to equity), and costs are debits. Table 5.5 provides some examples:

Table 5.5: Typical double-entry bookkeeping entries

Description	Amount	DEBIT	CREDIT
Purchase of computer equipment	£30,000	Equipment (increase asset)	Accounts payable (increase liability)
Payment to computer equipment supplier	£30,000	Accounts payable (decrease liability)	Cash at bank (decrease asset)
Cash sale	£3,000	Cash (increase asset)	Revenue (increase equity)
Payment of office rent	£6,000	Rent (decrease equity)	Cash (decrease asset)

This seems complicated, but it has a significant advantage when a company is processing thousands of transactions a day. If every item is recorded correctly, when all account categories are added up, total debits should equal total credits, and the balance of transactions should be zero. This is called a *trial balance*. If total debits are not equal to total credits, then an error has been made and needs to be corrected. A trial balance does not pick up all possible errors, but it is a vital check before drafting financial statements.

Another advantage is that double-entry bookkeeping creates accounts for particular profit and loss and balance sheet items, and the change in value of those items is clearly tracked as debits and credits are posted. The busiest account is often 'Cash'. A less-busy account would be a fixed asset such as a building, where the only movement in the year might be depreciation.

You may not get involved in the details of double-entry bookkeeping, but you need to know that it is the foundation for the accuracy and clarity of the financial statements. Auditors will check particular accounts and finance processes to ensure that they have confidence in the statement being made to shareholders.

Cash flow

Company directors like to see a healthy top line (revenue) as it is a strong indication that the company is making products and services that customers want to buy. If the company is growing, investors will want to buy its shares. Company directors also want to see good profits; without them, the company is not sustainable. Nevertheless, even with good revenue and profits, a company can go bankrupt. This happens when a company runs out of cash. The timing of cash flow differs from the timing of transactions recorded in the accounts. Making good sales is one thing, but the timing of customer payments is critical. Are they going to pay in time for the company to pay its monthly wages? If not, how is the wages cash to be generated? Can the company delay payment to its suppliers without incurring a penalty, or can it borrow from the bank? There are different types of cash flow, as shown in Table 5.6:

Table 5.6: Cash flow types

Cash flow from operations	Cash flow from investment	Cash flow from finance
INFLOW	**INFLOW**	**INFLOW**
Cash paid by customers	Sales of equipment	Cash received when shares sold
	Sales of part of the company	Cash from a bank loan
OUTFLOW	**OUTFLOW**	**OUTFLOW**
Cash paid to suppliers	Buying equipment	Paying a dividend
Cash paid to employees	Buying a subsidiary	Paying back a loan
Tax paid		

A simple cash flow statement is shown in Table 5.7. Negative figures are in brackets so they can be easily identified. This is a standard convention in financial reports. As you may have guessed, looking back at cash flow is not very helpful if you are trying to avoid a cash crisis. It is cash flow forecasts that drive the business. Directors want to see cash flow forecasts by month for twelve months ahead to make sure that the company can meet its obligations.

What you are selling to your customer affects their cash flow, whether they are a consumer or a business. Consumers are used to managing cash flow by using credit cards, but some consumers do not control them well. Credit card companies usually cover suppliers, but there are categories of purchase where you need to check customers' credit ratings. Companies also have credit ratings, indicating how well they can meet their financial obligations, and credit controllers undertake credit checks on companies.

To avoid putting your employer's cash flow at risk, avoid selling to a customer who may not be able to pay. Equally, it is not good for the customer if you sell them something which jeopardises their cash flow. There are some interesting grey areas, though; for example, a salesperson selling to a company with rapid growth was told by the credit controller that sales volume would have to be curtailed because they kept exceeding the credit limit advised by a credit rating agency. The customer's 'credit limit' is how much, and for how long, they can owe money to a supplier. The salesperson took the credit controller to meet the accountant at the customer. The accountant explained the customer's real financial health, which was somewhat better than the out-of-date information held by the credit rating agency. The salesperson and credit controller agreed to extend the customer's credit terms in return for a higher proportion of their purchases. This proved to be a 'win-win'.

Always discuss payment schedules, credit terms and cash flow impact with customers. There may be constraints, but there may also be opportunities to grow with an ambitious customer.

Table 5.7: Cash flow statement for Period 6 (ending 31 May 2020) in £000s

Beginning balance	200,000
Cash receipts from customers	100,000
Cash paid to suppliers	(50,000)
Wages and salaries	(50,000)
Purchase of equipment	(50,000)
End balance	150,000

Financial ratios

Companies measure their financial health with a number of calculations applied to their annual or quarterly accounts. These are important to shareholders and investment analysts. In accounting, several different categories of ratios are used, including:

- Valuation

- Dividends (returns to shareholder)

- Growth rate

- Financial strength (mainly focusing on cash availability)

- Profitability

- Efficiency

- Management effectiveness

The rest of this section provides more information about some of the specific ratios within each category.

Valuation

Earnings per share – This ratio is calculated by dividing the net profit by the number of shares held by investors during the year. For example, if the net profit was £20,000 and the number of shares was 15,000, the EPS was £1.33. This is an important figure for investors deciding whether to buy the company's shares, but it is only useful when compared to other companies and average sector performance. If you are researching a customer's financial status, do so alongside their competitors and/or market leaders in their industry sub-sector.

Price/earnings ratio – This ratio examines the relationship between the share price of the company (as quoted on the stock exchange) and the earnings per share. To calculate this ratio, divide the share price by the earnings per share (see above). If the share price is £20 and the earnings per share are £1.50, the P/E ratio is £13.33. A ratio that increases over time indicates that the company is popular with investors; one that goes down suggests that investors have lost confidence in the company's performance.

There are a number of other ratios involving the share price and annual performance measures, but the P/E ratio is the most commonly quoted. In your proposal to customers, consider how your solution will affect the valuation of the company. You cannot make claims about how it might increase the share price, but these ratios might look better in the future if you can help the customer to reduce costs or increase income.

Dividends (returns to the shareholders)

Dividend yield – This ratio shows how much the company has paid out in dividends relative to share price. For investors, this shows how much cash their investment is generating for them. The dividend per share is divided by the share price (x 100 as this ratio is typically expressed as a percentage). The company will have designated an amount from profit for distribution to shareholders, which must be divided per share to get the dividend per share. If the amount for distribution is £15,000 and the number of shares is 15,000, the dividend per share is £1. If the share price is £20, the dividend yield is 5%. If companies distribute most of their profit as dividends, they may do so to attract investors. However, the company also needs to build up reserves for investment in the sustainability of the business, so shareholders are sometimes expected to accept lower dividends in the short term to achieve more in the long term. During an economic recession, dividends may even be withheld.

Growth rate

Sales growth over time – It is useful for investors to track the sales of a company over time and the earnings per share of the company over time. To calculate growth, take this year's sales (or EPS), subtract the figure from last year and divide the result by last year's total. If this year's sales were £25 million and last year's were £20m, the difference of £5m is applied to the £20m to give us a growth rate of 25%. You need the last five annual reports to see what the growth trend looks like. Is there a steady growth pattern, a decline, or an erratic performance? Some companies report their year-on-year growth over the past five years, and many investment analysts' websites would cover such information. Remember that although investment analysts generally like growth, it has to be judged alongside other measures. Growth that was positive but costly, resulting in reduced profitability, does not necessarily reflect a smart strategy.

Capital expenditure – A company investing in capital expenditure is generally regarded as a positive indicator. Once again, the devil is in the detail. Some companies lease capital equipment and pay rental on a regular term rather than taking a big cash flow hit upfront. They would argue that this gives them more financial flexibility. Many companies now rent computer applications (software-as-a-service) rather than managing them in-house because they perceive that specialist providers can manage IT more effectively. How does your proposal to the customer affect their potential for organic growth (growth from within rather than growth by acquiring another company)?

Financial strength (mainly focusing on cash availability)

Quick ratio – This is also known as the 'acid' test of a company's liquidity. To calculate it, look at the 'current assets' on the balance sheet. Subtract 'stock/inventory' from the total and divide it by the current liabilities. If 'current assets' are £100,000 and 'stock/inventory' is £30,000, you have a remainder of £70,000. If current liabilities are £50,000, the quick ratio is 1.4. A ratio over 1 indicates that a company is well-placed to meet all its current obligations to creditors, which is a good thing. However, if this ratio is high, then the company could be holding too much cash in reserve rather than using it.

Current ratio – This is a simple division of current assets by current liabilities. In the quick ratio example, the current ratio would be 2. Remember that when a company buys something, this reduces its cash reserves; this means there needs to be counterbalancing improvements in other financial performance measures.

Debt to equity – It is important to know how much the company is borrowing. Excessive borrowing means that a company is paying a lot in interest, which reduces profits and can mean that it is vulnerable to changes in its lenders' policies. On the balance sheet, debt is itemised separately from shareholder equity. To get the debt-to-equity ratio, divide the debt by the equity. If the company has a debt of £10,000 and equity of £20,000, the debt-to-equity ratio is 0.5 (or 50%).

Investment analysts often refer to a company's 'gearing'. A proportion of debt to equity over 50% is considered a high gearing and high risk because lenders can call in debts and bankrupt a company. Debt is easier to access than equity-to-finance company expansion, so it can provide flexibility. A debt-to-equity ratio of 25–49% would be considered a reasonable balance. One under 24% would be regarded as a low gearing and an indication that the company avoids risk. As with all other ratios, comparisons with other companies and industry 'norms' are appropriate. Your customer may need to borrow to buy your solution. How does that affect their gearing?

Profitability

Gross margin (GM) – If you subtract the cost of goods sold from the value of sales, you have gross margin. If you divide that figure by number of sales and multiply by 100, you have the gross margin percentage. So, if sales are £100,000 and the direct stock and labour costs associated with those sales were £50,000, the GM is 50%. GM is important to companies as a management indicator, but it is the profit after overheads that attracts more attention on the stock market.

Operating profit/Net profit margin – If you subtract all costs from sales, you have the net profit (or operating profit); if you divide that figure from sales and multiply by 100, you have the percentage profitability. For example, if sales are £100,000 and all costs are £90,000, the net profit is £10,000 and the net profit margin is 10%. As with other measures, profitability is only useful when compared with other measures, such as the company's performance in the past, the norms of the industry sector, and analysts' expectations given the economic climate.

Profitability is regarded as a significant indicator of financial health and the success of the company's strategies. Investors also admire evidence of efficient cost control. Many companies find it easier to increase profits by controlling costs rather than increasing sales. Sometimes that is necessary, but the relentless pursuit of cost reductions can be harmful. Which costs get slashed first? Often it is training and marketing, both of which are investments for the future of the company even though they are classified as costs. If skills are eroded and communications with customers decrease in quality and quantity, it becomes even more difficult to make sales. In most cases, you will be explaining how your solution helps a customer to improve sales or reduce costs, both of which have a direct effect on profitability.

Efficiency

Asset utilisation ratios – These measure how effective the company is at using assets to generate cash. For example, the debtors or receivables turnover, which is calculated by dividing total credit sales (top line in the profit and loss account) by the debtors/accounts receivable figure on the balance sheet, indicates how good the company is at collecting money from customers and driving it back into the business. If sales are £3m and accounts receivable £400,000, receivables turnover is 7.5. If we divide 365 days in the year by 7.5, we get 48.7. This suggests that this company takes about 49 days to collect a debt. Given that the 'norm' for credit terms is 30 days, that could be a problem. Remember that problems are all contextual. If extended credit is common in the sector where this company operates, a sluggish receivables turnover may be acceptable. Alternatively, a company might offer discounts for early payment to gain a competitive edge on receivables turnover.

Another example of asset utilisation is stock turnover, which is a similar calculation. If sales are £3m and stock/inventory is £500,000, stock turnover is 6 (or 61 days). Is that good or bad? It depends on how perishable the stock is! For fresh food, this would be a disaster; for washing machines, less so. Fast-moving consumer goods companies would generally expect to get their products turning over within twenty to thirty days. In B2B manufacturing, sixty to seventy-five days is more likely. Modern thinking on stockholding is that it is expensive and improving stock turnover is healthy for cash flow and profitability.

Other efficiency ratios include turnover per employee and total asset turnover. Does your solution help the customer to get more from their assets?

Management effectiveness

Return on assets (ROA) – Dividing net profit by total assets is a way of assessing how good the management team of a company are at 'sweating the assets' to generate income for shareholders. If net profit is £10,000 and the total assets are £50,000, then the ROA is 0.2. This ratio needs to be evaluated by changes over time and comparisons with other companies with a similar asset base.

Return on equity (ROE) – This ratio is an indicator of the management's capability to generate profits. In this case, you divide the net profit by the shareholders' equity. If net profit is £10,000 and equity is £25,000, the ratio is 0.4. The higher the ratio, the better use the company is making of its assets.

Return on investment (ROI) – This can apply to any project within the company. Typically, if you are making a sales proposal, you must estimate the ROI to the customer of making the purchase. The ROI formula is straightforward:

$$\text{ROI} = \frac{(\text{Gain from Investment} - \text{Cost of Investment})}{\text{Cost of Investment}}$$

The calculation is easy enough if you are examining the investment after it has been made and fully utilised, but how do you estimate the gain in advance? If other customers have undertaken similar projects, you may have a good idea of costs and gains. Many companies explain ROI with online customer case studies. But if the product is new, there is a high degree of risk in estimating gains, especially as they constitute part of the promise to the customer.

You also have to take into account the product's life cycle. It may last for several years. ROI calculations use Net Present Value (NPV) to account for the difference in the value of money over time due to inflation. Even when inflation is relatively low, NPV is applied using discount rates to reflect the reducing value of returns over time.

Another consideration is comparing the product's ROI to the ROI of doing nothing or other choices that the customer might have (substitute products/services). Each ROI calculation is unique, so consult with colleagues in finance to make sure that you have covered everything relevant. Consider:

- Does this product enable the customer to get more from their assets (allowing them to reduce stock levels or debtor days)?

- Does it help them to improve productivity in some way (eg fewer machine breakdowns, faster throughput or reduced over time)?

- Does it have any indirect benefits such as improved sales or reduced sales costs through improved customer relationships?

- Does it help them to reduce administrative costs or legal liabilities?

It can take time to build a convincing ROI calculation. Make sure you cover the obvious and the less obvious, such as avoidance of the hidden costs of 'papering over the cracks' that are never captured in official records. Consider also that a return on an investment may not always be a tangible financial gain. Investments may be made to generate customer goodwill or to encourage support from local communities. Such returns are difficult to measure, but some attempt should be made to track the outcomes from any investment.

Where is the customer?

As business development professionals, we may wonder why company reports and investment analysts' calculations do not have specific sections for customer-related metrics. For example, where is customer retention and customer satisfaction?

Business consultant and author Frederick Reichheld (2003) has argued that the one number that an investor needs to know in relation to a company is a calculation of how many customers would recommend that company minus how many would not – he has called this the 'Net Promoter Score'.

A happy customer is more likely to buy from you again and recommend you to their family and friends or post favourable online reviews. In the case of B2B, satisfied customers might comment favourably on good suppliers to their business network. It is important to know if our customers are satisfied. How can we know? At this point, people often talk about 'word of mouth'. Think about the last time you were enthusiastic about a product, such as a computer game. You probably told your friends about it, and some may have started playing the same game, because your recommendation reduced the risk to them of trying it. That is word of mouth, and your actions have helped the company that makes the game to gain new customers. The reverse also applies. If you hate a product or service and tell your friends about it, you are generating negative word of mouth, which may result in the supplier losing potential customers.

For marketing and sales professionals, it is a challenge to try and quantify the value of 'word of mouth', even if, anecdotally, we know we are receiving recommendations. However, in recent years the Net Promoter Score (NPS)[7]

---

7 Net Promoter, Net Promoter Score and NPS are trademarks of NICE Systems, Inc., Bain & Company, Inc., and Fred Reichheld.

has emerged as a widely recognised measure of customer advocacy and is often quoted in company reports.

You may have experienced a typical customer satisfaction data-gathering exercise as a customer. After making a purchase, you may have received a text or email asking you how happy you were with the transaction on a scale of 1 to 10. Usually, this is followed by a second question asking how likely you are (also on a scale of 1 to 10) to recommend the product to your friends.

The results from the recommendation question are analysed cautiously by suppliers. Customers scoring 9 or 10 are considered 'promoters'; those scoring 7 or 8 are 'passives' or 'neutrals', and anyone scoring 6 or under is someone who might be likely to generate negative word of mouth about the product, so they are called 'detractors'. If a supplier has more promoters than detractors, the company has a positive NPS. NPS is usually expressed as a ratio of promoters to detractors. If it is above 1, then the company can be confident that they are doing a good job and are likely to grow sales (Reichheld, 2003). NPS is not universally acclaimed by marketing researchers. Customer satisfaction and advocacy is multidimensional and complex, so reducing it to a single measure is simplistic. However, simple measures have great appeal, as they provide an easy means of comparison between competitors. 'Our NPS is consistently 10–15% higher than our nearest competitor' is a strong message.

A measure like NPS is vital because satisfied and happy customers usually provide the majority of organic growth in established companies, and their recommendations are key to acquiring new customers for all types of organisations. Satisfied customers tend to stay with their chosen suppliers, so they become 'retained' customers, who buy more next time they have a need for the chosen supplier's category of products or services. Increasing the customer retention rate by 2% might have the same impact on the profitability of the company as reducing costs by up to 10%.

Tracking customer satisfaction through measures such as NPS makes business sense. By asking customers how they feel, suppliers gain valuable feedback and data, which enables them to improve customer experience. NPS can also provide reassurance for potential customers. If a purchasing decision-maker has access to this figure, they know how the prospective supplier is perceived by customers. A higher NPS than competitors could be vital in getting short-listed for a new invitation to tender.

Budgeting

So far in this chapter, we have looked at a company's financial performance from a historical perspective. Company reports are a record of past performance, not an indication of future performance, but companies do have to look to the future and plan for it. Business plans look forward to the asset acquisition, marketing campaigns and other strategies that are going to sustain the company in years to come. The business plan usually has a horizon of three to five years, and it precedes the production of a budget for the forthcoming year.

'A budget is a systematic method of allocating financial, physical, and human resources to achieve strategic goals… The fast pace of technological change and the complexities of global competition make developing effective budgets both more difficult and more important.' (Andersen, 2000)

A budget is a view of how much should be spent on what throughout a year. Each departmental manager will negotiate a budget for their activities – a budget for IT equipment, a budget for bonuses, etc. Accurate costing information is essential for setting reasonable budgets.

Activity-based costing (ABC) is regarded by many as best practice in working out what it costs to do something within an organisation. It is an attempt to attribute overheads to activities, rather than spreading the costs across all activities. If accountants can improve the accuracy of costing as a basis for budgeting, departmental managers will have more confidence in the budgets. However, ABC may require the implementation of new technology – such as radio frequency identification devices (RFIDs) on items in the warehouse – and it also requires employees to record how long they spend on activities.

Despite the financial performance advantages observed by some researchers (eg Kennedy and Affleck-Graves, 2001), ABC can be complex to implement and therefore tends to be used in problem-solving or process analysis, rather than for regular reporting. It can be useful to a salesperson in demonstrating how a product/service adds value to a customer's operations, but you will need a financial colleague to help you to apply it.

Variance analysis

Internal meetings and board meetings examine the actual performance of the company week by week against the budget set at the beginning of the year. This is called variance analysis. This analysis determines whether persistent variances in a particular cost centre are because of environmental factors (such as a shortage of skills in a region or increased recruitment costs), poor performance by the relevant manager and their team, or budgeting errors. Then decisions have to be made about how to address the variance.

The financial perspective in the sales role

Apart from analysing your customers, you also need to be financially aware in order to understand your own contribution to your employer's financial performance. Take into account the following:

- **The role of targets** – In the case of sales, each salesperson's targets are a sub-division of the overall forecast for sales. This is the budgeted 'top line' on which all other budgets depend. In many companies, there is also a 'bottom-up' consultation with salespeople about achievable sales targets in the forthcoming year. However, we are all human and likely to underplay what might be achievable to protect our bonuses. Expect 'stretch' targets which reflect the company's ambitions, with potential adjustment for the peculiarities of your own territory or customer set.

- **You are part of a team delivering the top line** – Without the top line, the company fails. You are also the standard-bearer of the company's reputation, which has a financial value.

- **Discounts are a direct hit on profitability** – You will need a good business case to reduce the list price for a customer. Discounts are usually associated with large orders, which may be appropriate if you work for a process manufacturer who needs to keep the factory running 24/7. Price reductions should always be an exchange of value, such as a discount for early payment which improves cash flow or a reduction if the customer takes on some stock-handling and distribution, which would otherwise be a cost to the company.

- **Customers often ask for more time to pay their bills** – Essentially, they are asking, 'May we borrow from you rather than our bank, because they charge us interest and you don't?' (Technically, companies are permitted by UK law to charge interest on unauthorised late payments, but it is rarely done in practice.) If you allow extended credit, you are increasing your employer's financial risk and tying up money that is needed elsewhere in the business by reducing the receivable turnover.

- **Your manager expects you to keep within your budget** – They also expect you to document your expenses and commission claims accurately and submit them on time. The administration is the least glamorous aspect of the sales job, but colleagues depend on your co-operation. It is a 'just do it' situation.

If you are working with large customers, embrace activity-based costing as a way of understanding what it really costs to serve your customer so that you can get an accurate calculation of customer profitability. The detail will help you in value mapping with the customer and in understanding value co-creation.

Summary

In this chapter, we have looked at the financial knowledge you need to be an effective salesperson who is able to analyse your customer's financial performance and your proposal's impact on it. We have also considered how salespeople affect the financial performance of their employers.

6

Digital Knowledge

Introduction

In committing yourself to any profession these days, you will likely wonder how much of the job you do today will be automated in the future. At the turn of the twenty-first century, the IT industry seemed to be willing the digitalisation of sales with the launch of sales force automation (SFA) systems, which made it sound as if salespeople would be turned into robots. Although on some websites you might be met with an avatar to help you to buy something, so far it seems that the digitalisation of the economy is complementary to selling and has not replaced it. In the 1950s, it was pronounced that marketing would make salespeople redundant, and in the 1990s it was claimed that the Internet would make salespeople unnecessary; in fact, the number of people in sales executive, account management and business development roles increased significantly in the ten years after the financial crash of 2008 (ONS, 2018). Consumers are now used to mechanisation and digitisation when they buy things. We are used to vending machines, self-service checkouts, and purchasing insurance and books online. It is convenient, and all buyers like convenience. Nevertheless, where there is complexity, whether it is a high level of technical complexity or the nuances of personal taste, most buyers expect suppliers to have representatives who can discuss a product or service with them. It is undoubtedly convenient for the buyer if those representatives are complemented by online information and if they can access information via a laptop, and if lots of the follow-up can be done electronically.

The idea of automation has been with us for a very long time – at least 2,000 years. One of the first examples of automating sales was invented by Hero of Alexandria (Tybjerg, 2003), who gave us the earliest known vending machine. His machine dispensed holy water for religious worshippers at shrines. The customer put a coin in the slot at the top of the machine. The coin fell into a pan attached to a lever which then opened the valve to let a measured amount of holy water flow out. The pan continued to fill because of the weight of the coin, until it fell off, at which a counterweight would move the lever back and turn off the valve.

The aim of mechanisation and digitisation is convenience for both buyer and seller. Everyone can buy into simple transactions being automated, but the potential to use embedded technology to do more and more in the buyer–seller interface is huge, and there are good reasons for it. For example, the automated analysis of website viewing patterns, telephone calls and buying activity can help diagnose needs more quickly. Many things are possible with data mining, but we still have our limits for absorbing information, so the more the computer can do for us, the less energy we need to expend.

In his technology acceptance model, Fred Davis (1989) stated that users must believe that using the system will improve their job performance (perceived usefulness) and they must think that using the technology is easier than not using it (perceived ease of use). These two concepts are fundamental in the application of any technology, and they are particularly pertinent in applying technology to the field of selling. IT companies have invested millions in trying to make systems intuitive so that users like them. There are still many outdated and clunky systems in use, but you should be optimistic about digitisation enhancing your job in the years to come. And be assured that customers still value human contact, as research from leading global consultancy McKinsey reveals: 'Companies that add the human touch to digital sales consistently outperform their peers. They achieve five times more revenue, eight times more operating profit, and, for public companies, twice the return to shareholders' (Angevine et al, 2018).

The external digital world

Information sources for buyers

In a later chapter, we discuss the value of the Internet for researching prospects and customers. It is wonderful to have so much information available, but you need to ensure that you are accessing quality information.

Consider where buyers go for information. According to research from CSO Insights (2018), buyers look for information from industry experts, the buyers' own experiences, supplier websites, industry events, peer/colleague comments, industry and professional online networks, industry publications, and trade media and general web searches before they would contact a salesperson. You need to be where they want to look, using similar sources, and trying to connect where buyers want to connect.

Automating transactional sales

It is likely that your employer enables customers to buy a variety of products online via an e-portal on the company's website or via e-marketplaces (also known as digital marketplaces). Typically, an online portal lets the customer quickly find the product category that they need and provides information with an option to contact an expert if needed, as well as the opportunity to place an order.

In 2015, BASF China announced the launch of its 1688.com store in China, becoming one of the first global companies to sell via Alibaba. Quoted in *Plastics News*

(Sun, 2015), Zheng Daqing, senior vice president of business and market development, Greater China, explained that 99% of Chinese companies are small and midsized, contributing 60% of China's GDP. BASF's aim in launching on the Alibaba platform was to provide a convenient and efficient platform for smaller companies to buy BASF products, and to provide faster access to information and support.

And B2B eCommerce company NuORDER has launched Online Trade Show, a B2B marketplace for wholesale buyers to discover new brands and place orders at any time from any device. The owner of one of the fashion brands involved in the pilot said that within a month she had been in contact with twenty new retailers. It had provided the opportunity for thousands of dollars' worth of new business (Savas, 2018).

As with websites, the expertise in making a company e-portal attractive to buyers lies with your marketing colleagues or their agencies. The principles of usefulness and ease of use are paramount. Content must be easy to read, relevant, compelling and up to date. Business users are just as likely as consumers to leave your portal if it is difficult to navigate or slow to respond. It is vital to generate trust online, and a strong offline brand will travel well onto the Internet. Buyers check the legal status of a company selling online along with their geographical location and trade reputation. Marketing may ask you for quotes from customers or case studies. Prospective buyers expect to see evidence of a company's current customers successfully using its products and services.

E-marketplace brands such as Alibaba and NuORDER are geared to driving even more categories of products and services to online self-service buying. These buying platforms are not your enemies. They can make you more productive and help you to focus on the innovative, risky and complex solutions where a purchasing decision-maker will value discussions with a salesperson.

As soon as a buyer hits the 'ask an expert' button on a website or portal, the door is open for a salesperson to have a conversation with an interested customer. The data that online trading generates will be fed into the CRM system, which will run analytics designed to pick up on buying patterns and send alerts when more relationship building could be helpful. Once again, technology is reducing your lead generation effort and giving you qualified prospects.

Social media

There are many advocates for using social media to find and nurture prospects. It is undoubtedly vital for B2C marketing departments to have a team trawling social media for consumer comments and making sure to help these customers find solutions as soon as possible. Social media comments also need to be analysed and fed into company strategy. There is evidence in B2C segments that relationship building with end-consumers via social media is beneficial for brands (see, eg, Wang and Kim, 2017).

In an article in *Computer Weekly* in 2014, the Head of Social Media at Marks & Spencer explains the importance of listening to customers on social media, noting that it enabled marketers to pick up on customer issues that would otherwise be missed. The article also mentions a significant increase in sales after the company spent two years on testing and analytics to improve its customers' experiences on its website (Baldwin, 2014).

To date, the main use of social media for salespeople has been to research customers and decision-makers. Following companies on LinkedIn and Twitter means that you see their statements about new policies, projects, premises or campaigns, and changes in company circumstances may present opportunities to offer a product or service. You can also use LinkedIn to research the names of key decision-makers within organisations, as well as information about their career path and interests. Not all companies use social media extensively in their communications mix, and some business decision-makers may prefer not to be on LinkedIn. There is no point trawling through social media, or posting blogs and vlogs to social media, if the contacts you want to make are just not there.

Some companies discourage social media use by employees as it is challenging to keep everyone's comments consistent with company communications policy. Nevertheless, research shows that use of social media in B2B contexts can improve sales performance and customer relationship quality (Schultz et al, 2012). Therefore, companies should use it proactively, provide infrastructure support for salespeople using it (eg marketing materials, links into the CRM system), and train salespeople in the best techniques. According to Schultz et al (2012), salespeople use social media:

- For awareness, prospecting and lead development

- To connect and develop relationships with current customers

- To ask for referrals from current customers to prospects

Be prepared to invest a lot of time in social selling. First, determine where your prospects are likely to be networking. While Twitter may help you to spot events that could open the door for a sale, general networking is also required. For B2B sectors, this is likely to be LinkedIn; for B2C, it may be Facebook or newer platforms. Note that Facebook is increasingly protective of users' privacy. There is advice about the use of social media in the Digital Skills chapter.

Digital infrastructure in organisations

Within your organisation, there will be a variety of systems which require your input and from which you can access data and analyses. Transaction recording, which used to be done by hand in ledgers, is now done predominantly at high speed by electronic equipment. Manual data entry persists but scanning and RFIDs are significantly reducing the need for it for everyday transactions. We tend to use our PCs and laptops for more creative work – drafting a report or a presentation or taking data out of the system for new analysis and discussion.

Most companies have automated financial systems, such as sales ledger, bought ledger, invoicing and payroll. For smaller companies, 'software-as-a-service' solutions are ideal. The software owner manages the software, so the company does not need its own servers to store data, nor does it have to maintain the hardware and software. The data sits in a secure data warehouse which could be many miles away, and the system functions are accessed online. This is often referred to as 'Cloud' computing. Larger companies are also renting process functions in this way. The availability, robustness, security and flexibility of IT systems are difficult to achieve from in-house management unless the company employs several experts.

Manufacturers have a system called material requirements planning (MRP) for production planning and stock control. Stock control will also feed into a more extensive network of supply chain management (SCM) functions, including logistics and purchasing. CRM – or account-based marketing (ABM) for B2B – organises and analyses data about customers. If you work in retail, the EPOS system is also a vital function for analysis of sales trends.

There will also be software devoted to making a sales rep more efficient and effective. It is sometimes called 'sales force automation' (SFA), but you may also hear the terms 'sales enablement technology' or 'the sales stack'.

SFA is designed to support sales activities, processes and administration. SFA will link with the CRM system to provide functions for lead development; its core functions are sales forecasting, sales reports and pipeline management dashboards. SFA may also include appointment scheduling, information gathering, needs assessment, online demonstrations, quote management, proposal building, contact management, channel relationship management, call reporting, expenses monitoring and much more.

The full portfolio of 'sales stack' software has been categorised by Gartner, the world's leading research and advisory company, and is shown in Tables 6.1 and 6.2 below:

TABLE 6.1: Gartner's five strategic categories of CRM sales technologies (Travis and Hansen, 2019)[8]

Stage in sales table	Description	Relevance
Plan	Systems that automate back-office sales processes	These technologies link a corporation's business objectives with its go-to-market plans. They often include processes such as demand planning, quote allocation, sales compensation plans and territory alignments. This work is often performed by operational resources, such as sales operations teams.
Enable	Systems that prepare users to sell by informing them what to sell and how to sell it	These systems most commonly involve sales training and coaching systems or learning management system (LMS) tools. They also include sales content management tools, where sales content is an essential tool for knowledge transfer to sales representatives. They may also include commercial data sources of firmographic and technographic information.
Execute	Systems for supporting and carrying out daily sales processes	Tools that are needed to execute the go-to-market plan. Includes a wide range of systems, from sales force automation (SFA) and lead management to less common tools like mobile sales
Monitor	Systems for monitoring and benchmarking sales execution against the corporation's KPIs, such as deal velocity or average pipeline growth	Commonly satisfied with the standard report and dashboard capabilities provided by SFA and lead management vendors
Optimise	Systems that use aggregated sales data to produce statistical insights about the quality of the organization's sales performance	New 'big data' solutions are emerging that apply advanced statistical techniques like machine learning to identify multidimensional correlations across a wide range of sales motions. This produces a complex set of performance benchmarks that identify the optimal mix of sales activities to affect outcomes. It also serves as a durable knowledge base that feeds the processes in the 'plan' category.

8   Used with kind permission from Gartner Inc.

Table 6.2: Example solutions within the Gartner Sales Technology Stack model (Travis and Hansen, 2019)[9]

Plan	• Incentive compensation management • Quota and territory management • Sales performance management planning • Strategic/key account management • ABM
Enable	• Sales engagement platforms • Sales training and coaching • Digital adoption solutions • Digital content management for sales • Data intelligence solutions for sales • Strategic/key account management • Partner data exchange platforms
Execute	• Sales force automation • Sales acceleration • Lead management • Partner relationship management • CPG, contracts, orders • Guided selling • Mobile sales productivity • Pricing optimisation • Digital content management for sales • Customer success management • Salesbots/VDSA • Social sales apps • ABM • Proposal management • Relationship intelligence
Monitor	• Sales analytics, with reports and dashboards • Customer success management • Gamification • Predictive sales forecasting • Sales engagement platforms
Optimise	• Territory and quota planning and optimisation • Sales advanced analytics • SPM modelling • Knowledge graphs for sales

Internal systems are usually integrated into enterprise resource planning (ERP) – the overarching system through which businesses collect, store, analyse and manage data.

---

9   Used with kind permission from Gartner Inc.

The business intelligence (BI) system is the interface between ERP and managers who need information to inform their decisions. As businesses accumulate more and more data, a sophisticated BI system that can deliver data in a usable format is essential.

Although BI systems with excellent query functions exist, you may be asked to gather some data and build a spreadsheet to do further analysis. Spreadsheets are derived from accounting forms; they are tables of data which can be added across horizontally and downwards vertically. The totals of the horizontal sub-totals and the vertical sub-totals should be the same. The benefit of computerisation is that formulae can be embedded into cells so that as a data change is made, the cells and totals affected by the change are automatically adjusted.

Spreadsheets are typically used for planning purposes so that the planning team can examine 'what-if' scenarios. For example, in sales forecasting, to see how a price increase could affect next year's sales, you could download current sales data into a spreadsheet and then apply changes. However, you may still need to draw data in from other sources, or make a judgement, to make your calculation robust. How many customers might switch away from your brand if prices are increased?

One of the first things a recruit into an organisation has to learn is the long list of acronyms used within the business, many of which are associated with internal systems. A basic understanding of all of them is essential. A detailed understanding of customer-related systems and how you can get value from them is worth learning as soon as possible.

How can we ensure that technology is useful? We all spend a lot of time with our electronic devices because they give us access to whole worlds of information and possibilities. The hardware speed and the software functionality improve continuously, so a textbook cannot advise on best practice as it would be quickly out of date. What it can provide is a way of evaluating what a system is achieving; Figure 6.1 shows an example of evaluation metrics for a sales application.

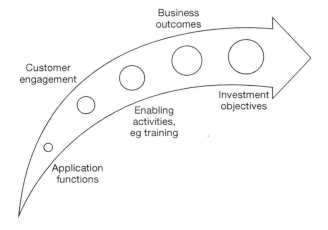

Figure 6.1: Factors involved in successful SFA implementation (adapted from Rogers, 2015)

Overall objectives for a sales-related IT investment include an increase in sales revenue or reducing the cost of selling, but if you jump from technology function to investment objective you miss the critical path between them. Unless the technology – either directly or via the salesperson – encourages the customer to engage with the company more than before, how can it increase sales? (Note: the customer has to agree to their data being used in ways which enable the company to make better-value offers to them.)

There have to be enablers for the salespeople, too. Meaningful outputs and measures are tangible indicators that using the system matters. It helps if the system is easy to use, but salespeople must also be able to access training so that they can continuously improve how they use it.

Customer benefits and enablers for salespeople are important, but we must consider one more factor before jumping to the investment objective. Business outcomes are different from investment objectives. If the system saves salespeople's time, improves their understanding of customers, reduces costs to serve the customer and enhances customer satisfaction, these are business outcomes which lead to the investment objective.

Historically, especially in the implementation of systems associated with customer management, companies have made mistakes by assuming that marrying poor processes with clunky software will reduce costs and increase revenue. Much has been learned about getting benefits from technology in the past twenty years. Systems in companies are likely to be more agile year-on-year and measured by the user satisfaction as well as financial and technical performance.

Customer relationship management and account-based marketing

Customer relationship management (CRM) did not start as an IT phenomenon. It is how a company manages its interactions with customers and prospects. Suppliers apply data analysis, initially the analysis of buying patterns, to help them make offers to the customer which are closer to their needs.

CRM systems were first launched in the 1990s, and for several years there were war stories of major failures in their implementation. The problem seemed to be that installing the software often made poor processes faster and more annoying for customers, and measurement of success was focused on internal efficiency and not the customer experience. A Morgan Stanley survey of chief information officers in 2002 reported that 55% of all CRM projects were regarded as failures and 20% might have damaged customer relationships (Rogers, 2003). The purpose of CRM should include the achievement of a positive customer experience, defined by Gartner (n.d.), the world's leading research and advisory company, as: 'the customer's perceptions and related feelings caused by the one-off and cumulative effect of interactions with a supplier's employees, systems, channels or products.'

CRM systems today are more likely to be assessed by a broad range of metrics which track cause and effect, from the efficiency of their functions and technical performance to customer satisfaction, employee satisfaction, levels of cross-selling, and reductions in cost per transaction. The value of CRM systems for the salesforce has been the visibility and accessibility of customer information. For example, it is now reasonably easy to see patterns in CLV, which provides an instant indicator of the customer's future potential rather than just current buying patterns.

A CRM system for a B2C company will be designed to interact automatically with reminders about regular orders, recommendations to try new products and information about special promotions. Many of these functions were pioneered by Amazon, which has always been online and needed to keep and grow business with customers entirely through algorithms that provided value to them, although some of the data going into the algorithm from customers' browsing behaviour could be random (a misspelling of a product name, for example) and generate unhelpful prompts. Nevertheless, we are now used to accepting prompting emails from brands that we allow to use our data.

In B2B, companies dealing with small businesses or offering standardised products can use similar techniques to tailor marketing messages using algorithms based on buying and browsing behaviour. RS Components (2016) are regular winners of B2B eCommerce awards:

> 'The company has made significant enhancements
> to search relevance and filtering, stock level visibility
> and quote functionality. In addition, site speed has
> been improved by 40%, over 120,000 new images,
> datasheets and videos have been added, and ongoing
> SEO has led to improved search engine visibility and
> ranking.'

With larger companies and larger customers, the terminology 'account-based marketing' has become widespread. The Information Technology Services Marketing Association (ITSMA) defines ABM as 'treating individual accounts as markets in their own right' (Burgess, 2016). ABM has the potential to integrate marketing, sales and service to ensure a better ROI for suppliers and better satisfaction for customers. According to research from ITSMA, 78% of B2B marketers say that ABM is important to their strategy, and demand is led internally by sales teams who want technology to generate better quality leads and help to prepare them for interactions with customers and prospects (Burgess, 2016).

ITSMA advises that there are four underlying principles for successful ABM (and they could apply equally to CRM):[10]

- **Customer focus and insight** – Understand the customer in enough depth to be able to create propositions that help them to achieve their objectives with their customers and stakeholders. Research and analytics are fundamental pre-requisites and co-requisites of ABM.

- **Focus on reputation and relationships** – Unsurprisingly, this is a complementary principle to customer focus. ABM objectives are usually focused on CLV and increased mindshare.

- **Partnership between sales and marketing** – Both sales and marketing share responsibility for improving customer understanding with a view to making more successful propositions that generate profitable revenue. They both have expertise to offer in prioritising the right accounts and designing integrated campaigns.

- **Tailored campaigns** – If customers are to be 'markets' in their own right, a variety of information sources have to be integrated:

  - The needs, opportunities and threats in the markets in which they operate.

---

10 Model originally published in Burgess (2016). Used with kind permission from ITSMA. For more than twenty-five years, ITSMA (the Information Technology Services Marketing Association) has led the way in defining, building and inspiring B2B services marketing excellence.

- The strengths and challenges of the organisation.
- The behaviours and preferences of individual buying decision-makers.

ABM systems should enable the analysis of these factors and lead to the design of effective marketing and sales activity that will engage the customer.

In major or key accounts, ABM marketing activity is designed to improve brand perceptions, build relationships and identify opportunities by generating account-specific thought leadership for meetings with the customer. It provides information for the account plan, and it helps the customer to perceive that this supplier understands their business needs in-depth and can offer tailored value propositions. Businesses judge ABM marketing activity by CLV and customer advocacy, contributing to revenue generation.

Digitally driven interactions

Digital systems drive much of our communication in the early twenty-first century. Any letter or report you write will be produced using word-processing software. Presentations get increasingly visually attractive as the software to create them becomes easier to use. Spreadsheets drive budgets and business cases. As our interactions with computers become more natural, it is likely that applications such as voice recognition will reduce the drudgery of typing and editing. In the meantime, use of these packages is a given for all professional jobs. The Digital Skills chapter offers some tips for enhancing your use of digital communications.

The Internet of Things (IoT)[11]

Since the turn of the twenty-first century, business analysts have been discussing the potential of sensor-enabled technologies. Imagine a future where customers' needs are met even before the customer or a salesperson has identified them. It is a future where the role of the salesperson is focused on high-profile change projects, rooted in idea generation and detailed knowledge, and supported by convincing analyses and what-if simulations. This sounds like an ideal scenario for the supplier – but what are the benefits for the customer?

Every day we co-operate as consumers with our favourite brands by accepting cookies on websites or sharing our location via our smartphones. Location and cross-device usage tracking are becoming a top priority for marketers because they enhance the consumer's shopping experience. We want to be prompted to take advantage of special offers when we are in supermarkets, even if that means being tracked around the aisles. If our favourite café chain knows that we are visiting a new town and directs us to the local branch with a voucher, we feel helped. We are grateful that RFIDs can tell us precisely where our parcels are in the delivery process. As more and more sensors are built into more and more products, we will share whatever information is necessary to take advantage of the potential of smart refrigerators, coffee machines, washing machines and televisions. This new wave of consumer value is powered by a concept called the 'Internet of Things':

> 'The Internet of Things (IoT) refers to a vast number of "things" that are connected to the internet so they can share data with other things – IoT applications, connected devices, industrial machines and more. Internet-connected devices use built-in sensors to collect data and, in some cases, act on it.' (SAS Institute, n.d.)

---

11   The section on the Internet of Things is adapted from an article by the author in the *International Journal of Sales Transformation* (Rogers, 2015).

The IoT is expected to reduce or replace human intervention in information flows with computer-to-computer interaction that will create new opportunities for convenience, efficiency and added value.

IoT is with us in business markets too. Jet engines, oil rigs, and mining and forestry equipment all benefit from embedded sensors to indicate how efficiently they are running and when they might need maintenance or replacement parts. Consultants IHS Markit forecasted in 2017 that the number of connected IoT devices worldwide would rise 12% each year, from 27 billion in 2017 to 125 billion in 2030 (IHS, 2017). Given events in 2020, that might turn out to be a modest estimate. Despite concerns about IoT being over-hyped, companies are innovating and developing solutions that improve their customers' experiences. For example, IBM's 2015 alliance with The Weather Company[12] combined cloud-based BI systems with data from over 100,000 weather sensors to enable customers to understand the impact of weather on business outcomes and respond to those opportunities and threats in tactical and strategic ways (Barker, 2015).

Who benefits? Utility companies, agriculture, fashion, horticulture, public services, food retail, media companies, the supply chain partners of these sectors, and more.

The adoption of IoT is driven by the degree to which *the customer* can realise benefits. Asset management is critical in sectors such as oil exploration, electricity generation and mining. Customers save money because machine downtime is reduced. In stock management, the cash benefits are faster responsiveness and less obsolescence. Companies can enhance product development, atmospherics, merchandising and sales promotions with the information generated from monitoring consumers' behaviour in a retail outlet or online.

---

12   The Weather Company became a subsidiary of the Watson & Cloud Platform business unit of IBM in 2016.

Potential benefits are limitless, but – as with previous waves of technology in the selling and buying processes – IoT applications must be designed to answer the 'So what?' challenge. In this wave of technology, something more than convenience is on offer. The survival of forestry businesses can depend on the uptime of equipment operating in harsh environments, the survival of logistics businesses can rely on optimum use of fuel, and the survival of food companies can depend on monitoring hygiene in their factories. Communities depend on enhancements to responsiveness in water management. The IoT helps suppliers and their customers manage risks and reduce costs, thus generating new waves of value creation.

The idea of co-creation of value between supplier and customer is often criticised as naïve, as customers control their operational environment and therefore how much or how little value-in-use they get from any supplier's products and services. Nevertheless, concepts such as vendor-managed inventory have succeeded where there is a mutual commitment to using shared information to improve joint-decision-making leading to mutual benefits such as better cash flows, less obsolescence and faster stock turnover.

Virtual reality (VR)

When we order a new kitchen, the sales representative may show us a virtual reality (VR) model of the design so that we can imagine walking into our kitchen after the work has been done. Similarly, in business markets, customers can see demonstrations of the machinery they want to buy, the office they wish to refit or the new product they want to develop.

VR can also be used in training. Scenarios delivered via VR headsets can help you practise generating rapport, negotiating with purchasing, giving presentations, dealing with customer complaints and working with colleagues. Like all technologies, it will get cheaper and easier to use so that it can be a regular element in training and development of salespeople over their careers.

Artificial intelligence (AI)

'Top sales teams, in particular, are realizing the power of using AI to craft compelling customer experiences, focusing specifically on automatically recommending products to customers based on their preferences. The technology has become the top growth area for sales teams, and its adoption is forecast to grow 155% over the next two years.'

— Devon McGinnis, Senior Marketing Manager at Salesforce (2019)

Science fiction has explored the possibility of intelligent machines for many decades. We love the idea of robots which can take on tedious tasks and do them better than humans. To do this, they need to be able to process visual and auditory input and make decisions. On the one hand, fiction has celebrated friendly robots such as Marvin, the paranoid android in Douglas Adams' *Hitchhiker's Guide to the Galaxy*, K9 in *Doctor Who* and R2-D2 in *Star Wars*, but there have also been robots or computers who have represented evil intelligence, such as HAL 9000 in *2001: A Space Odyssey*. This feeds on humans' fear that machines will take over their jobs and ruin their lives. This fear has a history in the Swing Riots of the 1830s, when agricultural labourers smashed up threshing machines, and the Luddites, who smashed up textile machinery around twenty years earlier.

We already use chatbots and avatars (both are essentially a computer-driven 'person' interacting with customers by text or voice) on websites to guide customers, but the future is not android salespeople.

Discussions about artificial intelligence (AI) in sales should be seen not as a revolution but an evolution from the software we see today. AI lets businesses apply more powerful algorithms and data processing to two core elements of the sales job – interacting with customers and analysing customer needs.

Interaction

User interfaces are improving and voice recognition is becoming widespread. It is now possible for algorithms to recognise speech patterns and respond with relevant actions or information. The hope here is not just that customers can have a frictionless response to a transactional purchase ('Send me six boxes of widgets, product number x3228, by Friday') but that salespeople can quickly access information. Instead of trawling through a company report to find a fact about a customer, a simple query of 'What was Rowin & Co's expenditure on capital equipment last year?' will call up the answer. Or, instead of trawling through your emails for customer interactions, you could ask: 'What was the last incoming query we had from Rowin & Co?' There are digital assistants available in the consumer world, and it is likely that more sophisticated models will soon be available on our work laptops or mobiles. AI can also augment meetings and presentations by making information and visuals available as you need them.

Analytics

Modelling and predicting the behaviour of materials is common in science and engineering, and many CRM systems already have some degree of predictive analytics based on customer buying behaviour patterns.

There are huge amounts of data about companies and individuals in the public domain. In the past, salespeople had to search manually for news about companies which might give up-to-date information about their immediate buying environment – news such as a merger or investment in a new plant. Tasks like this can now be automated.

AI's ability to process this data to identify buying prompts and indicators of sales success will become more sophisticated over time. This will benefit salespeople, who can offer value to customers before customers think of it themselves, as well as for customers, who can make faster progress with suppliers who anticipate their needs.

Summary

This chapter has reviewed some of the software and systems that you are likely to come across in your sales role and discussed how these systems are evolving. Selling remains a role which requires human judgement and empathy; therefore, all technology applied to selling should be usable and useful, delivering tangible business benefits by supporting salespeople and customer decision-makers.

PART 2

THE SKILLS OF A WORLD-CLASS SALES EXECUTIVE – PREPARING TO SELL

7

Sales Planning And Preparation

Introduction

Business involves a lot of planning. Although many companies' growth has been opportunistic, even that can be attributed to the unwritten plan in the entrepreneur's head to fill an observed customer need. A company needs to present plans to its financers – shareholders, venture capital companies and banks. Good planning ensures that a company makes efficient progress towards its goals, rather than wasting effort or doing the wrong things.

Salespeople have a role in planning. You have to help to implement the sales plan, but you also have to gather information to feed into the reviews of the plan and improving future plans. You should also have a plan for achieving your goals, both short-term and long-term. Where do these plans come from?

Understanding sales forecasts and targets

The sales forecast for the company and your individual sales target are outcomes from the business planning process which most sizeable companies undertake every year, looking three to five years ahead. There is some top-down planning – establishing what the company needs to achieve for shareholders and what it can achieve in the current business environment – and some bottom-up planning, where individuals and departments present their understanding of what can be achieved. All the granular plans at customer and territory level need to add up to what has been promised to the shareholders in the overall business or corporate plan, as shown in Figure 7.1.

In short, all business plans consist of what the company wants to achieve and how it will do it. The 'what' is summed up in 'objectives' and the 'how' is summed up in 'strategies'; for example, 'Over the next three years, we will gain a 5% market share in the affluent 50–65 age group car insurance segment by offering higher levels of personal service than our competitors.' Poor-quality plans mix up objectives and strategies or express them vaguely. Verbs such as 'maximise', 'minimise' and 'grow' are not specific or measurable. Managers will often refer to SMART objectives. SMART is an acronym for:

- Specific

- Measurable

- Assignable (to a person or function)

- Realistic

- Time-limited

People who work for an organisation need to know its high-level objectives and their role within it. There is an anecdote of doubtful origin about a politician visiting NASA (National Aeronautics and Space Administration) in the early 1960s and asking a man in overalls what he did. Instead of saying 'I mend the plumbing', he replied, 'I'm sending a man to the Moon.' Knowing the big picture and the big purpose of your employer can be very motivating. You may be asked to attend a 'kick-off' meeting where senior managers explain the company's overall objectives and strategies.

Company objectives are often expressed in terms of revenue growth, profitability and returns to shareholders.

Feeding into the corporate objectives will be marketing objectives, expressed in terms of market share, customer satisfaction or retention, and investment in new products/services. According to McDonald and Rogers (2017), 'Marketing plans… provide a rigorous approach to matching company capabilities to customers' needs and planning how value is delivered to the customer, as well as how it is communicated.'

Corporate plan								
Marketing plan								Other functional plans
Plans per division								
Key account management overview and plan			Major accounts plan	Plan for mid-tier		Consolidated segment plan		
Key account plan 1	Key account plan 2	Key account plan 3		Mid-tier sector plan 1	Mid-tier sector plan 2	Small customers segment plan 1	Small customers segment plan 2	
Action plans and links to functional plans			Plans per sales-person	Plans per salesperson		Territory plans		
						Plans per salesperson		

Figure 7.1: (adapted from McDonald and Rogers, 1998)

Marketing strategies are usually expressed as Ps:

- **Product** – launches, withdrawals, brand extensions, etc
- **Place** – which retail outlets or online, mobile or other channels to use to reach customers
- **Promotion** – what marketing messages, through which media
- **Price** – pricing relationship to costs, competitor prices and customer expectations

In the case of services, the marketing plan also covers the skills of **People**, **Physical Evidence** of the service and **Process** effectiveness.

Market share of a particular industry or consumer segment can be quantified as a sales forecast because the market will be sized (based on government statistics) and therefore a given percentage of it can be calculated. However, the dynamics between a market share objective and the sales forecast are subject to other tests.

Using statistical trends in forecasting

Companies can use statistical trends to test achievability. You don't have to be a statistician to appreciate that it is reasonable to examine what has been achieved in recent years with known resources and extrapolate what might be achieved next year with the same resources (or a measurable change in resources).

Moving average

A popular and straightforward trend calculation is the moving average. It involves taking sales data from particular periods, smoothing out anomalies through averaging and then carrying forward the trend. It is recalculated as new data becomes available. For example, the moving average of quarterly sales would be calculated by taking the sales average from June/July/August, then the sales average from July/August/September, then August/September/October, etc. This method has some value for short-term projections in stable selling conditions and provides a baseline of expected outcomes if nothing changes.

Quarterly revenue forecast

Table 7.1 shows a quarterly revenue forecast. It starts with a basic forecast based on last year's activity. However, 2020 was not like 2019, and by the end of March it was clear that business activity would be severely curtailed in most sectors. The second line predicts the impact of the lockdown associated with the coronavirus crisis (with the known effect at the end of March 2020 as an indicator). This company has historically lost customers at the rate of 5% of turnover, so this has also been calculated. The company has opened new online channels in response to the lockdown, which are intended to counteract loss of business. Once the model is established, the company is also planning a short-term advertising campaign. When these effects are calculated, the forecast is complete.

Table 7.1: Quarterly sales forecast in £000s at 31/03/2020

	Q120	Q220	Q320	Q420	Q121
Core forecast based on last year's sales	154	175	183	194	161
External impact	(5)	(60)	(40)	(20)	
Attrition at 5%	(7)	(9)	(9)	(10)	(8)
New channel activity		10	25	35	20
Radio advertising			5	15	10
Total	142	116	164	214	183

Most statistical methods involve 'smoothing'. This means that past performance is projected into the future in a straight line, assuming consistent growth. Business patterns can be volatile, though, and there are other methods which can predict spikes in sales figures through 'experiential roughing'. In other words, on the basis of past experience, the plan includes predictable peaks and troughs. Good forecasting involves a combination of evaluation of statistical trend information and professional judgement.

Scenario planning

Statistical analyses about the economy and trends in relevant industries (supplier and customer environments) must inform the sales forecast. You cannot sell more when customers cannot afford to buy more. Predictions should be subject to some scenario planning.

Scenario planning has been used for military purposes to ensure that a strategy can adapt to the surprising outcomes that may emerge from changing factors in war. Their use in business was pioneered by Shell. The oil industry is particularly sensitive to political shocks; business customers and consumers buy less in times of political and economic uncertainty. The exception is when hoarding behaviour leads to expected shortages. New technologies may inspire new waves of investment and/or change the way people buy. Social change is also worth discussion – television programmes can drive influential campaigns, such as aversion to single-use plastic as packaging.

Scenario planning can be complex, and companies would typically have about four scenarios to plan for, with one underpinning the core plan. Some organisations approach future scenarios in an exploratory and creative way, such as with a long-term outlook for twenty-five years. The process involves noting probable future conditions and their impacts (see Figure 7.2) and then considering how to respond to those conditions. This process will guide you in deciding which factors must be fed into the sales forecast and which might be side-lined or managed via contingency plans. Contingency plans are alternatives to the core plan; typically, they describe what to do in case of improbable but high-impact events. 'Although it is surprisingly hard to create good ones, they help you ask the right questions and prepare for the unexpected. That is hugely valuable' (Roxburgh, 2009).

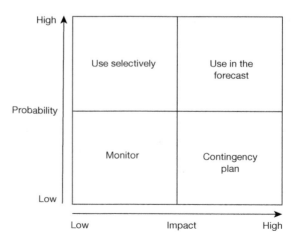

Figure 7.2: Scenario planning

Statistical analyses of company performance, extrapolating from the past into the future, must also be examined. Large companies are likely to use a variety of statistical techniques to explore future patterns of sales. The first outputs are based on steady-state resourcing. When a company chooses to employ more salespeople or agents, run an advertising campaign or offer a price promotion, the planners have to make assumptions about the positive impact of those decisions on sales performance. Judgemental factors must be analysed. What do experts in our field say will happen? What can we deduce from our experience? Most importantly, what do customers say they are going to buy next year?

A sales forecast figure is critical in business. It becomes a promise to shareholders about the value that their investment will generate. From the sales plan, the operations team can plan what needs to be produced and when, and the finance team plan for the necessary borrowing to keep cash flow positive.

There are also interdependencies between plans per key account or market segment. Value for customers is achieved through R&D, manufacturing, delivery and service. Whatever you plan for has to be delivered by colleagues across the business. You need to work with them to make plans come alive.

Prioritising customers to grow account value

When it comes to applying your own your time to achieve your personal objectives, first decide how much time to allocate to each of your customers. Beware of common pitfalls in customer portfolio management. The customers who are the biggest in terms of current spend are not necessarily deserving of the majority of your time. You do not want to be complacent about their business, or about spotting opportunities for further upselling, but you do need to consider that the future potential of smaller customers may be critical to building up your sales success. Equally, do not assume that all customers want to be 'key accounts'; some will be happy to buy in bulk over the Internet on standard terms. And if 'key accounts' are always asking about discounts, they are not key. Maybe the only way you can keep such accounts happy is by withdrawing your expensive time and persuading them to also buy in bulk over the Internet on standard terms.

Figure 7.3 shows a simple way of categorising your portfolio of customers. It is consistent with the matrices explained in this book, and it enables you to make some quick calculations about your own territory or customer portfolio.

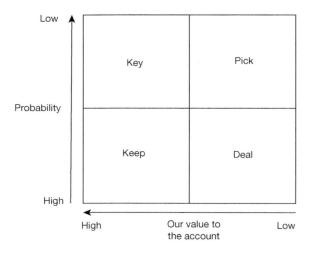

Figure 7.3: Strategic value of accounts

The strategic value of an account to a supplier will probably be measured by profitable growth potential. Companies often observe that where there is a joint investment in new projects, there is a 'key' relationship. Supplier and customer perceive strategic value. But there are other possibilities. The 'keep' account may buy from us but squeezes prices or is never going to do anything 'leading edge'. In the 'pick' account, we have to pick our moment to convince them of our potential. Where mutual strategic interest is minimal, we deal on an ad hoc basis. These stereotypes are simplistic, and circumstances in any account can change quickly, so the marketing department must be market sensing all the time to keep the sales team updated with news about customers.

To start categorising your customers using the portfolio, list your customers using the Table 7.2 template.

Table 7.2: Portfolio customer categorisation template

Customer	Value to us	Our value to them	Quadrant category	Time priority	Notes
Smith & Jones	H	H	Key	2	Extend strategic value
Green & Red	MH	VH	Key	3	Extend strategic value
AWQ Inc	L	M	Keep or Deal?	7	Find out if more can be done with this customer before conversion to online
Wright Ltd	ML	H	Keep	6	Maintain account share
L&B Plc	ML	ML	Deal	8	Convert to online
Sandi & Sunil	MH	H	Key	4	Extend strategic value
KED	VH	ML	Pick	1	Potential to gain account share
Moon & Sun	MH	ML	Pick	5	Potential to gain account share
East & West	ML	ML	Deal	8	Convert to online
Joe Bloggs SA	L	L	Deal	9	Convert to online

In categorising customers in your portfolio, ask yourself the following questions:

- Does the business environment for this customer look favourable in the medium to long term?

- Does the customer have a compelling need for the services and products you can offer?

- Is there scope for upselling and cross-selling a wide range of services and products?

- Is the customer well-managed, with a good reputation in their industry?

- Do colleagues report that the customer is easy to deal with (eg pays bills on time)?

- Have key individuals been working well together for a long time (eg technical teams from supplier and customer)?

- Is their geographical scope attractive, or is it too big or small?

- Do they like us? How do we know? Do we have a supplier evaluation from them that puts us ahead of competitors? Have there been any 'negative critical incidents' (such as a late delivery) recently that led to complaints from the customer?

- Are there any internal financial measures to be taken into account, such as CLV or account profitability?

Once you have completed your portfolio diagram, discuss your analysis with your manager or coach and defend your choices using evidence rather than 'gut feel'. If you have particularly valuable key customers or pick customers, you may need specific plans to secure their business over the next three to five years. Discuss these plans with the customer to gauge their commitment to you as a supplier, which feeds into better forecasts. You can also share them with colleagues in their functions to help them with their planning cycles.

Formulating and refining customer plans

'Individual key account plans appear to be of particular significance in driving customer satisfaction.'
— Davies and Ryals (2014)

The principles of planning to sell to a particular customer are the same as the principles for planning for any other aspect of business or life. However, you have to plan from the customer's point of view before you can apply your products/services to their needs. Assess the customer's situation, their capabilities and how they might apply them to meet their opportunities, and then you can assess how your products and services could enhance their capabilities. As McDonald and Rogers (2017) state, 'Key account managers are supposed to be "boundary spanners" who can see things from the customer's point of view. To ensure that thinking is embedded, key account planning must start from the customer's point of view.'

Step 1: Establish the customer's opportunities and threats

Opportunities and threats are external; the customer cannot control them. They come from the economic and industry contexts in which the customer operates. You will have come across PEST analysis and Porter's Five Forces in Chapter 2; apply them to the customer. What political, economic, social and technical trends are affecting them? How competitive is their industry sub-sector? Who exercises power in their supply chain? Assess whether each factor is an opportunity or a threat. Choose the high-impact factors that are most likely to affect the customer and think about what they might need to do to address them.

Step 2: Evaluate the customer's strengths and weaknesses

A customer's strengths are likely to be well-advertised, but weaknesses can only be established with deeper analysis. Look at what their competitors appear to do better or find media or social media commentary about the customer's performance. You might have also visited the customer and observed operations that need improvement. The customer's own opinion matters most, although investment analyst opinion is also relevant. Your thinking now can turn to how the customer might apply their strengths and weaknesses to addressing their opportunities and threats, and the nine-box SWOT diagram in Figure 7.4 will help you to organise those thoughts.

Step 3: Determine how the customer can move forward

Does the customer have a strength that matches an opportunity? For example, if an opportunity for a building firm is 'ageing population' and a strength is 'expertise/economies of scale in mobility adaptations', they will invest in applying their capability to seize the opportunity. Using the Figure 7.4 template, you would note this in the WIN box.

Does the customer have a weakness or a gap that matches an opportunity? In the case of the ageing population, if a building firm does not have much expertise in mobility adaptations, do they need to buy it in or develop it in-house? Alternatively, they might decide to concentrate promotional activity on another segment such as young families. Note this in the CONVERT box.

Turning to the threats, does the customer need to LEVERAGE a strength to overcome a threat? For the building firm, perhaps a new competitor has started up in their area, in which case they need to retain current customers and focus on their reputation when winning new ones. Endorsements such as being on the local council's 'buy with confidence' website will be important.

Finally, is there a threat which aligns with a weakness? If there is a 'credit constraints by banks' threat and the customer funds its expansion through borrowing, that is going to be a problem. Can they find alternative sources of borrowing? They need DEFEND strategies.

Objectives	Strengths	Weaknesses
Opportunities	Win	Convert
Threats	Leverage	Defend

Figure 7.4: SWOT analysis diagram (adapted from Weihrich, 1982)

Step 4: Where can you help?

Ideally, you would check with the customer that your analysis of their future strategies is reasonable, but you may not be able to do that in every case, especially if you are working under time pressures to make a bid to a customer who is a 'pick' rather than already 'key'. What you have written in the WIN, CONVERT, LEVERAGE and DEFEND boxes is now your raw material for establishing customer need. Some of it may be irrelevant, but the rest should provide excellent ideas about applying your products and services to helping the customer to succeed.

For the case of the customer who is a building firm, let us assume that you are selling a well-known brand of building materials. Perhaps you can help them to choose and promote the best range of mobility adaptations to offer to customers, offer some co-branding to enhance their reputation and arrange extended credit terms to help them to control their borrowing from the banks. Reflect on your proposals and consider, as one chief executive (a contact of the author's) used to ask his key account managers: 'Where's the spark?'

Perhaps the strongest argument for increasing the volume of business with this customer would be the extended credit terms, as decision-makers often spend a lot of time on minimising risks.

Bear in mind that the customer will have a view of your employer's strengths and weaknesses as a supplier. Just as you analysed the customer's weaknesses, consider your own and whether the ideas you want to offer the customer will be considered credible compared to what your competitors can offer. If the customer perceives that you are somewhat over-priced or inefficient, you will also need to explain how you are going to address their concerns.

Categorise the value you are proposing according to the following categories adapted from Ward and Peppard (2002). Is it:

- Strategic – something that contributes to the customer's long-term success

- High potential – something that has potential for future value

- Key operational – something critical to day-to-day operations which could help the customer to improve productivity, avoid costs or minimise risks

- Support – a useful support function which could help the customer to avoid disadvantage

Focus on the capability that you are offering (and its superiority to competitor capability) and the help it can provide for the customer. Remember to justify the price in terms of the customer's total cost of ownership (TCO) and value-in-use:

- **Total cost of ownership** – In addition to purchase price, consider the costs of operating, maintaining and disposing of a product when evaluating alternative solutions. For example, a ball bearing that costs £15 but lasts longer and uses less lubrication may be a better buy than a £5 ball bearing with a limited lifespan.

- **Value-in-use** – This can be calculated as the NPV of cash/benefits of a product in use, but usually there are also intangible perceptions of a product's usefulness that matter. For example, a user of a product may experience less stress because it is easy to use or gain status because it is an attractive item.

Step 5: Make sure that you can implement the plan

Customers love salespeople who bring them great ideas, but you have to be able to make them happen. You will have to negotiate with operations, marketing and finance to see whether the business can deliver what you want to propose. They will tell you what effort is involved, and you need to document it. You should also discuss risks with colleagues – what could go wrong, and how would you overcome it? Figure 7.5 shows a template to use for making sure that you can deliver on your plan.

Strategy	Actions	Who	When

Figure 7.5: Implementation template

Territory planning

In deciding what activities to plan for each customer and when, you need to assess not only their importance but also the current state of sales activity across your portfolio. How many sales have you made to date? How many deals need to close this month? Are there any open discussions with customers who need to proceed to proposal soon? How many qualified leads from your customers/prospects are on your radar? The company needs a pipeline of sales opportunities, and so do you as an individual salesperson. You must prioritise progress towards closing a sale which is time-dependent, but you need to develop new opportunities as well to avoid 'feast and famine' – over-focusing on closing one month and then having no proposals to follow up the next month. You are constantly trading off short-term and long-term activities, but it must be done to ensure the health of your sales performance.

In some sales roles, you will have a defined geographic territory to manage as well as a portfolio of customers. Much can be done by electronic media and phone these days, but you will still be expected to make visits to customers in your territory. You will need a routing plan. First of all, you must use your 'key, pick, keep, deal' categorisation to decide how much time you should spend with each customer/prospect. Which customers justify one visit a year? Which might need monthly calls? Remember that the customer has to want to see you for a purpose.

You may spend a lot of time on the phone negotiating for time with key decision-makers. You are selling from the minute you speak to a secretary to ask for a diary slot. 'Just catching up' or 'Just checking everything is OK' is not going to get you very far. 'Courtesy calls' can be short; 'Introducing our new XYZ range' or 'Ensuring the service level agreement is still meeting requirements' would be stronger reasons for a personal call and in-depth discussion.

Get a map of your territory and mark the locations you have to visit. Many CRM systems let you plot a time-efficient route, which can even take into account traffic patterns and roadworks. Allow plenty of contingency time – when you are on too tight a schedule, you will get stressed by traffic delays, and they are inevitable. Even if you have satnav, you can get lost or fail to find a parking space. When a routing plan has been agreed, remember to keep in touch with the customers about when you plan to be with them and notify them of any delays. Do not use your mobile phone illegally, though; even using your mobile hands-free increases your risk of having an accident (McEvoy et al, 2005). Observe your company code of conduct on driver safety and make use of service stations, lay-bys and other parking opportunities.

Make a plan of calls for the forthcoming month and discuss it with your manager. In the past, sales productivity was often measured by the quality of calls, and it still is in some telesales contexts, such as calling customers to ask for repeat orders. However, in these days of smart selling, especially in business sectors, it is more important that the meeting with the customer has a purpose which advances the business relationship. It costs a lot of money for an employer to put you on the road and cover your hotel and meals. These days it is far more likely that many of your meetings with customers will take place online, via software such as Zoom, Google Hangouts or Microsoft Teams. Do not be distracted by the apparent informality of online meetings. Whether you meet a customer face-to-face, over the phone or online, you should have a call plan.

Although most customers want to limit meetings with salespeople, some will ask for a lot of time which may not necessarily result in an advance. You have to decide whether you should make more calls or establish a different pattern of contact. Perhaps you could do more over the phone or in online meetings, or the delivery driver/service engineer could prompt for repeat orders.

Call planning

For each meeting with a customer, you should have a call plan. As with other plans, take into account the context for the call, what advance you want to achieve and how you are going to achieve it. Here is a typical call plan checklist:

- Call details – customer, person to meet and position, time and place

- Context for call (eg customer's equipment reaching the end of depreciation period next year)

- Call objective – Advance required (eg commitment to see a demonstration of a new product) and fallback position (eg secure another meeting on the same topic)

- Questions to ask

- Check facts

- Explore need

- Evaluate the impact of need

- Establish possible payoff from solving customer's problem

- Investigate budget and authority

- Questions to expect

- Customer's possible causes for concern about the change

- Responses

If you make a call plan beforehand, not only will your meeting have more purpose and be more likely to succeed, but it will be easier to write up your call report afterwards. Call reporting is required, and you will be expected to log a report in the CRM system shortly after the call. You will also need to add any new information you have acquired about the customer and their buying behaviour and to log and report your expenses in good time to have them reimbursed before your credit card bill arrives.

Summary

We have discussed how to establish the business plan and the sales forecast and how they guide your objectives and planning processes. Planning is important, but we must also remember the implementation and follow-up. The full process is:

- Plan

- Do

- Reflect

- Adjust

We might also consider that planning cannot anticipate every event. As the boxing quote says: 'Everybody has a plan until they get punched.' All sports players need plans, but they have to be aware that their opponent has one too. They have to adapt in the face of the tactics of the other player/s.

In any job, there will have to be some 'fire-fighting' as the unexpected hits your desk or phone. It is always uncomfortable and stressful. However, contingency planning does help you to manage the unexpected, even if the contingency that you plan for is not the one that occurs.

8

Gathering Intelligence

Introduction

In their early careers, sales professionals are often asked to be information gatherers for their account team or bid team. Of course, marketing also do a lot of information gathering and interpretation, but there is further work that salespeople need to do. Not everyone can love the research element of being a great salesperson, but it is necessary to learn about what information you need and how to turn it into actionable insight. You need to be a generator of insight in a sales role, and even more so as you progress into sales management and other leadership roles. You need information in order to:

- Develop your own opinion

- Present convincing recommendations to decision-makers (internal)

- Understand why customers do what they do

- Reassure customers that your sales recommendations are based on sound logic

Make sure that the information you use is high-quality information. We cannot always find large quantities of information about particular topics, so you need to be discerning about what sources you choose.

The following are some useful definitions related to gathering intelligence:

Business intelligence encompasses high-level information about customers, products and financial performance. This might include the total volume of products delivered, total sales revenue and total cash movements. If you are looking after a key account, you will need to manage business intelligence about your customer. Much of it may be in the public domain via their company report or registered with Companies House.

Market intelligence covers information about markets, customers, product categories and competitors. This information is vital across all sales roles. It can be more difficult to obtain than business intelligence. Your organisation may have a sophisticated marketing information system which uses external intelligence and internal information about customers and company activity to deliver accurate, up-to-date data and trends to enable data users to make better decisions. However, smaller companies can find this difficult to achieve internally and may bring in market intelligence from consultancies.

Formal intelligence is information which has been produced and published, often for a statutory purpose. Companies have legal obligations to publish information about their performance, which is designed to help shareholders and government bodies. Companies and individuals contribute information to databases maintained by government organisations, which can then be used by commercial analysts to observe trends in markets and sectors. In the UK, the Office of National Statistics (ONS) is the primary source of economic and demographic data. ONS produces a vast variety of data for the UK Government, most of which is freely available on its website.[13] Most countries have similar bodies, such as the Australian Bureau of Statistics and the Statistisches Bundesamt in Germany.

---

13 See www.ons.gov.uk.

Formal intelligence also includes data from professional institutes, such as the Chartered Institute of Purchasing's 'Purchasing Managers' Index' and the Chartered Institute of Personnel and Development's 'Job Quality Index'. There may be charges to subscribe to these data sources.

Informal intelligence does not come from official sources. It may come from anecdotes exchanged at a conference or comments on social media feeds. It would not pass many tests as 'good data', but when you hear the same opinion or perception many times from different information sources, or when it is clear that someone who influences others is promoting a strong opinion, you may need to share this information with colleagues and incorporate it into your analysis of a topic.

Another form of informal intelligence can be the absence of certain types of anecdote or social media comment. For example, if you were researching where to buy a stairlift for an elderly person, you would know to check social media for positive comments about companies which have simple, robust products and a sympathetic customer service department. You might also deliberately search for contrary evidence, such as complaints and negative reviews; none or few of these might indicate a company which generally does not get into disputes with its customers.

Information-driven selling

Second only to the opinion of colleagues, purchasing decision-makers trust independent sources of information about potential suppliers and their products (IDC, 2015). This is discussed in more detail in the chapter about understanding customers. In this chapter, we need to note that customers want to refer to independent sources of information, and it is important for salespeople to facilitate the customer's information needs. We expect marketing to load the website with information that potential customers want to find and to work with 'infomediaries' (websites that organise data and provide a platform for information suppliers to reach information seekers), online marketplaces and search engines.

In sales, we need to take a leaf out of the purchasing book. Our selling needs to be driven by information about the segments and customers most likely to be responsive to our product/service offering. The more we can use information to target effectively and to create an interesting proposition for prospects and customers, the more successful we will be.

A market intelligence system should aim to provide intelligence about:

- The business environment

- Market sectors

- Customers

- Competitors

- Channels

- Products

- Prices

- Promotions

  It should be able to draw data from:

- Internal databases (eg product catalogue, financial accounts)

- CRM systems

- External data sources (eg market research, industry analyst reports)

- Informal sources (including social media)

  It should support the following functions that users need:

- Generating analysis and insight from data mining

- Supporting planning (eg sensitivity analysis on price changes)
- Scheduling the application of resources
- Monitoring implementation

Accessing and evaluating external sources of information

It is so easy to go to Google or Bing, key in a few words, and get lots of hits. And, of course, there is Wikipedia. To senior businesspeople, however, a report based on casual web sources would carry little weight. You have to start somewhere, and Wikipedia often has links to more robust sources of information, but make sure that you dig deep. The majority of content on the Internet is opinion rather than fact. Bear in mind that this includes a business customer's website, which presents their view of what they do. You need to know how the customer sees what they do, but you also need to know how their customers and competitors see them.

Good sources of information can be difficult to use, and re-using data gathered for another purpose has risks. Nevertheless, we have to start by building our knowledge on the knowledge of others.

Google Scholar – research by academics

Google Scholar can lead you to robust research on topics which may be relevant to your customers. The academics who write the articles listed in Google Scholar have to convince their fellow academics that their methodology has been rigorous and relevant to their research topic. As with the search engines, not all search results are equal; check that whatever information you use from Google Scholar is published in a reputable academic journal since it will also pick up student essays. You can ask your tutors or the librarian at your college if they have access to databases which give more reliable lists than Google Scholar. Some academic articles are published in full by universities and research portals (such as ResearchGate), and you can link through to them from Google Scholar.

It can be helpful to start with a section in the article called 'managerial implications'. Did the research yield a recommendation that practitioners need to implement? Be aware that academic research can examine narrow topics in limited contexts, and it may take over two years to be published, so an article with a publication date of 2017 may relate to data gathered in 2013. Google Scholar findings that may be useful to you include case studies written about your key account, research about attitudes in a market or product segment relevant to your job, or research about technology relevant to your customer.

Government agencies and professional bodies

Governments produce large amounts of data, for example, statistical bulletins on manufacturers' sales. Data on government websites, such as that of the ONS in the UK, may include names and contact details for specialists at the agency who may be able to help you refine the data or find a particular item. If you are researching an international customer or segment, government departments in other countries also publish interesting data, such as the US Census Data and Statistics and the Ministry of Statistics and Programme Implementation in India.[14]

Professional associations are also a popular source of reputable data. There are many associations for all sorts of professions. Being 'chartered' conveys some prestige in the UK; while the terms 'chartered' or 'certified' are also used in other countries, they may not always indicate the same level of public scrutiny. Most professional bodies have publications or knowledgebase sections on their websites,

14 Available at: www.usa.gov/statistics and http://mospi.gov.in, respectively.

and the larger bodies have their own library services, which provide general or tailored industry reports. Many publications are of specific interest to their membership, but some have wider audiences.

Trade bodies publish regular reports for their members and wider stakeholders, which can be useful sources of market intelligence. Most trade bodies represent particular sub-sector interests, and your employer may be a member of a trade body. There are also generic trade bodies which may have a geographic focus, such as the Chamber of Commerce in the UK. They also publish trade magazines featuring articles focused on their sector. Although these are reports by journalists and consultants rather than research, they can draw attention to topics and trends of high current interest in the sector.

Examples of trade bodies include the Glass and Glazing Federation, which represents companies who make, supply or fit glass and glass-related products in the UK and internationally.[15] You may also be interested in the Society of Motor Manufacturers and Traders.[16] The SMMT is often quoted in the media as the voice of the UK automotive industry, and is widely regarded by its members, government and other stakeholders as authoritative and influential.

Consultants' reports

Some consultancies publish openly accessible papers; your marketing department or college library may also have subscriptions to regular surveys and reports about particular markets. The market research firms Mintel and Keynote offer a wide variety of reports about product markets, customer segments and geographical markets across the world. Some industry sectors also have specialist industry analysts – Thompson Reuters and Bloomberg

15   See www.ggf.org.uk.

16   See www.smmt.co.uk.

specialise in financial markets; Gartner and IDC in IT. Opinion from investment analysts and brokers about the shareholder value that particular companies generate is also worth examining.

Consultants' reports are usually easy to read and easy to use, and they are produced quickly. They may be sponsored, but this should not affect the core data presented. Check the methodology section to see how the data was gathered. Is it a reasonably large sample of respondents? IDC (2015), for example, conducted a survey of 200 businesses to gain an understanding of the process that companies use to evaluate and execute buying decisions; in this example, 200 businesses sounds reasonable. IDC's methodology statement also showed pie-charts of the value of purchases that the respondents managed and the number of decisions per year.

Press sources

We have all heard of 'fake news'. Most of it is on the Internet, but other media outlets have been found guilty of slanting 'news' in misleading ways. Much twenty-four-hour news content on television is journalists talking to other journalists about what might happen in politics today, rather than what has happened. Never jump to conclusions when you see a news headline – check other sources to assess how probable it is that the story is fact-based.

There are some media companies which have good reputations for providing high-quality journalism, such as the *Financial Times*, CNN, *Die Welt*, the *Washington Post* and the BBC. Check whether your customers appear on these websites. Are they making redundancies? Have they announced particularly surprising financial results this quarter? Has the CEO changed? If your customer is a big company, their fortunes will be covered by the press, and a newspaper like the *Financial Times* may be the first to report it. You might also use these publications and outlets as starting points if they feature interesting stories about a topic you are researching and could use illustrative quotes from reputable media sources in your reports, taking care to avoid fake news.

To evaluate the quality of the information, you can check the following. If the information fails the check then it may be suspect, and more effort will be required to validate it:

- **Web address** – Avoid websites that have uncommon URL endings. Common ones are .com, .co.uk and .ac. uk; ones which may be suspect include .lo and .co. This doesn't mean the information is definitely unreliable, but you need to check it with another source.

- **Author** – Who is writing this? If it is a single name or no name at all, check with another source. Unless it is a blog (which will likely be the writer's opinion), relying on a single source is unwise.

- **News sites** – Some news sites rarely fact-check and may even have guest contributors rather than reporters. Again, cross-check with another site.

It is best to consult multiple news sources, and remember, social media often contains opinion and paid adverts that may look like news.

Internal sources and CRM analytics

Researching the external world has enough challenges, so it is good to know that your CRM system should do a lot of analytics for you based on data it holds about products, customers, operations and financials. The science of predictive CRM analytics is advancing all the time. If you work in telesales, you have probably noticed how the system can prompt for making particular offers to customers when they call in, based on their past buying behaviour.

The impact of IT on selling is discussed in the Digital Knowledge and Digital Skills chapters; here, we are mainly concerned with your role as an intelligence gatherer. Whether your analytics system is running algorithms or not, there are some items in the CRM system which you should regularly check for yourself:

- **Is there any feedback from the customer?** If the customer has made a service call or responded to a survey or email, whether negatively or positively, this is a prompt to make contact and be useful to the customer.

- **Is there any new information about the customer?** Has a key contact changed? Have colleagues uploaded new details about the customer's branch network or recent financial results? If they buy online, what is the ongoing trend?

- **Are there any analytics about our share of the customer's spend or customer profitability?** Is there any satisfaction monitoring or indication of changes in satisfaction, such as the number of service calls? Try and follow the performance statistics for success with the customer and pick up any changes as soon as possible.

- **What does your sales pipeline look like?** For the opportunities you are managing at the moment, what do you need to do today to make something happen?[17]

The system will do a lot of analysis for you, and it will flag up things which, according to its algorithms, need attention. However, do not be completely passive. Look at the data yourself and determine what looks good and what looks worrying.

Sharing intelligence

You will usually gather information to share knowledge with colleagues or customers. Do not just dump

---

17 Questions developed and used with kind permission of Dr Zimdars.

information on them and expect them to sort it out for themselves. You need to present the information in a way that they can use.

Always quote your sources. The readers of your report need to know where the data and opinions you use have come from. It is a breach of copyright to present other people's work as your own. Some pressurised individuals have assumed that their colleagues or tutors will not have time to check work for originality, but they will check. Your college or university may ask you to check your own work through a software system such as Turnitin. They will also have checks in place for identifying essays which have been bought from 'essay mills'. Your credibility and your job are at risk if you present work which is not your own original creation and you should observe the courtesies of crediting sources you have used.

Many busy people have difficulties in structuring reports. You can ask your colleagues what they want out of the report, which will help you to structure it. It is also useful to remember the following generic way of presenting an analysis:

- What is this topic about? (Provide a clear definition.)

- Why is it important?

- What are the trends which are relevant to our business?

- How should we address these trends?

Alternatively, if you are asked to produce a profile of a prospective customer, a typical structure would be:

- Firmographics of the customer (size, location, turnover, number of employees, etc)

- Trends in the company's sales, market share and profitability

- Strategic positioning (versus competitors) as stated in their annual report and as observed by customers, investment analysts and the financial press

- Usage of products/services that we can offer

- Their current supplier for products/services that we can offer

- Any contacts or links with the company

- An assessment of the feasibility of making a proposal to the prospect

  Where possible, you should analyse information rather than just describe it (see Table 8.1).

Table 8.1: Sample customer firmographics analysis

Customer: Smith and Jones Plc
Date: 20 August 2018

Brokers' recommendations	Neutral	Buy	Sell
Brown & Green			x
Spoon & Miller	x		
Bloggs' Private Bank		x	
New & Oldster		x	
Next & Last	x		
First & Forth		x	

Sources: Websites of the brokers visited between 4 August and 8 August 2018.
Given that most leading investment brokers are recommending Buy or Neutral, the prospects of Smith and Jones Plc delivering positive shareholder value in the next one to three years seem reasonably good.

Here, you have not only shown what the analysts are saying, you have come to some conclusion based on the data.

When you are reporting back to senior decision-makers, they will ask: 'What decision do you want from me?' Perhaps you are arguing for time to develop Smith and Jones Plc as a prospect; if so, you will need a lot more information than one table. You need to build up evidence throughout the report, indicating that this company's custom would be worthwhile. You then need to provide a conclusion and summarise your recommendations. If the logical flow of your report is strong, you should find this fairly easy to do. If someone asks, for example, 'Where did recommendation 6 come from?' you should be able to trace it back to your data.

Inevitably, when you share information with colleagues and customers, there may be challenges to your analysis, and those challenges may not be fact-based. Many people in business have a 'gut feel', which may be related to past experiences or particular influencers in their sector, or they may even have access to information that you don't have.

When it comes to discussions about the information you are presenting, try to stick to evidence and do not feel that the questioning is personal. You may make simple mistakes in your early reports, and colleagues can help you to correct them. However, sometimes you have to stick to your guns and say, 'I think, based on these trends, that X is a real possibility, and we should plan for it.' Anyone who believed in the 1980s that the UK Government would raise the retirement age was generally thought to be a great pessimist. However, given the rise in life expectancy during the 1970s and 1980s, they were realistic, not pessimistic. Pension companies who helped their clients to realise that they might need to save more because their state pension would be postponed were serving their needs better than those who failed to imagine unpopular legislation. Your competitive advantage will come from good analysis based on understanding your business environment.

Contributing to the CRM system

When you gather data and produce reports, you should save and share them for posterity so that colleagues do not waste time trying to find the same information all over again. Even scraps of information you acquire doing your day-to-day work may have a value to others. Be a good corporate citizen and add information, formal and informal, to the CRM system. The CRM system is useful when you need information because others have bothered to upload data; if you do the same, it encourages others to keep up their efforts, and you create goodwill. Also, you cannot possibly remember everything you note on a customer call, so everything you add to the system is a reminder to yourself for the next call.

Some companies offer incentives for timely logging of call reports and other information uploads because they know that it can be time-consuming and slip down your 'to do' list. Even if your company does not do this, you will save yourself some hassle from your manager if you keep your administration up to date.

Summary

In this chapter, we have discussed the types of information that you will need to gather and manage. We have explored the best sources of external data and how to use internal sources.

9

Time Management

Introduction

Aeon and Aguinis define time management as 'a form of decision-making used by individuals to structure, protect, and adapt their time to changing conditions' (2017).

As an apprentice, you have taken on a demanding time management challenge. You have to achieve at work every day, and you have to gain qualifications. You also have to spend time with your family and friends to stay sane. It is hard. Employers often emphasise the importance of time management. They want employees to be productive. If you manage your time well, you are achieving for yourself, and you are also achieving for your employer and your customers.

Claims are often made about the value of productivity driven by better time management. Having reviewed the empirical research on time management, Aeon and Aguinis (2017) concluded that the link between good time management and job performance is not straightforward. It is interrupted by several variables in our working environments, many of which we cannot control. Some days you may feel superbly productive, and other days will be beset by distractions. However, we can be fairly confident that if you become a good time manager, you will have less stress to deal with and enjoy more 'me' time which will make you feel good.

'If you do not prioritise your life, someone else will.'
— Greg McKeown (2012)

There are five SCOPE elements to good time management:

- Setting long-term goals, and breaking them down into milestones over time

- Challenging bad habits that you may have acquired, such as putting things off until tomorrow, when they need to be done today

- Organising your months, weeks and days, in so far as they can be organised. You will always have to do some fire-fighting that you did not expect when you got up in the morning

- Protecting your time; such as ring-fencing sufficient study time and playtime

- Enjoying your time; because if you are not happy with the way you are using your time at work, at study and at home, you need to change something substantial about your life.

Remember that the purpose of time management is to give you scope to achieve the things you want from life.

Factors affecting how you manage time

No matter how good you are at time management, there are some things which will affect your plans.

Time structures

Many external formalities govern how we can use time. These include the timing of public holidays and religious festivals, academic timetables and your employer's and customers' official business hours and the time zones in which they operate. Many deadlines will govern your time, such as project schedules and the dates by which bids have to be submitted. These systems can help earmark particular activities for particular times, but they are also demanding and immovable. Make sure that you are aware of the time structures that affect you.

Cultural, social and organisational norms

How we use time is influenced by the messages we receive about its importance. Use of time has cultural influences. Some cultures like to spend a lot of time on meals, and some cultures value punctuality more than others. In the UK, there are even class-based norms about time, such as the concept of 'polite lateness' (allegedly about fifteen minutes) for dinner parties. In some youth subcultures, turning up late is considered 'cool'. It can get rather complicated.

Organisations have their own subcultures, and this is evident in their attitudes to time. Do meetings often go on for five hours with no discernible outcome? That suggests a cultural norm, and, even if you find it frustrating, you will be expected to endure it with a smile. Is it acceptable for a senior manager to arrive late to meetings, whereas they would be annoyed if a member of their reporting staff did the same? That is a power-play – 'My time is more important than your time'. Once again, it is beyond your control. Your customers may have different time cultures, and you need to find out what they are.

Some sectors and some companies have time cultures which have been described as encouraging 'workaholism' and 'presenteeism'. That means that everybody working for the company is expected to put in long hours, whether or not they are productive. Others may have 'work hard, play hard' cultures, in which periods of long hours are punctuated by company-sponsored leisure events.

Since the 1990s, there has been increased discussion about employees enjoying a healthy 'work-life balance'. While at work, some companies have introduced 'no email' days or 'quiet periods', to reduce some elements of work-based stress. IT has enabled many of us to work from home or hubs or while commuting. The problem with technology is that it can encourage expectations that you are available 24/7, and the need to control that makes time management essential.

Individual feelings about time

Do you prefer to do one thing at a time, or do you pride yourself on multitasking? Do you like to keep work time and family time separate, or can you juggle between them? Are you calm and accepting if something unexpectedly hijacks your plan for the day, or does it make you annoyed and unable to concentrate on either the new thing or the original plan? Are you more energetic in the morning or in the evening? There is no right or wrong way to feel about time, but you need to be aware of your feelings. As Peter Drucker (2017) has said: 'most people take for granted this unique, irreplaceable, and necessary resource. Nothing else, perhaps, distinguishes effective executives as much as their tender loving care of time.'

You may realise that your employer wants you to be good at managing your time, in part, because they pay you a salary every month and they want you to provide an effective return on that investment. Also be aware that, as an individual, your time is finite and you want to make the most of it. You need to budget for time in the same way that you would budget for money. Unlike money, however, you cannot borrow time and pay it back later, so be realistic about what you can do in the time available and don't take on more than you can do. All activities, from landing a major deal to soaking in the bath, cost time, which relentlessly ticks away at the same pace as it has done for millennia. The more aware you are of time as a resource which you have to use carefully to maximise your opportunities, the better you will get at time management, and you will experience less time-based conflict.

The elements of time management

Setting goals

We would all like to seize a bright future and bring it closer. First, though, we have to be specific about imagining exactly what that bright future should look like.

What you do day after day has little meaning unless you know where you want your activity to lead. Do you want to exceed your target this year? Do you want to be promoted within two years? Do you see yourself as the youngest sales director in the UK FTSE 100 within seven years? When you achieve a goal, you may look back and think, 'At that point in that week, the odds tipped in my favour.' Your goals have to be realistic, but they should be ambitious; otherwise, they will not motivate you day in and day out. Set SMART goals for your time management that are:

- Specific (rather than vague)

- Measurable (you must know that you are on the right journey and when you are making progress)

- Achievable (but ambitious)

- Relevant (career-oriented, in the context of your apprenticeship)

- Timed (ie with a deadline)

You have made a career choice and at the moment you may be full of excitement. You may not feel ready to plot out your career path in detail. Life and careers do involve luck and the force of human will, but most people need to pin down how they are going to achieve things in the long, medium, and short term in order to get anywhere. The following table may help you to challenge over-enthusiasm/over-confidence.

Table 9.1: Good practice in setting goals

Good practice	Sloppy thinking
I will transition from in-house sales to field sales.	I will conquer the sales universe!
Milestones with manager and relevant training in place.	The boss will know progress when I am acclaimed by others.
I have confirmed with my coach that I have the potential to move on to more strategic accounts.	I will shine, and then glory will be given to me.
Relevant to career goal of Global Account Manager.	I will see what's on offer at my next review.
I should be ready in 12 months.	This can happen soon.

You will probably discuss your goals with your mentor or coach and/or your manager. Setting them is one step; the next is trying to break them down into smaller chunks. Ask your coach, 'If I want to do X within two years, what do I have to do within the next few weeks to start the ball rolling?'

Challenging bad habits

One of the worst habits we can have when it comes to seizing the future is wanting to start seizing it tomorrow rather than today. There are so many enjoyable little things that can get in the way of starting anything substantial today, like a quick trawl through social media, or a snack, or a chat. We also get interruptions which can divert us from future-oriented activity – Jack needs information about customer X, or customer Y has a query about pricing. Putting things off is called procrastination – the delaying or avoidance of doing something.

Humans procrastinate for many reasons. We dislike tasks which do not have immediate value, even if the company wants them done. We dislike uncertainty, so we put off unclear tasks. We dislike boring tasks, so we delay doing them, however important they might be. As consumers, we avoid getting competitive quotes for insurance and banking because it is a hassle, even if we can save money. We dislike interacting with people who are not easy to deal with, and that will be the case with a number of customers – customers do not have to try to be nice in the way that salespeople do. Also, pleasurable tasks, such as enhancing our social media profiles, lure us away from the urgent and important tasks on our 'to do' lists.

Another bad habit which is common to a large proportion of the population is giving up too easily. Yes, some sales opportunities have to be dropped because they are improbable or impossible; however, many sales opportunities are achievable but hard to achieve. Just taking the 'low-hanging fruit' will not win you any prizes – anybody can be an order-taker. To be successful in sales, you have to persevere. It is easy to be put off doing something difficult because of the risk of failure, but in sales you are expected to try and fail rather than never try at all.

If your career ever involves line-managing staff, you will have a queue of people querying, 'Why does X have to be done as it does not add any customer value?' and 'Does Admin not realise how much time Y takes?' You may find yourself replying, 'Just do it'. As a reporting member of staff, you may want to clarify with your manager which tasks are urgent and important and which are just urgent. Be prepared to accept that in any job, some tasks are 'just do it' tasks, and you will be in a stronger bargaining position with colleagues if you do your 'just do it' work without having to be chased.

If you are daunted by urgent and important tasks arising from customer or employer needs, ask for guidance, but be prepared to get things started. Accept that you will make mistakes but you can learn from them. Be motivated by how good you will feel when you have completed a task that was both urgent and important.

Organising yourself

Most time management training focuses on the tools and techniques of organising yourself from day to day at work. We are urged to make lists of what we have to do by when. First, we have to remember all the things that we know we have to do. Then, we have to accept that our time is not our own, and every day our managers and customers will want us to do things that we had not anticipated.

Some time ago, a US politician was ridiculed for talking about 'unknown unknowns' in a press briefing. However, any scientific approach to investigating or planning requires us to note the following:

- Known knowns – what we know

- Known unknowns – what we know that we don't know

We also need to be prepared to find unknown unknowns – what we don't know that we don't know (Logan, 2009). How can we guess at what these things might be? It is worth the effort because a lot of time in a career can be spent dealing with the unexpected. Asking managers and customers in advance what they think might be needed this week or this month can reduce the 'double U' effect.

Prioritisation is key to managing 'to do' lists. A well-known tool for prioritising tasks is the Eisenhower Matrix (see Figure 9.1), named after the US president attributed with highlighting the problem of trading off importance and urgency.

To use this matrix, review your task list and:

- Identify tasks which are time-dependent, to assess urgency

- Consider which tasks are important to other people (your customers, your manager, your internal stakeholders), to assess importance

- Consider which tasks are important *to you* in terms of achieving your goals and plans
Then, prioritise the tasks as follows:

- Tasks which are urgent and important should be seen as 'must-do' items today or in the near future.

- Tasks which are important but not urgent should be scheduled for a later date (but do not let them slip – remember that they are important for a reason).

- Tasks which are not important and not urgent should be assessed to see if you can eliminate them. If these tasks impact other people, let them know that you are unable to help them in these matters.

- Tasks that are urgent but not important need some attention, but does it have to be yours? See if you can delegate them to a more appropriate person or negotiate the urgency with other stakeholders so that you can schedule time in the near future to address them.

Your manager will sometimes give you a task which you would classify as not urgent or not important. In those cases, seek clarification from your manager about why it is urgent and/or important. You may disagree with the reasons, but if your manager is clear about a task being urgent or important, it is a case of 'just do it'. Organisations are complex, and they can generate requirements which may seem trivial, but to constantly quibble about them will be exhausting and will not help your career.

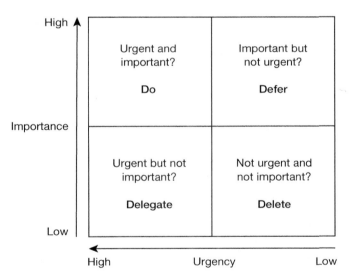

Figure 9.1: The task prioritisation matrix

Most people find it useful to work from lists, assign priorities and assess the time needed per task. One of the worst unknown unknowns in time management is how long a phone call or writing a report might take. Assume it will always take twice as long as your first guesstimate since people are generally over-optimistic about the passage of time.

You will need monthly lists (usually derived from your monthly review), weekly lists and daily lists. Tasks on the weekly and daily lists should be contributing to completing tasks on the monthly list. Table 9.2 shows an example of a good daily list.

Table 9.2: Sample daily to-do list

To-do	Priority	Time	Follow-up/linkages/ dependencies
Phone PA to Jim Smith to arrange needs analysis appointment	Top priority today UI – Try early and keep trying	10 minutes per call – up to 1 hour	Once in place, chat to the technical team about when demo can be set up
Talk to marketing about next month's prospect list	I	30 minutes	Start scheduling calls in the diary
Draft proposal for customer ABC	I – deadline is 10 days away, but want to check with coach	2 hours, but could drift if interrupted…	Send draft to coach for feedback (important development area for this month)
Discuss feedback about assignment 5 with my tutor	I – NB call tutor at 2pm sharp	30 minutes	Make a note of advice for the next assignment
Load call reports and analysis from last week to CRM	U	1 hour	Marketing needs to run a pipeline report tomorrow
Check LinkedIn for decision-maker updates to go into CRM system	Just do it	30 minutes	CRM system appears to be out of date – my job to check if decision-makers have changed role or employer
TOTAL WORK-FOCUSED PLANNED TIME		5.5 hours	
Time for 'KU's and 'double U's (eg incoming calls)	?	2 hours	
TOTAL WORK-FOCUSED TIME		7.5 hours	
Breaks/lunch		1-1.5 hours	
Travel time today?			N/A – day in the office
Estimated departure time from work		18.30	
Make a dentist appointment			
Phone Mum on the way home			
Pick up bread, milk and ready meal			
Total			

It is easy to fill a 'to do' list with important and urgent things but take care not to over-fill it. In a sales job, there are always known unknowns such as customers' incoming calls, and there will be unknown unknowns as well. If you tick off all your items and it is only 3pm, look ahead. Can you bring something forward or do something developmental (such as reading a textbook)?

Note that time-dependent things, such as a meeting starting at 3pm, need preparation time and travel time (even if it is only walking to another office). Table 9.2 includes a call to be made at 2pm. You would need to re-read the feedback from the tutor before making the call. You might need to prepare a list of questions or remind yourself of the questions you had when you first received the feedback. You will get more from the call if you are fully prepared and in the right frame of mind for it.

Remember to take breaks and lunch. If your company organises lunchtime walks or other informal get-togethers, try to make use of them to make informal contact with colleagues and to get some fresh air into your lungs and fresh ideas into your head. Also add in your personal 'to dos' (such as the dental appointment); otherwise, you might forget them as you get engrossed in your work, and they could be a cause of worry to you later.

Some tasks may get postponed to the following day's 'to do' list if your time estimates are over-optimistic but try never to postpone an urgent and important item. At the end of the day, give yourself a big tick for items completed – it feels good, and you have the reassurance that you are on your way to achieving your ambitious goal.

Most people end up with just one column on their daily list and asterisks against the urgent and important items, but as you train you may want to have more detail on your 'to do' lists so that you can discuss them with your coach or manager. Effective time managers start to draft their 'to do' lists for a particular week during the week before so that they can stay ahead of diarised commitments which may need some preparation and check urgency and importance with relevant colleagues and customers. Even if you have a personal assistant, you need to do a lot of 'to do' thinking for yourself.

Try to make tasks reasonably specific. For a home item, you might write down 'housework' and then be frustrated because you only cleaned the bathroom. If you only have time to clean one room, decide which room gets cleaned today and put it on the list.

Discuss your time management with your coach. It helps you to review how much you have achieved during the month, and they can give you tips for better time management or action planning in the future. A common principle in project management is Plan-Do-Check-Act (PDCA), also known as the Deming cycle after the guru of quality management and continuous improvement, WE Deming (1900–1993). You might prefer 'PDCI' for review meetings with your coach or manager:

- **Plan** – What I planned to do when we met last month.

- **Do** – What I have done (using evidence from 'to do' lists).

- **Check** – Does this look good or bad?

- **Improve** – What do I need to do to get further this month?

Protecting your time

There are a few things that you can do to protect your time as well as improve your work-life balance and how you enjoy both:

- As you plan your 'to do' lists, think about how your customers organise their day. If you call a decision-maker who always takes her lunch at 12.45, at 12.40 she is either not going to take your call or she will be grumpy. You will not know such details for all of your customers all of the time, but the more you can ask about the best times to interact with particular customers, the more likely you are to be successful with them.

- Have a contingency plan for your day in case a big unknown lands on your desk or into your inbox. Who can you ask for help with an urgent task if you have to rush out to meet a customer? If anyone is waiting for something from you, let them know that you have had to deal with an emergency.

- Try to schedule tasks that need more concentration when you are at your most energetic and try to deflect interruptions. If you ring-fence a time for similar tasks, such as outgoing phone calls, you can make them one after the other and deflect incoming calls as you do so. If you are writing a proposal, do not look at emails and hang a 'please do not disturb' sign nearby.

It would be nice if we could always eliminate things that waste our time in our working lives. What wastes a sales-person's time? Sometimes a salesperson will rush to say that it is customers who say 'no' who waste their time. Despite all the information in this book about qualify-ing leads effectively, you will sometimes be annoyed by investing time in a lead which fizzles out. Accept it and learn from it. In particular, learn how you might have seen the 'I'm leaning towards doing nothing' signals earlier and saved a bit of time.

The next thing that wastes everybody's time is meetings. Why do we have so many when they are often pointless? They are a ritual of business life which fulfils a human need to connect but does not necessarily fulfil the business need to get something done. There are fewer pointless meetings in sales than in other functions, but there are still some. As you become more senior and call your own meetings, adopt best practice: set and enforce an achievable agenda and a finishing time. If participants talk about irrelevant topics, or repeat other people's points, or say in ten sen-tences what only needs one, interrupt and haul them back on track. If there is dissent, take a vote. You cannot do this when the customer is in charge, but for your own account team you can make the point that you want to be an effective chair of meetings and eventually they will thank you for it, even if feathers are a bit ruffled on the way.

The '4 Ds' of email management

Emails are another huge drain on time. You may receive over a hundred a day, but only some need to be followed up. A common system that can be used to classify them is called the '4 Ds'. Emma Donaldson-Feilder, a chartered occupational psychologist, describes the system as follows (NHS, 2018):

'Making a decision the first time you open an email is crucial for good time management.

- **Delete**: you can probably delete half the emails you get immediately.

- **Do**: if the email is urgent or can be completed quickly.

- **Delegate**: if the email can be better dealt with by someone else.

- **Defer**: set aside time later to spend on emails that require longer action.'[18]

Effective use of time

Good time managers are usually tidy people. If your desk or inbox is a mess, you will waste time trying to find things. Keep paperwork, online and offline, to a minimum and file it logically.

Be aware if lack of time or misuse of time is stressing you out. Think back to your preferences about time. Can you adjust your use of time to reflect your preferences, at least in some ways? If not, what coping mechanisms do you need? Or, if you feel really ill, should you change job?

---

18 Quote used with the kind permission of Emma Donaldson-Feilder.

If you commute to work regularly, can you use your time commuting to save time at work? If you use public transport, can you read emails, listen to online learning, or prepare your day while on the train or bus? If you are driving, you have to concentrate on the road, but when you are stationary at traffic lights or in jams you can use that time to reflect on the day ahead or the day just gone.

Reflective learning is always worthwhile. What have you thought or felt about an issue that you might want to raise with your coach at your next meeting? If your reflections reveal that you have been avoiding a particular task, try to identify why. You may need to ask someone what role this task plays in the organisation. Try not to wait until the person who relies on it being done is angry because it has not been done.

Think about the things you do and what room there is for replication. For example, marketing may provide a 'boilerplate' for proposals. Are there still details that you find yourself typing again and again? Ask marketing if they can add these details to the boilerplate or if you can customise the boilerplate for your sector. Similarly, you are probably learning how you like to plan your sales calls – can you replicate your questioning strategy from one customer to another?

Enjoying what you do

The final letter of the SCOPE mnemonic is E, for enjoy. If you are not enjoying your time at work, at study or at home, you need to change something. Part of achieving enjoyment is striking the right balance between work and other interests, but it is also about having the right perspective in terms of what results spending time and effort on things will yield. Life has its ups and downs. As the poet Rudyard Kipling (2016) put it, success and failure are both 'imposters' that can deceive – a success does not mean that you cannot fail next time and a failure does not mean that you cannot succeed next time. You need to take time to celebrate the adrenalin 'highs' that come with sales success and you have to take some time to mourn lost sales. To ensure that over longer periods of time you feel overall enjoyment and achievement, make some time to reflect on both. Identify the learning points and apply them in the plan for your next meeting, proposal or campaign.

Summary

In this chapter, we have looked at some of the factors which affect time management, the elements that make up time management, and how you can improve your own time management.

10

Collaboration And Teamwork

Introduction

A team is a group of people who come together to achieve a common goal. In organisations, there are formal groups of people such as committees reporting to the board, there are constituted teams such as 'key account teams', there are ad hoc project teams/bid teams, and there are informal arrangements whereby individuals within an organisation form relationships to achieve mutual benefits.

A team depends on its members' individual expertise in what they do and how they work together. No matter how good the best striker in a football team might be, the manager cannot rely on that individual to score without other players also contributing their talent to the team effort. Portugal went out of the 2018 World Cup before the quarter-finals despite having Ronaldo, and Argentina went out on the same day despite having Messi. All creative teams need to have 'synergy' – a state where the collective effort is greater than the sum of its parts.

Effective teamwork is vital in a twenty-first-century organisation. Research findings support the value of high-quality teamwork to the performance of the team and its contribution to the company's objectives; it also points to the value of being in a successful team for an individual's personal success (see the discussion of Hoegl and Gemuenden's work later in this chapter). As a salesperson, you are a member of a functional team – the sales department. You are probably also a member of a cross-functional team, such as a key account team or bid team, which draws on expertise from finance, operations and research as well as sales. Whatever sales role you are in, your work is highly interdependent with operations and finance. What is made depends on what you sell, as does cash flow. There is evidence that performance is better when there are teams supporting major customers than where there is no formal teamwork (Salojärvi and Saarenketo, 2013). This is because knowledge sharing and use of information is better within key account teams.

As an employee, you may also be a member of a self-managing team which has evolved to solve a particular problem, such as a process failure, or create a particular outcome, which could be anything from the Summer Staff Sports Day to new product ideas. As an apprentice, you will be in learning teams, perhaps with salespeople from other companies.

Working in teams can be invigorating and enjoyable. They do sometimes fail, and this chapter will cover what is needed to improve the chances of teams succeeding. If you have mixed team experiences, see what you can learn from the failures.

The nature of collaboration

As Richard Branson (2017), founder of Virgin, says: 'The fundamental driver of our success at Virgin has, and will always be, our people working together. To be successful in business, and in life, you need to connect and collaborate.'

Collaboration means working together with someone else to produce an outcome. It can happen between two or more individuals or organisations. You have come across collaboration in the home, at school, in clubs and between friends. It is what humans do to feel human; history is full of examples of extraordinary feats of collaboration that helped people to survive or to achieve great ends.

Collaboration happens outside of teamwork as well as within it. It may be mutually beneficial, or one party may collaborate in a spirit of goodwill in the expectation of a returned favour at a later stage. It is never easy to know when to co-operate if there is no obvious benefit, but in an organisation that values co-operation there could always be indirect career advantages in having colleagues see you as someone who helps. Big organisations can sometimes present us with conflicting expectations such as, 'Yes, we would like you to co-operate with marketing on evaluating a new campaign message, but, by the way, you must meet your target this month.' Your colleagues in marketing might understand that you have to put your target first, and they'll try to ask for your help at a suitable time if possible.

Good communications can ensure that good collaboration emerges. The benefits of collaboration include a better understanding of who can do what, where and when, to best effect. This means productivity for the firm, but it also means that we, as individuals, can play to our strengths while benefiting from colleagues playing to theirs.

Creating teams

Diversity

'Every individual is a marvel of unknown and unrealised possibilities.'
— William George Jordan, American editor and author

You will sometimes need a team of experts in a specific field to solve a problem, but many solutions benefit from diversity in the team. As far back as 1961, multifunctional teams were found to be most effective in innovation projects (Burns and Stalker, 1961). Typically, companies with a reputation for encouraging innovation choose people from manufacturing, operations, R&D, finance, marketing and sales to take part in project teams, sometimes with representatives from channel partners, suppliers and customers. The concept of multifunctional teams is based on broad foundations in many contexts. Whenever you were asked to choose a team in sports, you probably based your choice on needing one natural defender, one person who is good at scoring, a good distributor of the ball in midfield, etc.

Diversity is not just a matter of picking people from different functions in the company, though. It can also cover people with different work experiences, such as someone who has worked for a competitor, someone who has recently joined the company and someone who has been with the company twenty years. Team designers should also consider demographic diversity (eg age, gender, ethnicity, educational background) and cultural variety. In global companies, teams are always international.

Diversity is associated with improved team performance for a variety of reasons. Team members can see a problem from different perspectives. They can offer a greater variety of solutions. They can foresee more consequences, costs and benefits. They have a broader range of network contacts within and outside of the firm so that valuable expertise can be accessed. However, it is a human inclination to seek out similarity and stereotype people who are dissimilar, so diversity in teams can be a source of conflict. Team leaders should note that the more diverse the team, the more necessary it is to encourage good and frequent communications and to manage the team in an inclusive way (Jackson and Joshi, 2004).

Roles

The most popular model for explaining roles within teams was designed by Dr Meredith Belbin (Belbin, 1993; see

Table 10.1 for an example). As part of your in-company training or education workshops, you may complete the Belbin questionnaire. Each of us has a natural preference for the role that we like to play in teams; we would find it easiest to play that role every time we join a team, but that is not possible, and it would not be healthy for career development. It is worth discussing with your manager or coach what development you would need to play a different role that interests you or seems necessary for a particular team assignment.

You are likely to be assigned to a 'selling team', which is the mirror image of the buying DMU discussed in Chapter 4. Deeter-Schmelz and Ramsey (1995) have defined the roles in a selling team as Leader, Seller, Internal Co-ordinator, Customer Service Representative and Extended Selling Team (functional experts).

Table 10.1: Belbin selling team roles

Belbin team role name	Role type	Potential weakness	Relevance to sales career development	Relationship to 'selling team' roles
Resource-investigator	Finding information, contacts or opportunities that are relevant to the task.	Enthusiasm at the idea generation stage wanes during implementation.	As an apprentice new to sales, you may be asked to be the resource-investigator for a key account or territory sales team.	Expressed as part of the role of the 'seller', but in most large bid or account teams it could be a market researcher.
Teamworker	Keen to get the team to co-operate; willing to take on tasks.	May avoid necessary conflict.	Everybody needs to play this role at some point in the life of a team.	Assumed that all members adopt this role to some degree.
Co-ordinator	Balances the need to complete the task with the need for people to feel fulfilled in the task. Delegates sub-tasks.	May not appreciate that they need to be seen joining in with some tasks.	Usually, a senior salesperson or sales manager, but anyone may be asked to lead a project if it aligns closely with their objectives, or if it is their idea.	In the 'selling team' there is a Leader, who is senior (probably a board-level team sponsor) and a Co-ordinator, who is administrative.

Cont.

Table 10.1 *cont.*

Belbin team role name	Role type	Potential weakness	Relevance to sales career development	Relationship to 'selling team' roles
Plant	Offer creative and unconventional ideas.	May be less keen on the practicalities of implementation.	Typically, R&D people are expected to be plants, but can they always be unconventional? Salespeople can be effective in this role.	Not a specific role in a selling team but could be an important player in the extended team.
Monitor-evaluator	Able to provide an objective review at any point.	May be perceived as too detached.	From a development perspective, you should always try out this role; salespeople can be over-passionate about their projects.	Not a specific role in a selling team – it is assumed that all members can step in to do this.
Specialist	Has in-depth knowledge of the topic at hand or a topic which is crucial at some stage (eg company law).	Can provide too much detail on technicalities.	This may be you if the project concerns your customer or the industry sector that you sell into.	This is the 'seller' – the person who is the primary interface with the customer.
Shaper	Someone who wants to drive the team forward towards its objectives.	Might drive some people too fast or hard and cause friction.	Sometimes a natural role for a salesperson – can you learn how to do this while managing friction?	Both the leader and the seller may play this role. The leader is responsible for gaining authorisation for things to happen.
Implementer	Someone who can turn ideas into actions.	Likes to stick to the plan, so can be inflexible at times.	In senior sales roles, you will be a planner and project manager, so you need to learn this role.	The 'customer service representative' is the installer of the product/ service.
Completer-finisher	Wants to see things done to a high-quality standard.	Can be over-concerned with achieving perfection.	Customers expect attention to detail. You may not be an engineer or a lawyer, but you need to respect their roles and understand what they do.	The 'customer service representative' is the installer of the product/ service and likely to take this role. However, it could also be a company lawyer perfecting the contract.

Although most people in business are familiar with Belbin team roles, they are not always consciously considered in team design. However, the principle that each member of a team takes responsibility for particular aspects of the team's effectiveness should be established when the team is set up. It would be a disaster if half the team wanted to be shapers and the other half wanted to be plants. When you are asked to join a team, ask the team leader about the role they want you to take on.

Size

Does the fact that Belbin identified nine team roles mean that all teams should consist of about nine people?

It has been argued that team effectiveness decreases as size increases because some members find opportunities to take a back seat in a larger group, and communication is more difficult as teams get larger (Hoegl, 2005). Teamwork is subject to many complex variables, so the context in which a team operates is important. One important factor is participants' confidence in being able to discuss difficult issues openly. A co-operative climate can enable larger teams to be effective (Peltokorpi and Hasu, 2014).

The problem or opportunity might be complex and require multiple players. One way to ensure that a complex task is managed productively is to make a multi-team project by establishing a core team and extended team or sub-teams and/or involving particular people at particular stages of the project (Hoegl, 2005).

How teams develop

There is a lot of cynicism about team-building exercises, but it is often useful to try solving a trivial or fun problem before moving on to business-critical situations. They also provide some social time for team members, which often helps them understand each other.

In an earlier book, I described an exercise which involves providing the team with several eggs. Their challenge is to design packaging that will protect an individual egg from a 4-metre drop. The team is set a reasonable time limit and budget. They are provided with an environment in which they can 'buy' and test materials and present their solution at the end (Rogers, 1996).

On one occasion, when I ran this exercise, a team noticed that the mud beneath the drop site was soft, so they tested dropping eggs without any packaging. They all survived. This raised the question, 'Is packaging necessary for every context?'

The facilitator of such an exercise will be expected to give the team feedback on their performance, using criteria such as:

- Quantity of ideas
- How they evaluated ideas
- Feasibility of implementation
- Allocation of sub-tasks
- Pragmatism (eg attitude to time and cost)
- Time management
- Cost management
- Focus on objectives set
- Mutual encouragement
- Analytical thinking
- Conflict management
- Quality and quantity of communications and interaction

This allows the team to reflect on how they might organise themselves for the serious task in hand.

Psychologist Bruce Tuckman identified four stages of team development. His model is widely used to understand team development (Tuckman, 1965).

Forming – This is the stage when the team is brought together, perhaps by a senior manager, and briefed about its objectives. At this stage, members may be apprehensive, and they will be careful about what they say and do as they try to adjust to their roles in the project. Because this can inhibit progress, exercises like the one above can help the members to get to know each other.

Storming – Not all teams experience a 'storm' shortly after forming, but many do, and it is important to be prepared for it. This is the stage when problems can occur as team members start to express opinions. If well-managed, differences of opinion can be constructive.

The team leader may set ground rules for group interactions, such as:

- Suspend judgement when we are discussing ideas and use it constructively when we are evaluating them

- Let everybody stretch their mind and take risks

- Listen to other people's ideas, and build on them if you can

- Keep our objectives in mind at all times

- Keep our stakeholders in mind (in sales, this is usually the customers and the shareholders)

Creating an atmosphere in which different ideas are welcome and team members can be patient with each other helps to build trust and let information and communication flow:

> 'Cultivating a psychologically safe climate can be effective in keeping conflicts in check. Also, providing training and workshops on a regular basis that underscore negotiation, listening, and communication skills can go a long way towards deterring the spread of conflict.' (Auh et al, 2014)

Norming – After the uneasiness of storming, teams settle down and start organising to achieve objectives. Members establish their own mutual norms and expectations.

Performing – Confidence and competence grows, feeding on incremental successes at project milestones. Performing teams are motivated, knowledgeable and proud of their tasks and each other. One indicator that a group of people really have formed a team is when everyone in the group is confident about their contribution and willing to praise the contributions of others (Tagliere, 1993).

Later in his studies, Tuckman suggested that a post-performing stage should be added, sometimes called 'Adjourning' and sometimes 'Mourning', describing how a team has to be broken up once its objectives can be achieved, leaving a gap in the working lives of the team members (Tuckman and Jensen, 1977).

You will take part in many teams during your career. You will observe good practice and bad practice. Even at the beginning of your career, you may be able to influence your teams for the better by considering some of the ideas about teamwork quality in the next section.

How teams succeed

Hoegl and Gemuenden (2001) developed a model of teamwork quality based on six factors:

• A high quantity of useful communications

• Closely co-ordinated working patterns

• A good balance of member contributions, based on acknowledged strengths and weaknesses

• Willingness to support each other

• Willingness to apply effort to the objectives of the project

• Strong attachment to the team and the project

Where such quality could be achieved, it was significantly associated with team performance (in meeting the effectiveness and efficiency objectives set) as rated by team members, team leaders and managers external to the team (although the perception of performance varied between these stakeholders). This research also showed a strong correlation between teamwork quality and the personal success of team members, especially with regard to their development and satisfaction with their work.

It may seem obvious that the quality of teamwork would lead to success in achieving team objectives, but in the heat of the moment much good practice can be lost, and teams can veer off track. Team members must make an effort to sustain quality teamwork throughout the project. Table 10.2 provides a simple tool to help you reflect on your contribution to your team's success.

Table 10.2: The Teamwork Quality Checklist (adapted from Hoegl and Gemuenden, 2001)

Element of TWQ[17]	Measurement	How can you help?
Communication	Is there enough communication? Formal and informal, direct and open?	If other team members aren't communicating, can you start circulating some ideas or questions?
Co-ordination	Are the efforts of team members being structured within a meaningful plan?	Can you ask who is doing something that needs doing? Can you offer to do something you think needs doing?
Balance of team member contribution	Is everyone able to contribute? Are they bringing their expertise to discussions and activities?	If someone seems to have gone quiet, can you ask them a relevant question to bring them back into the discussion?
Mutual support	Do team members help each other out in the completion of tasks?	If someone seems out on a limb with a sub-task, can you offer to help or encourage them to ask for the support they need?
Effort	Are team members stretching themselves to do the best they can for the team?	Exert yourself first. You may then earn the right to ask others what stopped them meeting their deadline.
Cohesion	Are team members motivated? Is there team spirit, such as members being proud to be in the team?	If you speak of your own pride in what the team is achieving, it can be infectious.

TWQ does not explain all aspects of team performance or always predict team success. Researchers have also explored

---

19   Based on the factors in Hoegl and Gemuenden's Teamwork Quality (TWQ) model (2001).

good leadership, good project planning, skills within the team, stakeholder support, availability of resources and organisational support, and all have some contribution to make. However, TWQ is something that the members of a team can adopt as team practice, and there are collective and individual reasons to do so.

It may also be valuable for teams to consider what techniques they can use to improve performance. In the case of idea generation, there are a variety of techniques available. The Ishikawa, or Fishbone, diagram has generic applications (Ishikawa, 1968). Have you ever been annoyed when the reason given for a late plane is 'the late arrival of the incoming aircraft'? It just begs the question, 'Why was that late?' Was it a technical fault? Air traffic control delays? Did someone forget that the pilot was on holiday? The Ishikawa diagram allows you to indulge every impulse to ask 'Why?', 'Why?' and 'Why?' again. You need to get to the bottom of a problem before you can solve it.

In Figure 10.1, the customer has reported a fault with your product. The product fault is broken down into a variety of factors, all of which contribute to the problem, and all of which need to be addressed before the product fault can be corrected.

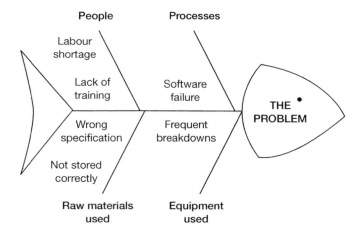

Figure 10.1: Product fault factors fishbone

Another technique is to reverse the problem. If our product was perfect, how would we ruin it? You can then reverse the ruination tactics to uncover potential solutions to product dissatisfaction.

A more abstract technique is to try to find a similar situation to the one on the table for discussion but from a completely different field, such as the military, medicine or nature. If you are investigating a product fault such as a tyre with a poor grip on hot roads, you might examine how animals in the desert deal with hot surfaces.

When it comes to implementation, there are a number of project management techniques which you can apply, some of which need qualified practitioners, such as Critical Path Analysis, programme evaluation and review technique (PERT), and PRINCE2.[20]

A simpler example is the Deming cycle. Although you will usually see 'PDCA' in common use, the addition of an 'O' in front emphasises the need for examination of the current state of the problem area before planning its improvement:

- **Observe** – examine the problem in depth

- **Plan** – identify potential solutions

- **Do** – test a potential solution

- **Check** – examine the results (do they help to some degree?)

- **Adjust** – improve this potential solution or try something else

If your team gets stuck, there may be a model which can help, at least by triggering the right discussions to move on to the next phase of activity. Ask your manager or coach for advice.

---

20 PRINCE2 is a registered trademark of AXELOS Limited.

How teams can fail

In his work on learning organisations, systems scientist Peter Senge observed that you can put a collection of highly intelligent individuals in a room to discuss a topic, but the outcome of their discussions demonstrates a less-than-average collective intelligence (Senge, 1995). How could that happen?

We have discussed good practice, and problems occur when good practice is forgotten or not observed. Typical causes of team failure include:

- **Organisational politics** – Not all teams can be above the game-playing that comes with organisational life. There is no easy answer to working around such difficulties; seek the advice of a manager and coach who has been in the company for a while.

- **Unclear or unworkable objectives or expectations** – The team needs to raise concerns with the project sponsor as soon as possible when they have examined a problem and found that the team's brief needs more thought. Equally, where objectives are clear, the team needs to stick to them and not stray into tangential issues. As Cespedes et al (1989) state, 'A close fit of sales goals with strategic goals, clearly understood, is essential'.

- **Poor information handling** – Too little or too much information are both difficult to manage. The resource-investigator should be able to manage the dissemination of information across the team.

- **Failure to resolve issues** – Conflict hurts team performance. Specifically, as conflict escalates, whether it's about the task at hand or a personality clash, team members lose sight of the interests of the customer and fail to communicate or share information (Auh et al, 2014). Team leaders need to step in and resolve the conflict as soon as possible. There is also an opposite phenomenon which is equally problematic. Psychologist Irving Janis studied dysfunctional teams and identified a phenomenon called 'groupthink', in which team members were so determined to achieve consensus that they ignored all uncomfortable truths that might create conflict, resulting in poor decision-making (Janis, 1971). Just as the team leader needs to resolve conflict, they may also need to flush out differences of opinion which are being suppressed.

- **Failing to complete sub-tasks** – Sometimes a team member does not do their bit. There may be a reason for it, but the other members cannot leave the work undone. A replacement may be the best way forward.

- **Personal attacks and win/lose attitudes** – Blame does not solve problems. Team members have to be accountable; however, stick to the facts of what did not get done and the consequences. The team leader should organise any change in team composition that might be necessary.

- **Insufficient planning and set-up** – Team design and team development must be considered.

- **Insufficient follow-up** – Is the team retained to review the implementation of its solution? At what point can it be adjourned?

You may feel scared when a team effort fails but move on to the next one with hope.

Sharing best practice

Whether you want to share an aspect or the outcome of your teamwork, be assured that sharing it will further your career development. You set yourself up as an expert on something, and you have helped other people avoid reinventing the wheel when they undertake a similar project.

You may have an opportunity to demonstrate your best practice at a meeting of fellow salespeople or another company meeting. Most people like to see something in action rather than just hear about it; however, you can also create a report for colleagues or a blog on the Intranet. You may just be asked to discuss your best practice with a specific group of your peers, such as other apprentices. You may informally share your best practice over coffee or lunch, or you can offer it to new contacts that you make. Remember to discuss it at a review meeting with your manager so that it contributes towards your observed career development.

Working with marketing

The most obvious example of regular collaboration and teamwork ought to be the relationships between sales and marketing. Many researchers have found that integrated sales and marketing leads to better company performance, better customer satisfaction and better employee satisfaction in the two functions (eg Guenzi and Troilo, 2007). Marketing and sales share responsibility for revenue generation and positive customer relationships. They share customer-facing processes and all the information held in the CRM or ABM system. They can achieve higher revenue generation when they co-operate on market sensing, new product development, supply chain management (particularly downstream management of channel partners), CRM, and the planning and implementation of lead generation and customer loyalty campaigns (Hughes et al, 2012). However, the relationship between sales and marketing in an organisation is often strained.

Marketing is responsible for raising brand awareness and encouraging brand preference, while salespeople have to work with individual customers to the point where they are ready to part with their money, and as they implement new products or services. Arguably, they take on more personal and professional risk. These distinctions create different cultures in different functions.

Marketing guru Philip Kotler and sales guru Neil Rackham explain cultural differences between marketing and sales as follows:

Marketers see themselves as focused on building sustainable competitive advantage for the future through market analysis and planning. To colleagues in sales, this can seem rather remote from the challenges they face in front of customers daily (Kotler et al, 2006).

As we have seen in this chapter, bringing different functions together in collaboration and teamwork is productive. It would not be desirable for marketing and sales to merge because they need different perspectives. Companies need a balance of interests because the over-focus on key accounts which might result from sales dominance would not be in the long-term interests of the balanced customer portfolios that they need. An over-focus on the future, which might result from a marketing dominance, could undermine the 'here and now' of customer demand which is critical to the quarterly results.

The principles of collaboration with marketing are the same as they are with all types of teamwork (see Table 10.2). Communication will help you to understand how colleagues in marketing can help you to succeed and vice versa. In some companies, part of sales training involves job-sharing with marketing. You will almost certainly be involved in many meetings with marketing colleagues, formal and informal, and be working on the same project teams. Avoid stereotyping and focus on those shared objectives of revenue generation and customer relationship quality. Never assume that you can do without marketing; on many occasions, you will need to ask for ad hoc information at short notice, and you will need goodwill to get what you need. Nevertheless, be prepared to challenge if you are not consulted on something – such as a marketing campaign involving your customers. Between marketing and sales, there is a lot of pre-planned high-duty strategic activity, but there is also a lot of give and take on day-to-day activities.

Summary

In this chapter, we have looked at the importance of teams in your career, how they are designed, how they develop and how their performance can be improved. Finally, we looked specifically at the relationship between marketing and sales and how it should operate.

11

Customer Experience Management

Introduction

Ultimately, competitive success is rooted in customer experiences. When customers trust a brand to give them a good buying experience, they will come back for more, profitable revenue will improve and shareholders will invest more. The 'customer journey' from enquiry to buying and using the product, along with post-sales service, needs to be smooth and pleasant. In many cases, for a variety of reasons, it is not. As a salesperson, you are the brand ambassador for the company, and if something does go wrong you will be in the customer's firing line, even if it was not something that you did or failed to do. However, managing the customer experience is not just about solving or avoiding conflict. With some customers, positive experience of a supplier involves regular contact for its own sake, although all meetings can be opportunities to upsell and cross-sell. Customers often see complacency about the customer relationship as a trigger to test the market.

The level of customer orientation and involvement that you need to invest will vary by product type and customer type. As we have seen in other chapters, many purchases are online and automated. Negative experiences such as missed deliveries, returns and technical queries will probably be dealt with directly by operational staff. It is when solutions are high value and complex that you will be the customer's first port of call, and you may be negotiating with operational colleagues on their behalf to arrange positive experiences or recovery from negative experiences.

Consider also that some customers have a high propensity to switch suppliers because they are sensitive to variations in their satisfaction and always aware of competitor offerings. They have higher experience expectations than customers who tend to stay with a satisfactory supplier, even when there are occasional problems (see Gustafsson et al, 2005). In some cases, the right thing to do with a 'switcher' customer is to help them to switch because they cost a lot of time and money to serve. As Homburg et al (2011) observe, the customer is not always king. However, if a 'switcher' customer is strategically important to the company, you will have to invest more time in managing their experience. Be proactive in planning positive customer experience activities and allowing contingency time for the reactive customer experience management you will face every day.

Customer experience – the big picture

Meyer and Schwager (2007) state that: 'Although companies know a lot about customers' buying habits, incomes, and other characteristics used to classify them, they know little about the thoughts, emotions and states of mind that customers' interactions with products, services and brands induce.' Although, as a salesperson, you must manage the customer experience, it is something internal to the customer or decision-maker in a corporate customer, so there are many factors beyond your control. The customer experience is affected by all events in their interaction with the supplier and 'touchpoints' (such as a telephone call or social media post). Perceptions build up in the customer's mind over time, and an accumulation of positive experiences can be rudely interrupted by a bad experience, causing the customer to rethink their view of the supplier.

Customer experience has been described as continuous – it changes over time as each individual customer has a variety of interactions with a supplier. They interact with people (employees and agents or dealers), systems, products and services. When similar products and processes are offered, it has been advocated that companies should compete on the quality of the customer experience. Systems, products, processes and employee training can be designed to provide the best customer experience at an affordable cost. However, in competing on 'customer experience', companies are engaging with many aspects of customer behaviour – and not all of them are rational.

Gentile et al (2007) identified that consumer experience is multidimensional, with six components:

- Sensory (the sights, sounds, taste, feel of products/services, locations, etc)

- Emotional (what mood is generated when dealing with a supplier)

- Cognitive (thoughts and ideas generated by dealing with the supplier)

- Usability (what use is derived from the product/service over its lifetime)

- Identity (using the brand has a meaning for the customer's lifestyle)

- Relational (connectivity with family and friends generated by the product/service)

They found that positive consumption experiences are at least as important as the usefulness of a product/service, even with simple products, and concluded that suppliers would benefit from innovation focused on the customer experience. In the B2B context, a deep understanding of

224 | CUSTOMER EXPERIENCE MANAGEMENT

customer experience is equally important and forms the foundation of proposals which engage the customer in 'co-creating' value.

Customer experiences: product, process, people

Product

For customers, the primary consideration in assessing their experience with a supplier is the functionality of the product or service. As discussed in Chapter 6 regarding technology products, Davis' Technology Adoption Model applies – the product must be useful and usable. It must be useful to the extent that it meets the specifications the customer set when buying it, and users judge usability by the intuitiveness of a product's functionality – can they learn how to operate it with minimum effort? A functional product which is easy to use can create a positive experience.

To maximise the potential for your customer to have a positive product experience, they must be able to test it before buying. In the case of a car, we usually rely on one test drive, but this could lead to 'buyer's remorse' when the customer is driving their new car in different driving conditions and discovers that the driving experience is not so pleasant. This does not mean that a month-long schedule of test drives is necessary, though – the customer may want their new car quickly. Instead, perceived product uncertainties can often be overcome with additional information, training or service; for example, the option to bring the car back in for testing at a later stage without financial penalty.

Despite the best intentions of operational manuals, the customer's experiences of purchasing services are much more difficult to control. The customer contributes themselves to the quality of a service experience; however, with the right corporate culture, some organisations have distinguished themselves for their good service, and they work hard to keep raising standards of consistency without losing the personal touch which customers value.

Process

Marketing and sales decision-makers can deepen their understanding of customer values and annoyances by looking at the complete process, from initial contact to completion of the sale and after-sales service. Best-practice companies aspire to what is sometimes called an 'outside-in' supply chain – designed to be agile and responsive to customers. From a process perspective, this means collaboration with the customer on stock management, forecasting/replenishment and logistics.

Customers, whether they are consumers or business decision-makers, get frustrated with suppliers who are difficult to work with because their processes are complicated and defy common sense. Company processes build up over many years, and sub-optimal routines accumulate as old processes try to accommodate change. It is particularly frustrating for customers when sub-optimal processes have been automated to annoy them more quickly. The early days of CRM were problematic for this very reason. Online experiences should be intuitive and efficient.

The elimination of waste in production and processes is often referred to as 'lean'. In lean manufacturing, the goal is to eliminate all wasteful routines which do not contribute to quality objectives. Waste includes moving things more than is needed, people or products waiting in queues, unnecessary actions (over-engineered products or services), and failure to eliminate defects in the earliest stages of production.

The Principles of Lean, which are observed by many leading manufacturers (Womack and Jones, 2003), are:

- Value is specified from the view of the end customer.

- All steps in the process of delivering a product/service to the end customer are mapped; any which are wasteful or do not create value for the customer should be eliminated.

- Process steps should be designed in tight sequence to ensure smooth and fast delivery of value (shortening the time from order entry to order fulfilment).

- Production is triggered by customer orders.

- Continuous improvement is critical – elimination of waste and focus on value creation is ongoing.

Successful 'lean' projects often involve integration with customer systems, which is good for closer relationships.

It is not up to you as a salesperson to implement 'lean' processes in your organisation, although you can always flag up a process that appears to add no value to the customer experience. However, you will often find that flaws in your employer's processes create problems for the customer, who will expect you to sort them out. Negotiate with colleagues to at least 'paper over the cracks' of a poor process to minimise annoyance for an important customer.

In shops, but more noticeably online, where over 50% of transactions that are initiated are not completed, suppliers are aware of the phenomenon of the 'abandoned cart'. There are several factors involved, but an important one is customer irritation. Difficulties in the process of buying and/or the service received during the process of buying can disappoint customers and cause them not to buy or to buy elsewhere (Bell et al, 2020).

People

You are not the only person in your organisation who matters to customers. Service engineers are popular as they are the people who sort out technical problems, and customers want to see engineers as quickly as possible within a convenient timeframe. Customers expect them to be competent and equipped with the right information and parts to do the job. They also expect them to be polite and to provide proactive advice.

Customers are equally dependent on competent and polite customer service representatives, whether in a call centre or a service centre. Companies are moving away from measuring call handlers on efficiency metrics (such as the number of calls completed) to measuring the quality of calls and their contribution to customer retention. Customers may also have 'touchpoints' with delivery drivers and accounts clerks.

Although many customers will have several interactions with colleagues in other functional roles, often the salesperson is the key 'touchpoint' for the customer, especially in complex B2B relationships. Throughout this textbook, you'll find many tips about the levels of knowledge and skills required to impress a business decision-maker. If you want every customer touchpoint with you to meet customer expectations, you need to demonstrate integrity, knowledge, high-level thinking skills, communication skills and the ability to 'get things done' for the customer. You will also need resilience and persistence.

One way to think about the customer experience is to remember their aversion to risk and appreciate that they perceive uncertainties about their experiences with suppliers. You can alleviate their concerns with frequent and high-quality communications. If you are proactive in contacting the customer to ensure that the value you intended to deliver is still being delivered, there should be fewer occasions when you have to deal with a customer who is grumpy or worse:

> 'A notable aspect of this customer uncertainty is whether the salesperson will continue to be accessible and committed to achieving agreed-upon solution outcomes in the future. As such, the salesperson's role entails assuring the customer of the supplier's intention to stay engaged, and ensuring that the supplier remains committed to delivering the performance outcomes wanted by the customer.'
> (Ulaga and Kohli, 2018)

No one can pretend that the demands placed on the salesperson to be a creator of and seller of new value, along with project managing the delivery of previously agreed value, are easy to balance. We know that 'role ambiguity' for salespeople detracts from their productivity; however, the twenty-first century is full of professional roles which entail some role ambiguity, so you need to be resilient in coping with it. Customer demands for service are escalating, and they can be immediate. In large key account teams, there may be a project manager who can take on most customer interactions about their ongoing experience, but the salesperson often has to manage concerns. This enables you to learn and to help the organisation adapt. According to customer loyalty analyst Frederick Reichheld in the *Harvard Business Review*, 'The lifeblood of adaptive change is employee learning, and the most useful and instructive learning grows from the recognition and analysis of failure' (Reichheld, 1996).

Managing customer concerns

It is never easy to deal with a customer who feels let down, but everyone has to do it from time to time, and salespeople have to do it more than most. Stay calm and remember that you would feel the same if you were disappointed with a product or service. Sometimes it seems that customers get angry about silly things. It is easy for you to feel angry when the customer is particularly difficult or has contributed to their problem by some omission or misuse. It is also natural to be frustrated if you feel that a colleague's blatant mistake has contributed to the problem.

When a salesperson (or engineer) devalues a customer complaint, it means that the opportunity to learn from it is missed. A typical example of devaluing a complaint is when you hear from the colleague who received the complaint that a particular customer takes up a lot of time on the helpline, implying that they are misusing products or failing to train operators properly. That might be true, but it is not a good reason for failing to analyse the customer's complaint (Reichheld, 1996).

Complaints are rarely personal. They are about missed deliveries which have not been sorted out, or inaccurate invoices, or a product failure. You are there to absorb the emotion and find a solution in the short term, and, in the long term, analyse the failure, learn from it and encourage colleagues to learn from it as well. Customers whose complaints have been handled well can become more loyal as a result, so it should be worth the effort.

If the customer calls you, they may have been wound up by recorded messages and difficulty in getting through to you, which will make them sound tense and aggressive. Face-to-face, the customer may be displaying negative body language and facial expressions, as well as sounding annoyed. In consumer markets, savvy customers are encouraged to make comments on social media so that their frustration can be seen by other customers. You may have a team of customer service colleagues monitoring social media for negative comments. They will be making sure to engage with the customer as soon as possible to switch the complaint to a telephone conversation. Early intervention will enable other customers to see that the company was quick to respond and concerned about the complainant's problems. Complaints can rarely be handled satisfactorily over email and social media; solutions come more quickly with the more personal interactions of a telephone conversation.

This is where your listening skills are most needed. The last thing anyone wants when they have a complaint is to be interrupted when explaining it. Whether your interactions are over the phone or face-to-face, listen first and then ask questions so you get a clear picture of what has gone wrong. Apologise without attributing blame to anyone because failures are usually more complex than just one person's fault. The customer will also expect reassurance that your employer can put things right, so ask what the customer wants – is it a replacement product, immediate repair, or compensation? Then, do what you can within your own delegated authority, followed by finding the colleagues who can solve the problem and getting their commitment to do it. Finally, follow up throughout the full process of recovery.

You should never be on your own in resolving the problem; even consumers see the bigger picture of 'corporate' complaint resolution, including the retailer/dealer's and manufacturer's brand. Unless there is comprehensive support to help resolve the problem, the consumer may switch brands:

> 'The individual's overall satisfaction with the salesperson, dealership, and manufacturer all demonstrate a significant impact on the consumer's level of commitment to repurchase from the dealership. However, with regard to the level of commitment or repurchase from the manufacturer, only the individual's overall satisfaction with the manufacturer had a significant impact.' (Mansfield and Warwick, 2002)

Proactively minimising customer concerns

Many websites you visit and emails you receive may invite you to feed back to the company. Phrases such as, 'We're here to help,' 'Feel free to contact us,' or 'Please send us your queries or comments,' are common. You may have noticed that every organisation that you deal with asks for feedback. On your supermarket till receipt, you may be asked about your shopping experience and invited to take part in an online survey with the reward of entry into a prize draw.

It is many years since Frederick Reichheld began writing about the profitability to be gained by keeping customers, pointing out that 'a climbing defection rate is a predictor of a diminishing flow of cash from your customers' (Reichheld, 1996). He urged companies to measure customer defections and complaints. We love to learn from positive feedback, but much can also be gained by eliminating even small causes of annoyance in the customer experience. Reichheld argued that losing customers was an indication of erosion of value which would lead to loss of cash flow from customers. However, if companies were eager to learn from dissatisfied customers, they could improve and be more competitive.

Reichheld's arguments are now widely accepted, and his Net Promoter Score is an important metric for many companies. Many other studies of the value of customer retention have been undertaken, and statistical models have been built to predict retention and defection patterns with a view to proactively managing them. There are still some sectors where service is poor, and 25% of customer defection is considered acceptable, but this approach is in decline. Most organisations are now focused on improving customer retention and encourage customer comment.

CASE STUDY: A NATIONAL CHARITY

An example of good practice is a national charity in the UK which devotes a whole page of its website to encouraging customer feedback:

- They invite positive feedback and provide a form for it.
- They make a pledge to supporters to treat complaints and comments seriously, to resolve them quickly and to learn from them in order to improve services.
- They define a complaint and explain what is not treated as a complaint.
- They explain their complaint process and provide a form.
- They explain their adherence to standards set by the Fundraising Regulator.
- They provide a link to their Supporter Service Charter.
- They supply comprehensive contact information to make it easy for the supporter to choose a way to contact the charity.

How does this case study relate to your role in sales? In interactions with the customer, you need to check that everything is going well with their purchase. Encourage positive feedback, but make sure that the customer knows that you welcome negative feedback and will use it for improvement. You can even prompt for slight annoyances (eg 'Is there anything that is not working as well as you expected?'). If you can demonstrate early on in a customer relationship that you want to improve on small things, the customer will trust you more if something major occurs. Also, it prevents small annoyances accumulating to become a general dissatisfaction which will prompt switching behaviour.

Most people know that things can and will go wrong over time. If they feel reassured that the person and company that they are dealing with will help them when that occurs, conflict is less likely to arise in the business relationship. By prompting for comments and feedback, you may be saving yourself stress at a later stage.

Summary

In this chapter, we have looked at aspects of customer experience management and the salesperson's role in it. We have considered the relationship between customer retention and profitability and observed the value of learning from both positive and negative customer feedback.

12

Digital Skills

Introduction

People learn about new IT almost every day. Systems are becoming more intuitive, but we may groan every time a supplier introduces a new code or function which we have to negotiate to use their website. The best way to learn is by doing and getting used to it.

'When digital transformation is done right, it's like a caterpillar turning into a butterfly, but when done wrong, all you have is a really fast caterpillar.'
— George Westerman, Principal Research Scientist with the MIT Sloan Initiative on the Digital Economy (quoted in MIT Management, 2014)[21]

Effective and efficient communications via digital media is an essential life skill and business skill. A textbook cannot help you to learn a system any better than the handbook or training available from the manufacturer, but this chapter offers some points to bear in mind as you master the systems you need to use in your job and in your learning.

---

21 For further reading, see Westerman et al (2014).

Using digital tools for research purposes

This section offers tips on finding useful material online. Refer to the Digital Knowledge chapter in this textbook for more detailed guidance on using electronic libraries and databases.

Google searches

What keywords might authors writing about your topic have used? Often, you can be searching for something using one term, and the best sources have used another. If your searches are too broad, you will be swamped with lists of irrelevant items; if you search too narrowly, you may miss what you want.

For example, if I search in Google for 'sales software', I get millions of results. If I search for 'sales software best expenses management function', however, I may get too few results. Changing the search to 'sales software expenses management reviews' still brings up thousands of results; adding 'best' to Google's predictive search string 'business expense tracking software' yields some relevant advertisements on the first results page, although there are still thousands of results in total. Add 'industry analyst report' to the same Google predictive text string, and you find some news items which provide links to reports you may be able to use.

Google provides a free alerting tool that allows you to easily set up and monitor useful public-domain information.[22] HubSpot offers a guide to setting up these alerts for sales purposes (Powell, 2015).

Wikipedia

Wikipedia is not a popular source of information with senior decision-makers as enthusiasts for a particular topic create the content about it. To be fair to Wikipedia, most of its users genuinely want to share information, and many

---

22   See www.google.com/alerts.

provide references for the text you see. Use Wikipedia for signposting and read the referenced sources before making any assertions in your reports. Always attach quotation marks to direct quotes, and, however you use someone else's findings to support your report, always list your sources in case you are asked 'Where did that come from?'

Evaluating search results

Be discerning about your data sources. Asking the following questions will help you develop searching skills and judge good and bad information and sources:

- **Where does this information come from?** Is it from a well-known academic journal? Is it from a professional association or government department? Is it from a respected newspaper or industry website? Is it from an expert in this field? If the source is none of these, avoid using it. An unsubstantiated opinion will not help you in your quest for good information about a topic or customer.

- **How relevant is this information?** Why was it created, and does it suit my intended use?

- **How objective is this information?** If it is survey data, how big was the sample size? If it involved interviews, how many and how were they conducted? The method used to create the knowledge being discussed is relevant in assessing its value.

- **How recent is this information?** Generally speaking, the more recent the better.

Using digital tools to generate new business and engage with customers

Researching sources of new business is one aspect of a salesperson's role, and proactively seeking new business can take place online.

Social media

Many companies have policies about social media use, but researchers have observed that it can be successful (see the Digital Knowledge chapter). As a professional, people will be searching for you on professional social media sites such as LinkedIn, so it is worth considering how you develop your profile and make proactive use of the sites.

Create a strong profile so that anyone interested in what you do can find out more about you. Your profile is a personal branding statement, and it needs to appeal to buyers. Write about how you have helped customers solve problems, not how many sales targets you have achieved, especially in your profile summary. Include keywords that might be in customer search strings. It may be worth including information about your interests or volunteer activities and your education, to show that you are a person and not just a brand ambassador, but these details should be brief. List your skills thoughtfully and ask close contacts for recommendations to endorse them. Provide links to helpful information, podcasts or videos. Provide detailed contact information so someone who has looked you up can easily connect.

Join communities in the social networking site, and you may wish to create a community around your product interests (or ask marketing to do this) so that you have a direct place in which to be active. You will also need indirect ones for people who do not currently know about your product. Spend time listening on social networks before you start posting to get a feel for what interests the users of particular communities.

Extend your connections through contacts and introductions. There is power in a second-degree connection. If someone recommends you to one of their contacts, then your new contact will be reassured about your value. Having connections is not enough, though; many social media users have lots of connections and generate little activity. Connections become prospects when you start to interact. Respond to their posts, and post information and opinion that is of interest to your prospects to try to start a conversation about it. Information can be found from third-party or company sources, but if you want to be seen as a thought-leader you have to comment on it, at least briefly. Use hashtags (#) in the content so that people searching on keywords can find you. Many successful social sellers create blogs or vlogs to share with their connections, or run webinars.

Email

Every company has an email policy. Learn yours and keep to it – it is all too easy to hit 'send' and regret it later. It is possible to be sacked for inappropriate use of email, and there have been many high-profile cases covered in the popular media.

Most well-known cases involve using company email for personal purposes, so keep your personal email for friends and your work email for colleagues and customers. Keep terminology suitable for personal emails out of work emails. Some people join the workforce thinking that they can use texting/chat abbreviations and emojis in their work emails, but you are expected to maintain professional communications at all times. Stay on topic – emails should be short, clear and about something specific – and remember to check your spelling and grammar.

Another common error is inappropriate forwarding. If you think someone might be interested in an email you have received, think twice. They probably have a long list of unread emails which were of marginal interest already. If you still want to forward your email, perhaps indicate why you thought so in a covering note, rather than sending it out of context. Make sure you read to the bottom of the email before forwarding it – perhaps there is other material attached. It is annoying that some email systems send whole conversations rather than just the latest item; deep in those conversations there may be something you do not want to send.

Take care with 'reply' and 'reply all'. Sometimes it is necessary to communicate with everyone on a distribution list, but more often you just want to send a reply to the sender, such as: 'Hello Hayley, Thank you for the invitation. I can do Monday at 3pm. Regards, John'. Everyone else who received the invitation does not need to know your attendance.

A company email has a legal status. Assume that anything you write could make a public appearance; for example, if you say something unkind about one colleague in an email to others, it could be used by the person you were disrespecting at an employment tribunal.

Writing reports using word-processing software

When faced with a blank screen, it may be easy to type first and think later, or you might prefer to draft your document with pen and paper and then turn to the computer. Whichever way you work, be sure to edit your report several times to ensure that it has a good structure and that the people you need to read it can use it.

However detailed your report needs to be, remember that most readers will have made up their mind about it on the first page. A one- to two-page executive summary explaining what your report is about and what decisions you need is essential. You then need a contents page demonstrating a logical structure.

Helpful structures generally include:

- An introduction (the context of the report)

- What is proposed

- Why it is important

- Why it is justified

- How it can be implemented

- Conclusion and call to action (budget to be signed off, project team to be appointed, etc)

Your report should include tables, diagrams and models as some people prefer visual representations. Use paragraph spacing and bullet points to break up the text. If possible, ask someone to proofread the report for you as it is difficult to see your own typographic errors.

Delivering presentations using digital media

Before PowerPoint, there were slide shows. Visual prompts to information are valuable to most decision-makers.

- **Your presentation should be visual**. Slide after slide of text will send your audience to sleep. Audiences expect photos, diagrams and embedded videos, but use the slides as a backdrop for discussion, not the focus for discussion.

- **Ensure that there is a logical progression** from slide to slide and that the design, colours and fonts are consistent.

- **Make titles and headings meaningful and interesting**, and ensure the content of every slide is easy to see and understand.

- **Less can be more**. There is a limited amount of information you can convey on one slide.

- **Take it easy with slide builds and animations**. They can be distracting rather than helpful, and they are time-consuming.

- **Your presentation should have pace**. Your audience has a short attention span.

Salespeople have to give a lot of presentations, and the best advice is to practise, seek feedback and practise again. Learn from the people in your organisation who produce PowerPoint content, such as the graphic designers.

Using your company's CRM and associated IT systems

We have discussed CRM and other systems which support sales in depth in the Digital Knowledge chapter. You may have a personal objective to keep certain bits of the system up to date, such as logging call reports or noting a customer's contact changes. Each system will have its own updating processes, and some are more intuitive than others, but you have an obligation to the company's collective customer knowledge. Set aside time each week to make sure that you are up to date with reporting. To avoid it feeling like a chore, make a list of the things that you want out of the system, such as customer buying trends and incoming calls to the service centre, and make sure that you explore them after you have completed your updates.

Summary

Professional salespeople have to be digitally literate. You may not enjoy every information system function, but you have to invest time in mastering the systems that you use and contributing to them as well as taking from them.

PART 3

THE SKILLS OF A WORLD-CLASS SALES EXECUTIVE – THE SALES PROCESS

13

Customer Engagement

Introduction

You will have many sales conversations in your career, and the early stages of engagement with customers are crucial. Your progress towards making a sale and building a commercial relationship with a customer depends on you making a favourable start, by demonstrating common understanding and appreciation of the customer (Kaski et al, 2018).

This may not stop the sales, but it makes it difficult to progress. Like most skills, customer engagement takes practice. You need to practise in scenarios enabled by your employer and learning organisation, and you can even practise the art of talking to strangers in bus queues. This chapter includes advice on what to practise and what to avoid.

Self-awareness

To get better at engaging customers and developing your style, you need to know your starting point. It is difficult to ask for feedback on how you open conversations and build rapport with people. It is also difficult for the people you ask to give you feedback. They may feel that their views are personal and that to give an honest opinion might cause offence.

You may feel that your engagement skills are OK because you have spent many years connecting with your friends. However, when you enter the workforce you will be engaging with a wide variety of people. In particular, many of your workmates and customers will be older than you and have different communications style preferences, so ask your coach or manager for advice. As a business professional, you do not want to blunder along happily with unconscious incompetence. What is your communications style now? Where does it need to be? You can then try to make improvements – perhaps small ones at first, such as practising greeting people more formally.

Self-awareness is also important in dealing with a common reaction to stressful situations, such as meeting new people: 'stage-fright'. Remember that you have done your homework and you have a solution that would help them to succeed. Age-old advice about focusing on breathing deeply can also be helpful. Control your concern, but do not relax too much. If you are too casual about engaging with the customer, you may come across as indifferent.

Opening customer conversations

Face-to-face introductions

Business conversations have to start somewhere. Although some purchasing decision-makers may wish to dive straight into the topic of a meeting, in most cases they invite you in, let you hang up your coat and offer you a cup of tea. Some like to talk about anything but business long enough for them to know who they are dealing with. So, how do you 'break the ice' when meeting someone new?

First impressions

You will have done your homework about the company and the person you are visiting. It is surprising how much you can find out about people online, so take care not to sound like a cyber-stalker! You might not go into a meeting asking them about their love of mountain biking, but you could prepare a question about sport that might lead them to volunteer their interests.

'Small talk' is often described as a conversation without purpose; in fact, it is useful when we meet new people. It is a polite and indirect way of trying to find common ground from which to do something together. When you join a class or club, you have to make small talk with strangers whom you hope to befriend. Perhaps you want to establish if they have the same taste in music so that you can go to festivals together. In the case of salespeople meeting buyers, it is a way of exploring whether you feel comfortable doing business together.

First impressions are important, ensure that you have a business-like appearance, which in the UK means formal suits, unless you know that the customer has a more relaxed dress code. Show respect, which includes putting your phone in your case and on silent. Try to convey openness and interest in the person you are meeting by smiling and making eye contact as soon as they come to pick you up from reception. Remember to greet the customer with a 'Good morning/afternoon' followed by their name, using their title and last name (eg Mr Jones, Ms Smith, Dr Ali) until you have permission to call them by their first name. Shake hands and thank them for making time to see you. Then what?

Businesspeople in the UK often start conversations with a comment about the traffic they have encountered or the weather. Conversation starters about holidays, cars and sports are also common, but might not be useful unless the customer has a clear interest in any of these topics, perhaps indicated by photos in their office.

These are not usually controversial topics, and they enable some toing and froing to find common ground. Maybe you both like holidays in Italy or playing golf. Unfortunately, much advice about business small talk has emerged from assumptions that both people are male and from the same country or subculture. In the diverse workplaces of the twenty-first century, sometimes you may feel at a loss trying to identify a mutual personal interest. You could instead offer a compliment about the company premises, such as, 'These are impressive new offices. What is it like working here?'

Offer information about yourself as well as listening attentively when the customer talks about themselves. For example, golfers compare their handicaps, their clubs and the courses where they play. You need to prepare for this part of the meeting as well as the rest of a sales conversation but try to develop your own style: 'Original personal styles appear to be much more effective than clichéd small talk, which can be perceived as false friendliness. Both short and extended episodes of small talk can assist in building rapport between the salesperson and buyer' (Kaski et al, 2018).

Non-verbal communication

There is a lot of dubious quasi-psychology about body language. There are whole books about it, usually from a North American or Northern European perspective. Remember that body language does not always cross borders well:

'The thumbs-up sign is equivalent to the middle finger in Greece and Sardinia. Tapping your finger to your temple is a gesture to show memory in North America but suggests insanity in Russia. Even nodding yes or shaking one's head can be misunderstood abroad. The yes-no gestures are reversed in countries like Bulgaria and Albania. In Turkey, "no" is gestured by nodding the head up and back. It's not just the individual gestures that can cause miscommunication, but the rate of gesturing. Some societies, like Italy and Spain, are known for talking with their hands. Others are more reserved with body movement as a form of politeness. In parts of East Asia, gesturing is considered boorish behaviour, and would be rude in a professional setting.' (Merritt, 2013)

In a face-to-face meeting, our head movement, facial expression, eye movement, body posture and hand gestures are important. We understand from an early age what 'good' and 'bad' body language is like. We know not to slouch in our chairs, rolling our eyes at customers. It is important to look interested in what the customer has to say, which is normally conveyed (in the UK) by leaning forward and occasional nodding. If the customer leans back and crosses their arms when we say something, we will deduce that we have made them feel defensive and they do not agree with what we have said. In seeking approval, we usually try to adapt to the style of the other person in the conversation. For example, if they use expressive hand gestures, then we feel that it is OK to do so too. If they are particularly conservative about physical expression, then we also rely more on tone of voice to convey emphasis.

As with other communication skills, seek feedback from colleagues and coaches on what you do well and not so well. Practise whatever improvements they suggest. If you work across cultures, research body language and take care not to cause offence. Body language can help to make connections, but it can also be irritating. For example, the use of hand movements to emphasise points can be a useful visual cue that something important is being said, or it can distract the customer away from eye contact with you while they wonder why you think using a chopping motion is necessary or clever. If in doubt, minimise your body language until you are familiar with the customer's expectations.

Verbal communication

Whether your meeting is face-to-face or over the phone, you need to concentrate on your words and those of the customer. It is important to avoid problems with coding messages (a customer may hear your communication differently from what you intend) and decoding messages (you may hear a customer's communication differently from what they intend). The immediate challenge in starting conversations is the sheer volume of words in English, some of which can cause confusion. Factors that can cause misunderstandings include:

- **Word meanings** – English is littered with words that sound the same or similar and have different meanings. If in doubt, ask the customer for clarification.

- **Slang and jargon** – English is also full of regional, age group, or subculture slang and jargon in every field of technology and business. 'Wicked' can mean that something is truly horrible or quite clever. A slim chance is the same thing as a fat chance. Stick to plain English, especially in a first conversation.

- **Assumptions** – Sometimes we stereotype people or jump to conclusions. The art of successful conversation requires open-mindedness, listening and concentration.

- **Inattention** – We may fail to ask enough questions to generate understanding. We may fail to pick up on cues from the customer, such as urgently needing to get to their next meeting, which will cause annoyance. Our minds may drift when we are trying to listen to people because of a distraction or if we've made a tangential connection with something the customer has said.

Communicating by phone is particularly important for busy professionals, which includes your customers. Initially, they may not have time for a face-to-face meeting or they may like the relative privacy and anonymity of a telephone conversation for the first communication with a potential supplier.

You need more concentration for small talk on the phone since you have more distractions (as does the customer). Because you cannot see if the customer is looking bored, annoyed or happy, you have to listen for verbal cues. However, a telephone conversation can be just as revealing as face-to-face interaction, as academic researchers have found:

> 'Respondents provide verbal cues – hesitation, sighs, for example – that can indicate that a follow-up question or probe is in order. Even though the telephone interviews precluded probing the interviewees based on visual cues, it was still possible to probe participants.' (Sturges and Hanrahan, 2004)

In telephone conversations, you need to speak clearly, and you may need to ask the customer to repeat sentences because of signal problems. Polite greetings, remembering names, thanking them for their time and conveying enthusiasm to speak to them are just as important as in face-to-face meetings. There may be less time for small talk on a telephone interaction, and the customer will expect you to focus on the purpose of the call and maintain a reasonable pace in the conversation.

Here is a short checklist (adapted with kind permission from McDonald and Rogers, 2017) to help you prepare for meetings and calls:

- **Appearance** – Dress formally for in-person meetings unless you know that the customer has an informal dress code.

- **Body language** – Think about hand movements, eye contact, facial expressions, personal space and sitting positions during face-to-face meetings. Be reserved when you first meet someone.

- **Greetings** – Most cultures appreciate time being taken over greetings and introductions.

- **Language** – Speak clearly, without jargon or ambiguity. Think about the balance between speaking and listening. Give the customer time to talk and an opportunity to demonstrate their understanding, as well as checking your understanding of what they have said. Do not rush to answer questions if they clearly need some thought.

- **Humour** – Avoid it until you know someone well.

- **Concepts of time** – 'Now' and 'soon' mean different things in different cultures. Be specific when discussing time.

- **Directness versus small talk** – Getting to the point is highly valued in some cultures; in others, it is considered rude. Try to get the balance right. Do not ask people things that you should have researched yourself, such as their status. Assume the person's status is higher than it might appear.

Written communication

How on earth can we make small talk in an email, LinkedIn message or letter? We do not usually engage people in small talk in an email because we have to assume that all emails are either deleted before reading or skimmed. Written communications are usually focused. The title of the email must arouse the interest of the customer (to prevent the recipient from deleting it), and your opening line must specify who you are and why you are contacting them; for example:

> *From: John Smith*
> *To: Hayley Brown*
> *Topic: Improving ROI in your logistics hub*
>
> *Dear Ms Brown*
>
> *My name is John Smith from SuperLog Systems. You kindly agreed to connect on LinkedIn after an*

invitation from James Green. I am e-mailing to
tell you a little bit more about what we do here at
SuperLog...

First emails or LinkedIn messages need to be short and have a call to action, but how many of us act upon emails from contacts we don't know well? A message that is short and simple, such as a link for further information, is likely to be most effective. If you have the analytics, you will know if the customer clicked on the link and followed up. If they did not, follow-up emails or messages might help, in which you can acknowledge that now may not be the right time for their company and include a calendar invitation for a call or follow-up at a convenient time. If the response comes after one year or never comes, you know you have a cold lead.

Building rapport

Rapport is a stepping-stone on the way to establishing your credibility and trustworthiness. Your actions are important, but recent research (Kaski et al, 2018) demonstrates that successful salespeople do not drive forward with all their learned rapport-building techniques; they are sensitive to the customer's efforts at rapport building and respond to them with a personal example or empathy:

> 'Relying on an authentic focus on the customer along with collaborative, responsive actions, rapport building can lead to shared positive feelings between participants. In turn, these interactions may result in feelings of being heard and appreciated as professional individuals, leading to overall positive attitudes toward collaboration and possible business relationships.'
> (Kaski et al, 2018)

This important research finding, based on empirical cases, offers a model to explain the best practice; this model is simplified in Table 13.1.

Table 13.1: Simplified rapport-building actions (author's own examples based on Kaski et al, 2018)

Timing	Rapport-building function	Actions		
Before the meeting	Gain customer insight	Understand customer needs	Understand decision-maker	Prepare potential solution
	Personal preparation	Understand your motivation for the call	Reduce personal stress	Concentrate on decision-maker as a person
During the meeting	Ice-breaking	Concentrate and listen	Offer small talk with a confident pace and tone	Look pleased to be with the decision-maker
	Find common ground	Listen to customer's small talk	Respond to customer's small talk, giving examples from your own experience	Be yourself (avoid sounding scripted or trivial)
	Make a connection	Adapt and build on what you appear to share	Accentuate positive connections	Address any negative issues that arise
	Reinforce the connection	Confirm points of agreement	Check for positive mood	Move on to the purpose of the meeting

Adapting to customer preferences

Many books on rapport building suggest that you agree with the customer and reflect back their stance on the topic you're discussing; however, customers say that they value salespeople being original and authentic. It is not rude to agree to differ on something like the weather. If the customer loves cold weather and you prefer hot, explain your preference and explore theirs with polite curiosity with questions like: 'Do you take holidays in colder climates in the summer?'

Cultural awareness

As mentioned earlier in this chapter, ideas about body language, ice-breaking and rapport building vary in different cultures, and you need to adapt to the customer's preferences in this respect. There are many cultural factors to consider, including national culture, the customer's demographic and interests, and the business culture in which they work.

Consider your own sense of belonging. Do you feel you 'belong' to the country where you were born? When you are at work, do you feel that you belong first and foremost to your employer? For example, many people who worked for IBM in its early days had a strong identity as 'IBMers'. Perhaps you feel that you are part of a global community of sales professionals. For some of us, identity with a sport or hobby is important, such as being a proud fan of a football club or stamp collecting society. Many would also say 'family first' and identify strongly with their family name.

Although we live in a globalised world where English seems to be everyone's second language, we cannot assume that there are universally successful ways to engage customers. Many cultures around the world, and some subcultures in Europe and North America, are profoundly different from anything you will have experienced to date. For example, there are specific relationship-building customs in some regions, such as Guanxi in China, Ubuntu in Kenya and Wasta in the Middle East. They are complex, and it is prudent not to assume that you can use them; mistakes are likely.

You should research the culture of the customer but be careful in making assumptions about it.

Enhancing and sustaining customer relationships

Once you have established rapport with a customer, you need to keep it up. Follow up on all sales calls quickly, and when a sales call has been particularly pleasant, make sure you follow up quickly so the customer remembers the positive atmosphere and you can move the sales process on as soon as possible. Whatever the customer told you about their love of holidays in Iceland to escape summer heat should be logged in your mind or in a notebook so that you can discuss it again next time there is personal contact.

You must do your bit to demonstrate a commitment to the customer, but you must also sell internally to colleagues to ensure that there is a company-wide commitment to your new contact. Across all cultures, it is not only your personal credibility that matters to a customer but also the credibility of the supplier brand. The whole company needs to focus on keeping its commercial promise (ie delivering goods to a certain specification on a given date). Contractual performance is at the core of all business relationships. The goodwill that you generate with customers is important, but it is the competence of the company overall that will sustain a business relationship in the long term, as you can see in Figure 13.1.

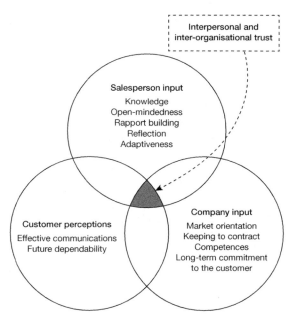

Figure 13.1: Business relationship factors (based on research by Harich and LaBahn, 1998)

Summary

Your success as a salesperson is not dependent on rapport building in its own right. There are plenty of amiable people who can build rapport, but not all of them can move on to potentially challenging business discussions and negotiations to make a sale. As we have discussed in this chapter, recent research emphasises the value of rapport building with new contacts. If you get it wrong, you will face difficulties later on in the business relationship – if it progresses at all. Follow up on the suggestions in this chapter, practise and seek feedback from your manager, coach and/or tutor.

14

Customer Needs Analysis

Introduction

One of the most important skills you will ever learn in sales is analysing the needs of a variety of customers. Sustainable sales success for a supplier depends on providing solutions to customer needs.

Customer needs are not always explicitly stated or even top of the customer's mind when you start a conversation with them, and there are many anecdotes about how new inventions would have failed if salespeople had relied on the customer's articulation of their needs. For example, in the 1900s, road transport users might have imagined they needed a more comfortable carriage with faster horses because they were not yet familiar with cars. A 1920s homeowner might have longed to afford a maid when vacuum cleaners and electric cookers were newly affordable to make housekeeping easier and faster. In the 1950s, as financial services companies struggled with the administration of large numbers of new customers, it took a brave purchasing team to realise that computers (previously only used for military purposes) could automate many processes.

'Customers are your best teachers. Learning about your customer's beliefs, values and priorities teaches you which selling points you should emphasize.'
— Mark Goulston, psychiatrist and business author (2018)

The salesperson is the interpreter of needs, helping customers to see how the solutions available can be valuable for them. Bear in mind that the customer has to agree that the analysis of their needs is correct. If you start your interaction with a customer by extolling the benefits of your product, you might get a 'So what?' response quickly. If you take time to ask questions about the customer's outlook and how they use their current solution, you are more likely to present the product in a way that makes 'Aha!' more likely than 'So what?' James Hotson (2017) of the Forbes Business Development Council writes: 'Your pitches should be all about your prospect. Forget about yourself, forget about your product features and capabilities, and start the conversation with a genuine interest in the customer.'

In this chapter, we will discuss how you can analyse needs, starting with the research you can do ahead of customer interactions and then explaining questioning strategies for emails, calls or meetings with the customer.

Desk-based needs analysis

To start understanding customers, get into good habits such as following the business news. This way, you will pick up on factors in the business environment that are affecting each customer and their industry sector (B2B) or market segment (B2C). In fact, it is worth following your whole supply chain from demands in consumer markets through to factors influencing the production of raw materials – such as weather affecting the growth of crops or political unrest affecting the mining of raw materials. Hancock, John and Wojcik (2005) explain:

> 'In a best-practice example, one consumer durable-goods manufacturer engages in thorough end-consumer research, including efforts to understand the preferences and buying patterns of shoppers at its important retail customers. The supplier can thus

collaborate with customers to conduct long-term category planning, manage changes in the mix of products, tailor marketing campaigns, and improve in-store sales and service execution.'

Consumers

In Chapter 2, we looked at multiple methods of segmenting consumers into target groups and how marketing can provide personalised profiles which are relevant to your company's products and services. You can generally rely on your marketing colleagues to keep you up to date with the needs of target customers, but it is still useful to do your own background reading. To do so, you need to be aware of the socioeconomic classification of consumers which is generally used by the government and in the media. The ONS socioeconomic classifications are shown in Table 14.1.

Table 14.1: NS-SEC Analytic classes (ONS, 2016)

1	Higher managerial, administrative and professional occupations
	1.1 Large employers and higher managerial and administrative occupations
	1.2 Higher professional occupations
2	Lower managerial, administrative and professional occupations
3	Intermediate occupations
4	Small employers and own-account workers
5	Lower supervisory and technical occupations
6	Semi-routine occupations
7	Routine occupations
8	Never worked and long-term unemployed

The new classification was established in 2010. You should also be aware of other classifications, such as the National Readership Survey (NRS), started in 1956 and now owned by PAMCo (2020), which many organisations use. There is also a more descriptive socioeconomic analysis called ACORN, developed by a company called

CACI Ltd.[23] Acorn uses a variety of data sources to classify consumer lifestyle, behaviours and attitudes. The data can also identify needs, especially public service needs, in specific neighbourhoods (CACI, n.d.). ACORN is common in fast-moving consumer goods and retail sectors; for example, it helps retailers plan the location of shops and micro-market their stores. Each of these classification systems is unique and based on different datasets, but there are similarities.

We explore examples of classification methods in Table 14.2, which shows how the various classification systems align with each other. The NS-SEC uses something similar to type 1. Socioeconomic analysis would use descriptive phrases similar to type 3, eg ACORN. Type 2 uses a similar approach to type 1 but may use different rules to establish at which level the prospective customer is classified. The key is to identify which classification method your business uses and understand where each of your customers fit into it.

Table 14.2: Similarities between classification approaches

Type 1	Type 2 (PAMCO method)	Type 3 – Descriptive phrases (ACORN method)
1	A	High achievers
2	B	Established
3,4	C1	Comfortable
5	C2	
6	D	Struggling
7,8	E	Facing adversity

You may also find that general sources of consumer information will use age-based or lifestyle-based segmentation. Jargon may emerge when sub-segments become popular media themes. Examples of the jargon include 'the grey pound' to describe the spending

---

23   See https://acorn.caci.co.uk.

power of the over-sixties, 'millennials' to describe people born between 1982 and 1996, and the 'pink pound' to describe the spending power of the LGBTQ community. You may find some stereotypical comments about market segments, and you may find reasonable sources which make you challenge those stereotypes. For example: 'Millennials have a reputation for doing everything with their smartphones, but the reality is strikingly different. A majority of millennials make most of their purchases offline' (Kestenbaum, 2017).

High-net-worth individuals (HNWIs)

This term is often used in the financial services industry to indicate extremely wealthy clients. Their wealth is well above that of 'affluent achievers'. Some very wealthy people are featured in the media; if you are selling to the aristocracy, Premiership footballers, television personalities or chief executives of major firms, you may be able to find out about their personal likes and dislikes and their lifestyles. Not all wealthy people are famous, though, and some pay people to preserve their privacy.

An interesting angle on researching the needs of the very wealthy is that over time, their needs become more mainstream. Even if you do not sell to HNWIs, their spending patterns might give you ideas for other customers. Colin Lewis, CMO at OpenJaw Technologies, observed in 2018 that 'once, rich people used their money to buy bling, now they use it to buy customised goods and services that give them back their time – and one day, so will we.'

Organisations

The main generic business market segmenting factor is called 'firmographics'. It is based on the characteristics of the firms, and it is the equivalent of demographics for consumers. The characteristics included in a firmographic analysis will be:

- **Industry sector** – This is usually according to a classification system such as the UK SIC (standard industrial classification).

- **Company size** – This may be measured by turnover, market share in its sector, number of employees, value of assets or number of locations. Many measures of size can be misleading; with employees, for example, the company could have an army of subcontractors and relatively few direct employees. Generally, turnover is the most comparable indication of size.

- **Location** – This may not just be a matter of a geographical region; it can also be whether the firm is in a city or a rural or remote area.

- **Ownership and structure** – There are different legal entities for firms, such as limited companies, public limited companies and partnerships. Some firms are decentralised; others are hierarchically run from group headquarters. Some are owned by a single entrepreneur, and some sizeable organisations may be owned by a large workforce or a variety of small shareholders.

- **Customers served** – The portfolio of customers that a company serves may be relevant in its firmographic. Does it focus on government departments or one particular industry sector? In some cases, you will need to analyse the customer's whole supply chain to understand what drives their needs.

- **Financial performance** – Some financial ratios can vary significantly from year-to-year and are not particularly comparable across sectors. Nevertheless, a company's profitability and credit rating are likely to be included in a firmographic analysis.

For the purposes of desk research, you will find specific trade magazines in sectors which discuss industry trends, specific organisations to represent firms in particular regions (such as Chambers of Commerce per city or county) that may produce research or newsletters, and pressure groups or co-operatives that represent small firms.

They may have some bias, but these reports will be instrumental in giving you an understanding of how firms with a particular firmographic perceive their needs.

Needs analysis in customer interactions

Most major sales training organisations have methodologies to help you to prepare and conduct interactions with customers which will help you to understand their needs and make a value proposition to them. Although your connections may be indirect in many cases, these methods are manifestations of the theory of adaptive selling, which has been empirically tested hundreds of times since its articulation in 1990 by Rosann Spiro and Barton Weitz. Adaptive selling describes the process of establishing the customer's situation and adapting the sales proposal to it. The research tells us that you are more likely to succeed by using adaptive selling techniques (Spiro and Weitz, 1990). In this section, we focus on establishing needs, and the questions and question sequence that will help you to impress the customer.

First, a few reminders of what needs to be in place before you ask questions to establish need:

- Do your homework and revisit your research before you meet the customer. If you are having a telephone call or online meeting, it may be acceptable to work from notes; if you are meeting face-to-face, you need to have your facts and figures about the customer in your head as you converse. You can take notes as a prop if it helps you to feel less nervous; however, if you keep referring to them the customer will think that you are not serious about understanding what they do.

- Establish rapport, as discussed in the Customer Engagement chapter.

- If appropriate, ask permission to start asking about their needs. In the case of a consumer sale, 'May I ask you a few questions about how you might be using this product?' would probably gain a positive response.

In a B2B sales meeting, there will likely be some overlap between establishing rapport and asking questions that help you to identify the need. Your questioning strategy will be a combination of open questions and closed questions:

- Open questions start with 'what', 'why' or 'how'. They are an invitation to the customer to give you a long answer explaining their opinion on the topic. These questions will help you to understand the customer's perceptions about their current product and potential new products.

- Closed questions are intended to get a 'yes/no' or a specific answer. For example, the question 'When did you buy your last car?' may receive a reply of '2012', and the question 'Have you had a large repair bill in the last year?' may receive a reply of 'Yes'.

Purchasing managers have little time to spare so they will not want a barrage of questions, and they will not want to be asked about things that they think you should already know. Many consumers also take this approach and are infuriated by the slow sell. Particularly if you are visiting a customer's home for any reason, be careful not to out-stay your welcome; it could be interpreted as an aggressive commercial practice under the Consumer Protection from Unfair Trading Regulations 2016. Strike the right balance between a meaningful conversation and boring the customer into submission.

Sales representatives who have been found guilty of illegal sales activities have been fined personally, and their employers have had to pay fines too. The fines are designed to outweigh any gain from the sale to a substantial degree. In such cases, both the salesperson and the company have to pay costs and a victim surcharge (see, eg Tegeltija, 2016).

Question types

Most sales training organisations have acronyms and formulae for helping you to understand which questions to ask and in what order. The acronym SPIN[24] was developed by Association for Professional Sales patron Neil Rackham and is described in Table 14.3 and Table 14.4 below. Although these models are primarily aimed at complex sales in the B2B sectors, you can also apply them in consumer scenarios. They tend to explain situations in which you are trying to unseat an incumbent supplier, but they can also guide other sales scenarios.

Table 14.3: A B2C example of SPIN (Rackham,1988)

Question type	Purpose	Examples
Situation	To establish facts about the context of the customer's business need	'What sort of car do you have at the moment?' 'How long have you had your car?' 'What do you use it for?' 'What sort of job do you do?'
Getting it right: Try to get a good picture of the person in front of you. Do they fit any of the consumer profiles developed by marketing? Can you deduce which general socioeconomic trends apply to them?		
Problem	To probe for problems or dissatisfaction with the current situation	INDIRECT: 'What prompted you to come into the showroom today?' 'What new trends in car design and technology interest you?' DIRECT: 'You mentioned that you go on family outings in the car. Is your current model big enough for every occasion?' 'You mentioned a lot of business mileage. How comfortable is your current car on the motorways?'
Getting it right: Try not to disrespect the customer's previous choices. Their current car may be an old heap, but it may be a much-loved old heap. We can all get very fond of our cars, and some of us are sad when we must change them. Remember that you are introducing the idea of change by drawing attention to the customer's current problems. This is uncomfortable territory. In some cultures, it is particularly impolite to start talking about problems too soon. At the other end of the spectrum in the UK and US, you need to get to your point quickly. A customer may volunteer their problems, which is helpful, but make sure that the volunteered problem is the real problem – sometimes we disguise what is really bugging us by focusing on something else. For example, introducing a technical problem such as 'poor performance in low gear' might be a symptom of a desire for a more powerful car.		
Implication	To establish the implications for the customer if the problems are not solved	'Does that mean you have to make a lot of stops at service stations?' 'How does that affect your weekly budget for journeys?' 'Are your MOTs becoming more expensive?'

Cont.

---

24   SPIN is a registered trademark of Huthwaite International.

Table 14.3 *cont.*

Question type	Purpose	Examples
Getting it right: Much subtlety is required when you are pointing out to the customer how much their current solution is costing them in terms of money and hassle. Implication questions are essential; asking the right one will tip the customer into thinking 'Yes – I've got to do something about this unsatisfactory situation and sooner rather than later.' Practise implication questions with your coach. The more you have tried, the more likely you are to find the right one when talking to a customer.		
Need-Payoff	To explore what value the customer perceives in investing in a solution to the problem	'How much could you save on your weekly budget by switching to a hybrid car?' 'How much easier will family outings be if all the kids feel that they have enough space?'
Getting it right: If the customer is reluctant to do any financial calculations for themselves, you can prompt them for amounts, but take care not to assert that they will make savings at a particular level, particularly where third parties are concerned (eg insurance companies). While you should be prepared to discuss the cost of ownership in detail, intangible benefits such as peace of mind, more comfort and environmental impact can be deciding factors, depending on the customer's profile.		

Table 14.4: A B2B example of SPIN (Rackham, 1988)

Question type	Purpose	Examples
Situation	To establish facts about the context of the customer's business need	'I read that you had record growth last year. Is this year going to be another record year?' 'So, this new plant has been open six months. It looks very impressive! How is everyone settling in?' 'I read about the appointment of your new CEO. Is he likely to take the company in new directions?' 'I believe you use XYZ equipment at the moment. Are you on Version 8?'
Getting it right: Do not walk in and start asking 'How many employees do you have? What is your turnover?' You should have done your homework. Make the point that you have done your research and then ask an associated, qualitative question that could lead to discussions about business need. In a North American/ Northern European culture, you would not ask too many situation questions, but for other cultures you might have to manage many meetings full of situation questions before earning the right to ask a problem question. Start with high-level questions and then get more specific.		
Problem	To probe for problems or dissatisfaction with the current situation	INDIRECT: 'May I ask why you agreed to see me?' 'Would you show me around your current canteen/ other service environments?' DIRECT: 'What kind of performance are you getting out of this machine?' 'Is your current service level agreement meeting your productivity needs?'

Cont.

Table 14.4 *cont.*

Question type	Purpose	Examples
Getting it right: As with consumers, you have to make a judgement call whether to cut to the chase and ask for facts which reveal the incumbent supplier's underperformance or whether you need to be more subtle. If you are selling a service, a tour around the current service enables you to ask some detailed follow-up questions.		
Implication	To establish the implications for the customer if the problems are not solved	'How much are those breakdowns costing you?' 'Are users frustrated with that level of service?' (Or ask about specifics such as queuing bottlenecks, waiting for computers to be fixed, etc.)
Getting it right: As with consumer scenarios, implication questions are very important. Asking the right one will tip the customer into thinking 'Yes – I've got to do something about this unsatisfactory situation, and sooner rather than later.' With professional buyers, you can usually be specific in asking buyers to quantify or estimate cost implications, risk and hassle.		
Need-Payoff	To explore what value the customer perceives in investing in a solution to the problem	'How much would it be worth to the company to have more reliable machines/ software/ services?' 'How many hidden costs would be saved if there were less hassle involved in getting PC upgrades installed?' 'How much would it be worth to the company to reduce that financial risk/ technical risk?'
Getting it right: Purchasing decision-makers may have detailed analyses of what savings they want or which service improvements will save them hassle, but they may ask you to suggest what is available in the market or from your firm. An invitation to switch into your pitch is not what you want at this stage. You need to probe for the payoff that the customer is seeking or you may never establish that they have a need urgent enough to kick off the buying process.		

A system for designing follow-up questions

The guru of opinion polls, George Gallup (1947), provides a format for questioning which he calls 'quin-tamensional' – it has five elements. This can be used to probe for the real 'pain points' that a customer is experiencing, which can lead to better-tailored proposals and greater confidence in establishing how ready a customer is to make a purchase.

• **Information** – Check if the customer is informed about something relevant to your needs-related conversation with a question such as: 'Have you heard about the latest XYZ regulations?'

- **Breadth of knowledge** – Try to establish how much they know with an open question such as: 'What do you think are the most important elements of XYZ, as it affects you and your company?'

- **Seek an opinion** – Ask the customer what they think about the XYZ legislation and how it might affect them or their company.

- **Seek reasons** – Ask the customer why they hold that opinion.

- **Seek intensity of feeling** – Ask the customer how strongly they feel about XYZ legislation.

The answers to questions like these will give you an in-depth view of the customer's perceptions on any given topic. However, all this question planning would be futile unless you are able to listen and interpret the customer's responses to them.

Observation and listening

As Singh et al (2018) have identified:

> 'Customer interest plays a critical role in the sales interactions in that it captures the ebb and flow of customers' state of (positive/negative) activation, which in turn influences other aspects of the sales interaction (eg, persuasive appeals) ultimately contributing to the sales outcome.'

In any conversation with a customer, you must check their reactions to your questions. Have they understood them? Are they evading them? Are they responding enthusiastically, or with caution, boredom or cynicism? If some questions miss the target, try to rephrase them. Does the customer counter-question? They will have their own questioning strategy, and you will have to respond openly and honestly to their questions because you want the same in return. Take care not to over-do empathy about the customer's query; recent research suggests that informative answers are more likely to impress. Singh et al's (2018) research identified that customers' questions and objections are motivated by the need for more certainty (about features, costs and performance claims) and for reassurance that the product fits their needs. At this point, if the salesperson offers empathy, it can be annoying. The customer just wants a clear, specific and honest answer.

Most importantly, do you listen to the answers to your questions? One of the most frequent complaints about salespeople is that they do not listen to customers. Academic research with sales managers found that they rated listening skills as most important in sales success (Marshall et al, 2003). Effective listening takes concentration. As we discussed in the Customer Engagement chapter, you need to pick up not only what the customer explicitly says they need but also what they imply about their needs. Be prepared for a period of silence while you think about what the customer has said. If in doubt, ask them to repeat it or explain in more detail. Most importantly, once you are sure you have understood the customer correctly, adapt your answer or next question to include that knowledge. For example:

SALESPERSON: What sort of driving experience do you get with this car? (Indirect problem question)

CUSTOMER: Well, it's OK overall, but it bugs me that my car stutters in low gear.

SALESPERSON: Can you describe that to me? (Seeking clarification)

CUSTOMER: I put my foot down, and it seems to pause-lurch-pause-lurch into action.

SALESPERSON: How does that affect your daily commute? (Open implication question, expecting discussion about stop-start traffic)

CUSTOMER: I don't feel entirely confident that I can slip into a gap at a roundabout.

SALESPERSON: Is that something you have been able to do with other cars? (Follow-up/probing question)

CUSTOMER: Yes, when I had a company car with a decent-sized engine.

SALESPERSON: Have you downsized your car recently? (Follow-up/probing question)

CUSTOMER: Yes. I think I may have downsized too far.

As this example shows, you can have a normal conversation and establish needs. By asking a few relevant questions, listening to the answers and adapting the next questions, the salesperson has uncovered that the customer is uncomfortable with their current car model and would probably like something more powerful.

Listening for explicit and implicit expressions of need

Explicit needs

Dictionary definitions of 'explicit' focus on clarity and precision. Something which is explicit leaves no room for doubt, so if a customer states clearly what they want, that is what they want. 'One kilo of baking potatoes' is clear. Even in our age of choice, many simple needs can be easily fulfilled through self-service retail or via online catalogues. Even in more complex consumer sales, while a customer might want some advice, there will also be some explicit specifications, such as 'I must have a butler sink in the utility room' or 'I must have an automatic gearbox'. Complex business sales are likely to cover a variety of needs within one overall need, some explicit and some which require exploration.

It is often helpful if you can ask customers to be explicit about what *outcome* they need, rather than what gizmo they need. Many business purchases fail to satisfy because something specific was requested, and something specific was supplied, but the need had not been thought through. For example, if you have a flawed business process which is frustrating for customers and you ask an IT supplier to automate it, they will automate it. The outcome of this explicitness is that customers are still frustrated – just faster. This is what happened in the early days of CRM systems, many of which cost millions of pounds and failed to deliver any benefits. Customers want value-in-use but do not always know how to get there, which is why sales-people have to interpret needs.

Implicit needs

Implicit needs are not expressed, but you might guess them from what the customer says. In the example above, the customer moans about performance in low gear, but she has not yet said that she wants a more powerful car. Without some probing questions, she might never realise that she does. If that can happen with buying something as familiar as a car, think how much a consumer will not know about their needs in a one-off complex purchase such as a pension. So, if the customer does not recognise their implicit needs, how are you supposed to guess them?

If a customer can be explicit about the outcomes that they want in terms of value-in-use, then you can probe for how they would like to get there. Maybe they are unsure or can only say what they do not want. You can still work with that. If you ask problem questions such as: 'What do you like and dislike about your current product/service?' you open the door to a statement of dislikes which you can probe. Listen to the statements of dissatisfaction. These are the starting point for uncovering implied needs. In a complex business sale, it could take a long time to explore every stakeholder's implied needs, but it could be time well-spent in making sure that the solution you propose will be successful.

If you question well and listen well, you will start to form a good idea about what sort of product proposal will interest the person in front of you. However, before you get over-enthusiastic about having thoroughly analysed need, remember that this person's buying decision affects other stakeholders. Who are they? Do they have the power to over-ride the buying decision?

Asking about the DMU

Few people make a major purchase without consulting someone else. For a consumer, the DMU usually consists of family members, but they may also ask friends for recommendations. In business, as discussed in the Customer Knowledge chapter's section on purchasing behaviour, several stakeholders in a company may be involved in a buying decision. Never assume that the person who presents to you as the one with the need is also the one who has the authority and the budget to buy. Always ask who else has an interest in the purchase and endeavour to meet them or speak to them if possible. They may have different perspectives on the need for your product/service. You also need to establish the balance of power among decision-makers:

> 'There are few business activities more prone to a credibility gap than the way in which executives approach organizational life. A sense of disbelief occurs when managers purport to make decisions in rationalistic terms, while most observers and participants know that personalities and politics play a significant if not an overriding role.' (Zaleznik, 1970)

You may have developed a great understanding of one person in the DMU, such as the purchasing manager in a major company or the primary earner in a family about to buy a new boat, but how much do you know about the decision-makers who are less interested in engaging with you? You can, of course, ask, 'What do your colleagues think about this?' or 'What do other family members think about this?', but that only gives you a second-hand view.

Remember to establish who else is involved in the decision-making process. Your advance from one sales conversation to the next may be to secure a dialogue with more decision-makers by asking: 'Please, would you arrange for me to talk to the chief operations officer?' or 'Would you like to bring the family along to see the boat tomorrow?'

When you understand all the needs of all the people in the DMU, there will be conflicts to try to resolve. Who has the power in the DMU? Sometimes it is obvious; however, many people in companies try to give the impression of power when they do not have it, or they may be using you and your solution to play politics against someone else. All may not be as it seems. Be sensitive to any hints from any conversations about the balance of power in the customer's organisation or family.

In the case of an organisation, you may be able to find out about formal hierarchies by finding director names in company reports. Informal ones are trickier. Is a member of a DMU concerned about how their team will see the change? They probably see their power as vested in the people reporting to them. Does someone worry about how this affects the power balance with another department? They may feel that they are undervalued and will be prepared to scupper anything that does not help them to gain some power. Is the chief executive friendly with the incumbent supplier's senior team, even if the users of their products think that they are under-performing?

To remain as the trusted advisor, you have to be an objective mediator and solve as many people's problems as you can. If someone is bound to lose out from your solution, be honest about it and try to encourage your allies in the DMU to think about mitigating that situation. You will not win in situations where the politics are against you, or where they are so poisonous that the organisation itself is heading for a major shake-down, so it is best to explore a prospect's political landscape before investing too much time in designing a solution. Bear this in mind when you are evaluating bid/no-bid situations.

Budget availability

One of the buying decision-makers will see their role as the 'budget-holder', and nothing can happen without the budget-holder's approval. Buyers always aim to stick within their budgets, but they also aspire to solutions which are beyond their budgets. It is important for you to ask questions about the budget because the more a customer is outside of their financial comfort zone, the more likely they are to suffer buyer's remorse after they have signed the contract. Consumers are protected from buyer's remorse to some degree by the fourteen-day cooling-off period stipulated in the Consumer Credit Act 1974 (GOV.UK, 1974). The implication of the cooling-off period is that contracts will be cancelled if the customer feels that they cannot afford what they have bought, and making lots of sales that get cancelled will affect you financially and harm your career. Companies are less likely to cancel after an extensive buying process, but they will lobby hard for extra services which erode profitability if they think they need to claw back value.

Companies set their budgets at least a year in advance. It is important for them to estimate the required cash flow and make the best use of company funds. To many organisations, these budgets become straitjackets. Despite changing circumstances and new opportunities or threats, they must keep to budget. Managers who save in one category of spend but exceed another may be in trouble even if they have balanced the budget overall. This is why your super-duper solution, which saves operational cost, will be delayed or turned down if it exceeds a critical capital budget. Many large organisations help customers to manage the finance associated with making a major purchase, either with a finance offer to accompany the product/service or by varying payment terms. Make sure you fully understand the customer's budget issues and talk to your finance colleagues about incorporating an attractive financial offer into the solution.

Summary

In this chapter, we have looked at the homework you need to do and the questions that you need to ask to understand your customers' needs. We have emphasised that thoroughly understanding customer needs is of primary importance in progressing sales opportunities.

We will close this chapter with a quote from recent research on this topic: 'Buyers' expectation of in-depth customer insight did seem not to align with the sellers. Sellers identified this requirement but did not recognize the height of customers' expectations' (Kaski et al, 2017). However much you think you know about the customer and their needs, they expect you to know more!

15

Preparing And
Presenting Solutions

Introduction

An influential market research study conducted in the USA in 1973 has led to a popular myth that people fear speaking in public more than death. A more recent study found that 62% of students cited speaking before a group as a fear, but when asked about their top fear, it was ranked second – after death. Nevertheless, 18% of the students surveyed ranked public speaking as their top fear (Dwyer and Davidson, 2012).

As a salesperson, you will prepare and deliver hundreds of proposals and presentations in your career, so you will be taking on that fear and conquering it. It does take bravery, but it is a lot easier than armed combat or fighting disease, so do not let it overwhelm you. It feels terrible when a presentation has flopped, but like falling off a bike, you just have to pick yourself up and get on the bike again. Resilience is vital. From all mistakes, you learn.

While some concern about public speaking is sensible, if you prepare properly, as a salesperson you will be comfortable with an audience. This chapter provides an initial guide to presentation best practice. It starts with the written proposal, moves on to presentations (live and via the web), and ends with a discussion on demonstrating value.

The information about communication models and customer orientation in this textbook will also inform how you propose and present solutions which you want the customer to buy.

Writing good proposals and making good presentations takes practice. Seek feedback from your coach and tutor, and if you can focus on one new improvement every time you propose or present you will be doing well. Never be complacent; it is easy to lapse into poor practice, especially after time off for a holiday or sickness. None of us can be perfect, and your style may not suit everyone in an audience; however, enthusiastic effort is often well-received.

Deciding to write a sales proposal

Customers ask for written proposals to compare suppliers' offers, get detail about complex products and ensure the buying process is objective. The more complex the sale and/or the organisation you are selling into, the more likely you are to need a detailed written proposal.

Invitations to tender and requests for quotations

Every branch of government is legally obliged to advertise for suppliers when they have a contract to offer. They post an invitation to tender (ITT) or request for quotation (RFQ) in relevant journals and on relevant websites. The first stage in responding may be a pre-qualification questionnaire. The organisation will provide specifications for the information that must go into it. Public sector bids probably involve the most paperwork, but quotations are also expected for small items in B2B markets.

An organisation sending out a pre-qualification questionnaire will usually explain why and how the PQQ is part of their supplier evaluation process. Typically, they will ask for the following information:

- Details about your business – what it is and what it does, how long you have been established, key stakeholders, etc

- What you have done in the past – contracts, customers, technical experience

- Accreditations from professional bodies

- Financial accounts for the past three years

- Company policies, such as health and safety, equality and diversity

- Details of insurances, such as public liability or professional indemnity

A period of time for review of the PQQs may be specified, after which you will be asked to bid if you are successful. If you are not, you may receive some feedback about why the PQQ fell short of requirements.

Bid/no-bid reviews

The cost of preparing a written proposal can be enormous, and there are no prizes for coming second. It is an opportunity to compete and to demonstrate value, but you should only embark on preparing a written proposal when you have a reasonable chance of winning. Unless your marketing department has done a good job of positioning your company in the customer's market sector as a worthwhile player in your industry, you are on the back foot. Being 'unrecognised' signals 'risk' for buying decision-makers. There are exceptions, though; if you are a small, growing company, bidding for business via online marketplaces might get you recognised.

Just as buyers want PQQs, you and your colleagues should have done a rigorous qualification of the opportunity in an objective bid/no-bid review. In fact, there may be several reviews, depending on the size of the bid. Salespeople should not be afraid of a 'no-bid' decision. If a competitor picks up business that your team considered unprofitable or high risk, the competitor will have the hassle of a failing customer relationship later on, and you will not. In some cases, the no-bid decision may open up a conversation with the customer, which can lead to a better ITT.

Nick Oulton, CEO of m62 visual communications, stated in a *Forbes* interview that 'Purchasing need to run a process, and in order to run a process, they need you to bid. So, for any potential supplier, and especially if you are the market leader, saying no generally gets an indignant "Why not?" – which gets you in at the C-suite[25] to talk' (Searcy and DeVries, 2013).

A bid/no-bid review should first consider how qualified you are to meet the specification, in light of competitor activity. You can understand the need in depth and be a credible supplier of the product/service required, but that guarantees only your right to be on a shortlist. If the customer is an advocate of their current supplier, you can assume that the probability of them changing to you is low, but merely 'satisfied' customers do sometimes change. If you are the incumbent supplier, or one with an improving relationship with the customer, your chances of winning are good.

You also need to work out the profit and cash flow that winning the work would generate and offset the costs of bidding. You need to be confident that you can deliver the work if you win the bid. You also need to consider how committed your company is to winning the bid. Strange as it may seem, not every sales opportunity is embraced by all stakeholders because winning significant chunks of business introduces change into your organisation as well as the customer's. Landing a major deal is an operational and financial challenge. Companies must often over-resource bids to improve the chances of winning and then over-resource implementation to improve the probability of a successful start to the customer relationship.

---

25 In American companies, senior decision-makers are either chief (functional role) officers or vice-presidents. The 'C' in 'C-suite' stands for 'chief'; a C-suite is the offices of senior managers.

Each company will have its own bid/no-bid criteria, but they should cover the following:

Customer

- What is the nature of the current relationship with the customer?

- Is this a strategic customer or a prospective customer in our portfolio?

- Is the company able to deal with the change needed?

- Are they financially viable?

- Are they interested in price or value?

- Are they after information or ready to make a decision?

- Are there any external stakeholders who are going to influence this project?

Competitors

- Which competitors are also going to bid?

- What are the states of their relationships with this customer?

- Can we compete against their strengths or exploit their weaknesses?

- Will winning this bid enhance our strategic position in the industry?

Costs

- How much profit is feasible from this bid? Over what time frame?

- Will the cash flow be manageable?

- Would this bid create a resourcing challenge in any part of the business?

Organisational fit

- Is it the right time for us to undertake a bid like this?

- Are we committed to this prospect? This type of solution?

Once you have undertaken a bid/no-bid review and you are authorised to proceed to the proposal, the bid team can digest the ITT again and prepare the proposal. You may need to ask the prospective customer to enter into a non-disclosure agreement (NDA) to emphasise that the contents of your proposal are to remain confidential.

Writing major proposal documents

The content of a proposal document

Proposal documents are formal and constitute a legal offer in contract law, so they have to be accurate. Customers expect them to follow their technical specification. However, there will usually still be room to exercise some creativity and include differentiating statements. These days, most documents will be managed online and may contain a variety of electronic data, including video clips and 3D simulations. Table 15.1 provides some ideas for structuring a proposal document (inspired by Sant, 2018).

Table 15.1: Proposal document components

Category	Items
The business case	— Cover letter
	— Title page
	— Table of contents
	— Executive summary
	— Customer needs (restatement of information provided in ITT)
	— Customer objectives
	— Overview of the solution
	— Key differentiating points of our solution
	— Overview of pricing and ROI

Cont.

Table 15.1 *cont.*

Category	Items
Proposed solution and proof	The solution in detail: — What is to be delivered — Operational features, advantages and benefits (applied to this customer's needs) — Training, change management and other services — Value mapping and value analysis specific to this customer, including total cost of ownership
	Implementation programme: — Scope of work — Project plan — Timescales — The project team, including contractors
	Risk management: — How risks will be managed — Contingency plans
	Proof: — References, case studies and testimonials — Technical benchmarking with relevant professional institutes — Guarantees/ service level agreement
Governance	— Company accounts for the last three years — Equality statement — Environmental impact statement — Other legislative requirements, licences, etc
Attachments	— Terms and conditions — Relevant marketing material including a video demonstration of equipment, a video tour of our factory, etc

On a major bid, the salesperson is not responsible for writing every section of the proposal; relevant engineers, accountants, marketers and corporate lawyers will complete much of it. However, its overall 'look and feel' will be the responsibility of the sales lead, and it is essential to include '3 Cs' for all the members of the customer's decision-making team (Kleiner, 2016):

- **Confidence** – Here is a company that knows how to do this.

- **Comfort** – This supplier knows what I need, and I could sleep at night with this supplier implementing this change.

- **Credibility** – This supplier has a good reputation, looks after its customers and complies with relevant standards and legislation.

That is the big picture, but there is also a lot of detail to consider. Some of the points may seem obvious, but the checklists in the following sections will help you when you are writing important proposals and your deadline is looming:

The principles of proposals

Put customer need first – Technical features may have to be listed somewhere, but the purpose of the document is to establish how your products and services can be applied to meet the customer's objective. That should come through on every page.

Proof – References and endorsements from loyal customers can be powerful, but you also need objective evidence such as the results of tests by independent third parties (such as environmental health inspectors if you are a catering company). You will need to include spreadsheets indicating the customer's expected ROI. Include as much information as possible to explain why the figures in that spreadsheet are realistic and not a mere theoretical estimation from a supplier's laboratory conditions (rather than the real, imperfect world).

Discuss costs and value in depth – This part of the proposal will get the most scrutiny. Understand that the customer will have to invest in the change beyond just paying your invoices. The customer will incur costs in switching from current suppliers (or from doing nothing) and faces changes in operating expenses. As Friend et al (2014) state, 'Value is determined not only by perceived benefits but also by perceived sacrifices a buying organisation might incur.'

Differentiate – Show comparisons with the competitors' performance where there are public-domain benchmarks.

Offer choices – This is a way of opening negotiations about value.

Discuss risk – It will be in the customer's mind.

The structure of proposals

Give particular thought to the cover letter – It can seem like a tick-box add-on, but a cover letter creates a first impression. Make sure that it includes the customer's reference numbers (eg ITT number), your internal reference numbers and contact information. Thank the customer contacts for the opportunity to tender and provide a brief (one-paragraph) summary of the solution proposed. Make sure that the cover letter is signed by someone senior (not an electronic signature, unless it is an electronic submission).

Consider what the customer would like to read – If your proposal fits the way the customer wrote the ITT, they can find their way around it easily. They like the compliance elements, such as annual accounts and governance statements, to be covered by a checklist or matrix so it is clear that they are all present and correct. They also like clear, specific statements throughout. They will want an overall summary and section summaries as reminders of key points. They will want you to say – and prove – why you are the best supplier they could work with.

Create a logical flow for the document – We know that every document starts with an introduction, moves on to the body of content and ends with a conclusion. Each section and each paragraph also need an introduction, a 'middle' and an end. There also needs to be 'signposting' between sections so that the reader understands why we are moving from topic X to topic Y.

Consider document length – A proposal needs to be a thorough response to the customer, but the customer is not going to weigh it. Be concise where you can.

The language of proposals

Check for simplicity – Short, everyday words and short sentences convey meaning quickly. 'Cost optimisation evidence' may sound impressive, but 'proof of cost reduction' is more powerful.

Make your meaning as clear as possible – Clarity is not just about avoiding jargon. English is a flexible language, but there are a few rules. We can all construct sentences with garbled meaning, perhaps when we are distracted or in a hurry. You can get away with it in conversation, but not in writing. If you write: 'After pressing the pause button for twenty seconds, the machine will shut down', you may assume that the meaning is clear; however, the sentence implies that the machine presses the pause button. This would be particularly confusing to someone whose first language is not English. Be exact, especially when explaining how technical equipment works. Also, when you use descriptive terms make sure that it is obvious which noun or verb they are describing. 'The operation may suddenly end' is not clear; write 'The operation may end suddenly' instead.

Use active rather than passive statements – The 'passive voice' has its place in particular types of writing, but it puts the object of an action before the subject, which means that it takes longer for the reader to understand the statement. 'Your factory was visited by our engineer' (passive) is correct but sounds awkward. 'Our engineer visited your factory' (active) is better.

Spellcheck and proofread – Word-processing tools such as spellcheck and grammar-check are handy, but they do not pick up everything. Because they are algorithms working on combinations of letters and words, their suggestions for alternative words or phrases are not always logical. Spellcheck will also miss words that are themselves correct but used incorrectly, such as 'affect' (a verb) instead of 'effect' (a noun). Similarly, it will not flag 'principal' instead of 'principle' or typographic errors such as 'in' instead of 'on'. Proofread your own document and ask a colleague to check it, too. They will pick up things you are likely to miss.

Avoid using expressions which sound like hype – For example: 'state of the art'. How often do we hear that? What does it actually mean? Professional purchasers are likely to screen out this sort of terminology.

Use diagrams, charts and tables – These can reduce word counts and make an idea easier to understand.

Quality control

Edit yourself and find an independent editor – you need to check your proposal, and it is vital that someone else checks it as well. Even small documents need checking; for example, a decimal place error (such as 00.98 instead of 98.00) in a price is an embarrassment you would wish to avoid. Someone else reading your work can make their own judgement on its accuracy, readability, clarity, structure and customer focus. You may also ask them to check the fit to the customer's ITT and compliance with legal requirements as well as sufficient proof of competence, credibility and competitive advantage.

Submission

Following quality control, make sure to deliver the proposal on time. Do not leave things to the last minute and allow more time for delivery than you think you need. If you deliver via a courier, what happens if they get stuck in traffic?

These days, proposals are often delivered electronically. Make sure that the technology has worked and that the customer has received the proposal. Continue to check with the customer during the reviewing process; they may need more information or may revise the date for feedback. If you are shortlisted, you will be called in for more discussions and presentations.

Giving presentations

If your proposal is shortlisted by the customer, you will be invited in for negotiations, and you may be asked to make a presentation to the DMU. This section explores factors to consider when giving presentations.

Expect snags

When you give a presentation, people are looking at you. In a business presentation, they expect you to turn up on time, smartly dressed and smiling, but even doing that can take some effort. On one occasion, I (Beth) was presenting after a coffee break. Before the break, I had been quietly expecting to network or check the technology during the break. Then, the hem of my skirt got snagged on a chair, and I spent the coffee break improvising a sticky-tape repair to the hem. Be prepared for wardrobe malfunctions and anything else that might distract you and the audience from your message.

Your personal style

Once you stand up to speak, what do people expect? We know that they do not like speakers to use a script or read from the screen. You need to know your stuff. Should you speak quickly to emphasise your enthusiasm, or slowly to make sure that everyone hears you? Varying the pace might be a good compromise, but what is your style? Most television presenters and politicians these days use their hands as well as voices to emphasise a point – does that mean that you should, or does it look too staged? Could it irritate someone? Should you tell jokes to break the ice, or would that be too risky? Discuss presentation style with your coach but remember that your audience needs you to be 'authentic'. If you are naturally serious, you do not have to be humorous. If you are usually calm, you do not have to wave your arms around.

Practise, practise, practise

Practise in the presentation venue if you can, using the voice, pace and movement that suits your style. Practise looking at your audience and smiling at them. Remember to thank them for the opportunity to present to them before you start. Bill Rosenthal, the chief executive of Communispond, offers the following advice: 'It's much better to rehearse the presentation the way you'll deliver it – standing, aloud, and with the passion, pacing, and movement you'll actually use' (Rosenthal, 2013).

Content and delivery

A presentation is a means of conveying understanding to the customer. The content needs to be right, and the delivery should enable understanding of the content.

Check the relevance of the material to the customer – As with proposals, check that customer need comes across on every slide.

Actively engage the customer – Encourage interaction and questions from the audience throughout; otherwise, their thoughts might drift off. Make most of your slides visual rather than textual; the picture will be remembered better than words. If possible, embed a short video demonstration of the product, or, better still, pass something around for the customer to handle and examine. One student pitching waste management in an assessment brought the examiners a model tipper truck to handle. In an academic context, that demonstrated learning about 'feel' in presentations. It might be perceived as a gimmick in a business context, but you would prefer the audience play with something that helped them to remember your pitch rather than their mobile phones.

Get professional design help – Draft your own presentation or customise the company's standard materials but do get a graphics expert to edit it and make the slides look neat, attractive, appropriately branded and memorable.

Enthusiasm and belief – Even if you are anxious and tired, find some authentic enthusiasm to convey to your audience. They are curious about what you have to say. They want you to succeed so that their time is well-used. If you can start confidently with questions to get the audience talking to you (even something like, 'Did anyone else get stuck behind the hay lorry that shed its load?'), you can lay the foundations for a productive discussion.

Online presentations/webinars

Every day, millions of meetings and presentations take place online so that highly paid professionals can save travel time and costs. There are three types of online presentation:

1. **'Live' online** – where you connect and present via meetings software

2. **Webinar** – where the content rather than the presenter is the focus and invitees dial in to hear the talk

3. **Slideshow with commentary** – which can be accessed by the customer at their convenience

Many of the rules of presenting person-to-person still apply, but the technology adds new elements. People can be impatient online and are more likely to try to multitask (eg checking emails while listening to a webinar). Here are some extra considerations for online presentations:

Make it easy – If the customer cannot join the meeting with two or three clicks, they will lose interest. Some meetings software is easy to use, but there can be problems with compatibility across different corporate systems. See if you can politely persuade the customer's secretary or assistant to run a short test with you beforehand. If there is any potential for a missed connection, send the customer the slide-pack and have a contingency plan to discuss it over the phone.

Timing – Online, twenty minutes is plenty; thirty minutes stretches the concentration. Make sure that the content is not overly detailed.

Use analytics on the site, particularly in the case of webinars – This will give you some idea about audience reaction to the webinar (eg when they joined, how long they stayed). You may find that a particular slide was a turn-off, and then you can work out how to make it more useful to the audience next time.

> 'The best salespeople learn from their mistakes. They go through their previous presentations in detail so they can find out what worked and what didn't. They are not afraid to make mistakes. In fact, they welcome mistakes because they know they can learn from them.' (Agarwal, 2016)

One of the most challenging things to present is the justification for buying a product or service. You will have learned already that this has to be quantified in the customer's terms. The following section offers some thoughts on conveying value in a presentation.

Presenting value

You will discuss 'value propositions' within your organisation, with customers and with other stakeholders. Prepare a short statement of value to headline any proposal or

presentation to the customer, including the elements outlined in Table 15.2.

Table 15.2: Elements of a value proposition (adapted from Davies, 2017)

Questions that the value proposition must answer	Possible answers
What will the customer look like in the future if this item is bought?	More efficient? More market share? Higher cash turnover? International potential? Lower carbon footprint?
Therefore, what customer needs are fulfilled?	Improved operating performance Better offering than competitors Greater financial flexibility Global expansion Environmental compliance
What is our offering?	Innovative product Robust services Expertise
What evidence do we have that we can deliver the desired change in the customer?	Case studies and references Benchmarking Accreditations Professional standing
How are we going to measure value capture (customer success)?	Customer's key performance indicators System-captured operational metrics

Even a fairly small-scale consumer sale should have these
elements.

What is value?

A customer might greatly appreciate a hot drink on a cold
day. Their future state would be warmer; the supplier has
met their need to avoid the discomfort of feeling cold.
The offering could be a choice of hot beverages made in
modern, safe equipment, enhanced with milk and sugar if
wanted. There is visual evidence that the drink is hot – the
drink is steaming. The customer can measure within a few
sips if they are going to get value from the whole drink.

Value is what the customer perceives it to be, but it
is multifaceted. In the case above, the hot drink might
have high perceived value, but the consumer would not be

prepared to pay much more than they know a hot drink costs on a mild day. Because they know that there is a general range of acceptable prices for a hot drink in their location, they would find paying more a rip-off.

Customers define value using their measures of success and their concept of a 'fair' price. You create value collaboratively with customers. Whatever you sell them with however many implementation services, they have to use it to contribute to its success. A typical analogy is a gym membership. A gym can provide premises, equipment, classes and trainers; but to get the best value from their membership, a member has to turn up and use them.

Value does have to be quantified, even if the benefits are qualitative. For example, how much monetary value is there in 'peace of mind'? If I gain peace of mind when I install a burglar alarm, better sleep should lead to better productivity, which means that I can earn more (if self-employed) or bring forward a promotion (if salaried). This is stretching the point, but in B2B you will be expected to try to quantify all benefits. When 'perceived value' is higher than cost, a purchase is justified. The question then becomes, 'Which solution offers the best value?' As Hinterhuber and Snelgrove (2016) state: 'If… value can be expressed monetarily; it will be a harder value than a perceived value that is not.'

How is value quantified in a business context? A simple model is:

Value = Impact – Total Cost of Ownership
(Davies, 2017)

What is the impact? Your solution will change the customer in some way. It may increase their revenue, decrease their costs, enhance their business reputation/position, or improve their strategic or organisational abilities. The total cost of ownership (TCO) is discussed in more detail in the next section. It encompasses the initial purchase price and the ongoing costs of using the purchase.

Value is relative – both to what life will be like without buying something and to alternative solutions from suppliers and substitutes. Buying one's first car is a financial challenge. There are many choices for someone considering that purchase, including: keep using the bus, buy a bicycle, buy a motorbike, buy a second-hand car privately or buy a car from any of several local dealers. The bus would probably always be the cheapest option, so the buyer has to quantify the value of flexibility, availability at all hours, time saving and reliability, as well as the reputation of particular local dealers versus a private deal for 'peace of mind' and other factors.

Value has to be substantiated with evidence. We have already mentioned that references from loyal customers are not enough. If you are buying a car, you check reviews by motoring experts as well as asking anyone you know who owns a model that you are considering.

The total cost of ownership

As mentioned earlier in this chapter, TCO is a financial calculation which includes direct, indirect and hidden costs of a product or service over time, which can include social and ecological costs. Some experts talk about the 'priceberg' (Vitasek, 2016), as depicted in Figure 15.1.

The price is the bit you can see, but below the water there are the costs of implementation, the costs of using or running the product in your operations, the costs of maintaining and repairing it, and the costs of disposing of it. A ball bearing may seem like just a round piece of metal, but one that needs less oil for lubrication and has a longer life (thus causing fewer machine breakdowns) has a lower TCO than one that could be one-third of the price.

A high-quality product can deliver better lifetime performance on operating costs even before adding considerations of safety and environmental compliance, which reduce risk. Best practice in manufacturing companies involves working with the customer to identify the best data that can reproduce a simulation of normal (and abnormal) use and then apply the supplier's solution to estimate potential cost savings. When the customer supplies their own data, they can be reassured that the scenarios and outcomes are realistic and reliable.

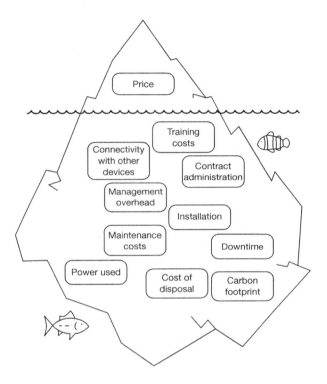

Figure 15.1: The priceberg

Many companies (such as Microsoft and Nissan[26]) provide online TCO tools so that customers can do their own calculations. According to Snelgrove, 'a good TCO tool is not a sales tool in and of itself. It's a process and methodology for benchmarking, finding, prioritizing, customizing and quantifying expected values in financial terms so that the customer can see if it makes sense for them to invest in your solution' (Hinterhuber and Snelgrove, 2016).

---

26 See https://azure.microsoft.com/en-us/pricing/tco/calculator and http://corporate-sales.nissan.co.uk/fleet-cars/tools/tco/full/passenger, respectively.

Total cost of ownership is a similar concept to the financial definition of value-in-use, which focuses on future cash flows generated by company assets. It is important to quantify things in a way that customer decision-makers appreciate, but, besides 'better before cheaper', try to also introduce 'revenue before costs' and other elements of positive impact into your proposals. How does your solution help the customer to grow? As Raynor and Ahmed state, 'By an overwhelming margin, exceptional companies garner superior profits by achieving higher revenue than their rivals through either higher prices or greater volume. Very rarely is cost leadership a driver of superior profitability' (2013).

As mentioned earlier in this section, the positive impact of a product or service on a customer comes before the TCO consideration. The offer wheel shows the full picture of this impact (see Figure 15.2).

Figure 15.2: The offer wheel (adapted with kind permission from Davies, 2017)

Even when you have a longstanding relationship with a customer, mapping and discussing value is an important agenda item for every catch-up meeting. Supplier-customer relationships can leak value over time, leading to adversarial discussions about complacency and price negotiations. Always be prepared to present value, as Davies explains: 'Organizations often have significant potential value that could be delivered to the customer, but due to a lack of focus on the concept of value-in-use in the customer's business, this value is not discussed, captured or realized' (2017).

Anticipating objections

The more you build customer needs analysis and value mapping into your proposal and presentations, including evidence, the less likely you will be to hear objections from the customer about the validity of your proposal, but these are not the only type of objection that customers may raise. While objection handling is discussed in more detail in the Negotiation chapter, this section provides some high-level considerations for objection handling within proposals and presentations.

Changing supplier or buying something new from an existing supplier means a change in the customer's life or organisation. Even with the best value proposition, you may still hear concerns about timing and terms. Given that 'do nothing' is always a strong competitor in complex sales, showing that you are serious about risk management is as important as value delivery. Remember that customers pay more attention to their sacrifices than what they gain from change.

Although it may mean adding cost into the proposal, it's advisable to engage a risk management expert on the bid team. If you can show the customer that you have anticipated the challenges of implementation on their behalf, the objection-handling element of negotiations is likely to be much more constructive. One way of showing your thinking about anticipating risk is a probability/impact diagram, as shown in Figure 15.3. This is a simple risk diagram for installing new software or software-as-a-service.

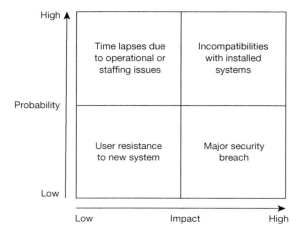

Figure 15.3: Software risk probability/impact

Showing that you know all the typical risks of the change you are proposing to the customer is one thing; you must also explain how you deal with them via contingency planning. The customer will want to know how much resource you would allocate to making sure that problems are resolved quickly.

Answer as many questions as the customer might have before negotiations, but they will have many more throughout the sales cycle. Be open about what you know and do not know. Find answers from colleagues or facilitate a discussion between the relevant colleague and the relevant customer decision-maker.

Summary

In this chapter, we have looked at best practice in proposing and presenting to customers, including written proposals, various presentation types and a discussion on the concept of value.

16

Negotiation

Introduction

You have discovered the customer's needs and made a value-based proposal. The customer now will expect some negotiation. This is taken for granted with a professional buyer in a company, and it will also be the case with 'savvy' consumers. In some circumstances, you could say, 'That's what my company offers – take it or leave it.' If your offer is so standardised, it will soon be online only; professional salespeople are usually deployed where there is some customisation of product/service offer and terms. A negotiation is a discussion undertaken between two (or more) parties to establish common ground and reach an agreement. Possibly the most difficult element of negotiation is putting aside emotion and focusing on the facts.

There is sometimes an expectation that negotiation is about somebody winning and somebody losing; this is not the case. Negotiation, whether in diplomacy, commerce or everyday life, should be about both sides winning. The concept of both sides gaining advantage without one or the other side losing can be challenging to grasp, but it is possible. For example, a supplier may deliver to customer branches as standard. If the customer wants centralised deliveries in return for a price reduction, the supplier has not lost because they can reduce costs by having fewer delivery points. Negotiation should be a problem-solving discussion.

Customers may not like aspects of your offer and want to negotiate for changes, or they may not be convinced that the price and risk balance is right for them. Professional buyers will expect discussions about pricing, contract terms and service level agreements, and it is prudent to engage in some detail. If the customer needs to check the contract after the sale, it is usually when they are thinking about complaining or talking to the legal department. At minimum, they will be annoyed that a user department has raised a query about levels of service, and they will carry that annoyance into their next communication with you. Suppliers must not over-promise or under-deliver.

We must be realistic in this textbook about what you might expect in the real world. Unfortunately, often even the best-trained buyers will resort to short-term price negotiation tactics, even with strategic purchases. Always be prepared for the best calculation of long-term value to be challenged:

> 'Buyers, even at senior levels, more clearly identify value as the result of price negotiation, a functional perspective, than as the construction of sustainable competitive advantages, the shareholder perspective. They do not discriminate sufficiently between short-term transactional value transfer and long-term shareholder value capture.' (Philippart, 2016)

The background to negotiation

Professional buyers are trained (and sometimes have income incentives) to reduce prices and get better terms. Every price advantage they gain goes straight to boosting the company's bottom line – in the short term – and they will play competitors off against each other. If you offer a margin-skimming price early in negotiations, they might offer it to the competition as a target and return to you to beat the competitor's counteroffer.

Consumers are urged to do research online, including price comparisons. They may complete their transactions online because they do not want the bother of dealing with a salesperson in a retail setting or over the phone, but if they do their research online and their shopping in-store they will negotiate. Other consumers want to seek advice and to deal with a person because they are confused with the mass of information online. It may be reasonable to assume that many consumers who do not do business online may have some kind of vulnerability, so salespeople must be particularly careful not to exploit that by over-specifying products or inflating prices.

Although negotiation is generally placed between value proposition and closing, sub-negotiations on particular points can take place at any time during the sales cycle. Professional buyers may try to jump to price negotiations before you have even proposed a solution with statements such as, 'By the way, whatever it is, I'm not going to pay more than £100,000 for it.' Acknowledge their statement but explain that you want to explore the possibilities and give them options so that they can get all the functionality they want.

Planning to negotiate

What buyer concerns, often described as 'objections', might you anticipate? Your marketing department will hopefully have gathered data on common queries from customers, and they can prepare answers you can give or options you can offer. You will have also listened carefully to the particular customer you are negotiating with, so you may have your own ideas about what their negotiating tactics might be. You will be asked about price repeatedly, so prepare lots of information about value. Understanding whether you are selling a commodity or value can be established by running through a short self-assessment checklist, as shown in Table 16.1. This will help you to determine whether you are negotiating on price or value.

Table 16.1: Value or price negotiation checklist

Question	Yes or no	Outcome
Does the company you are dealing with have a professional buyer involved in the negotiation?		If yes, a value negotiation is relevant.
Is the negotiation via an auction process (eg a web auction where the value of the bids decreases in each round)?		If yes, it is a price negotiation.
Is the market leader a low-cost provider with a massive share of the market?		If yes, it is a price negotiation.
Does anyone apart from your company have a price premium?		If yes, a value negotiation is relevant.
Is this customer interested in the total cost of ownership?		If yes, a value negotiation is relevant.
Does the customer want additional elements over your standard offer (eg extra services, personalisation)?		If yes, a value negotiation is relevant.

It is common to feel commoditisation pressure from the company. A two-year study across nineteen countries (Dietmeyer, 2018) found that the most common buyer tactic is saying, 'I can get the same thing from your competitor cheaper.'

This statement may be true; remember that the buyer is searching for the best deal for their company, not yours. However, it is often accepted too easily, often without challenge from the salesperson, thereby costing companies millions in lost profit, as the standard response is to offer a discount (Dietmeyer, 2018). Using a checklist can help you prepare and avoid the knee-jerk reaction of offering price cuts.

Another key aspect, discussed in Chapter 15, is the total cost of ownership. This is very useful in moving a price commodity negotiation towards a negotiation on value. Establishing TCO means 'buyers and sellers make decisions on who is creating the best value and what someone should be willing to pay for it. Anyone who can demonstrate and document the greatest value surplus is the one delivering the best value' (Snelgrove, 2017).

In your preparation, remember your homework about this customer and different points of view in the DMU. You also need to have information about the relevant competition and what they are likely to be offering. They may have a reputation for certain negotiating tactics, so expect them to be deployed. Explore the Internet for recent news about your company and products, and take any good news with you. If there are negative stories, talk to marketing about how you can present a positive side to them. Ironically, there is a perception that a company that has recently made a mistake is more likely to be learning from inspections and improving its practice than one that has not been exposed to such scrutiny.

Check that the person you are negotiating with has the power to make a decision. You may have established that in the earlier stages of the sales cycle, but if there is any doubt try to clarify by directly asking them the scope of their authority and whether other members of the DMU need to be involved.

Is the negotiation a team effort on your side of the table? The scope, size and scale of a solution will usually dictate how many people get involved. Talk to colleagues in operations, finance and legal departments as aspects of any negotiation will affect them. You need to understand what financial flexibility you have. There are two calculations that you need to learn, perform and memorise before each negotiation:

- **ZOPA (zone of possible agreement)** – The gap between the point at which you must walk away from the negotiation and the highest price the buyer is willing to pay. For example, if you have to walk away at £40,000 and the highest price the customer can pay is £45,000, you have a ZOPA of £5,000. A ZOPA could be negative, in which case both parties should walk away.

- **BATNA (best alternative to a negotiated agreement)**
  – At what point do you have to walk away and lick your wounds?

  What are your options if this negotiation fails? List them, do some calculations to evaluate them and choose the one which has the best value for you. Try to pursue this option if the customer's demands have taken you beyond your ZOPA.

  Try to estimate your customer's BATNA. What will they do if you refuse to give in on something important to them? Does the procurement professional have a different view from other people in the DMU? Remember that BATNA may fluctuate in a negotiation as each party gets more information about concerns and expectations.

  Your awareness of several alternatives may make you feel more determined to get something out of the deal but take care. The investment of time in assessing alternatives will stand you in good stead for future negotiations; in each negotiation you should focus on looking for goodwill rather than the worst-case scenario. The Program on Negotiation at Harvard Law School produced a management report in 2012 entitled *BATNA Basics: Boost your power at the bargaining table*, and it advises that 'By remaining vigilant about negotiating in good faith and reciprocating goodwill, you should be able to emerge from the shadow cast by sunk costs.'

  Finally, have an agenda and use checklists and worksheets in your negotiation meeting. Cover all agenda items and keep your working papers close at hand.

Good practice in negotiation

We can learn good negotiation practice from other fields which use it. Police departments often have experts trained to negotiate with criminals who have taken hostages. Staying calm when you are trying to reason with someone who does not have socially conventional ideas about being reasonable is a great skill. Although your sales negotiations will never be as dangerous as theirs, it is worth drawing some parallels:

- Listen carefully to the other person
- Try to understand where they are coming from (develop empathy)
- Develop rapport
- Suggest/prompt behavioural change (influence)

In an interview with Eric Barker referenced in *Time Magazine*, former head of FBI international hostage negotiation Chris Voss explains: 'Business negotiations try to pretend that emotions don't exist... Human beings are incapable of being rational, regardless' (Barker, 2014).

You are not in an adversarial hostage situation. The customer has voluntarily invited you to negotiate a deal with them, and you will probably have already had constructive conversations about the customer's needs and how your product/service could be applied to them. Nevertheless, you can apply the suggestions above.

Listening

Listening is most important in negotiation. You have to be sure that you have heard the customer's concerns correctly. Active listening requires concentration; you have to put aside your underlying drive to make the sale and make the conversation all about the customer. Don't jump in with a 'yes, but' or start trying to evaluate the customer's objection in your head. If you contradict someone, they may get defensive. You can only (politely) deny an objection if it is based on 'fake news' or blatantly untrue.

Acknowledge the customer by nodding or saying something like 'OK' occasionally to indicate that you are listening and concentrating. Summarise what has been said and ask for confirmation that you have heard correctly. If you don't understand where they are coming from, say something like, 'I haven't heard that idea before – can you help me to understand what leads you to say that?' Ask open questions to get more background to the objection so that you can understand it in more depth, and listen through pauses. In addition to the objection, the customer may indicate a favourable attitude to your company or offer an 'If only you did X, I would be more interested', and that is something you can work with.

Ask yourself:

- Have I understood correctly? (Pinpoint the cause of the buyer's concern.)

- Has something been under-explored? (Is it a point on which you can agree to disagree and move on?)

- Is it a showstopper?

- What solutions, options or workarounds would be acceptable?

Table 16.2 offers some ideas about possible objection workarounds.

Table 16.2: Potential workarounds to objections

Typical objection	Which means...	Possible responses
'I need time to review other offers/ talk to other people. How long is this quote valid?'	'I have to make comparisons.' It could also be a stalling technique for a buyer who is considering doing nothing.	It is reasonable to time-limit the quote. If you have comparative data (eg independent performance statistics), share them. Provide customer references so the buyer can talk to people who like you. You may have to give the customer some time, but keep communications going. Ring regularly to check how the comparisons and/or consultations are going.
'Your company is not well-established enough. What service do I get to minimise the risk?'	'It is too risky to go with a new company. What service do I get to minimise the risk?'	Use endorsements from customers and professional accreditations. Explain the financial backing that the company has. Discuss any insurance they may wish you to take out. Explain how you would handle the scenarios that are worrying them.

Cont.

Table 16.2 *cont.*

Typical objection	Which means...	Possible responses
'This proposal does not meet my needs.'	This could be a play for extra services or better terms.	Ask for specifics but try not to annoy them by asking for too much detail. Ask what needs to be fixed to keep the door open to further negotiations.
'This product/ service is not tried and tested.'	'I want leading-edge technology, but not "bleeding edge". What service do I get to minimise the risk?'	Provide opportunities to test and pilot. Reassure the customer about how well your company does risk management in installations and how much support will be available to make the system work. Remind them of the advantages of being a first mover.
'Your company has mucked up before.'	'I don't want any hassle.'	Admit any fault and explain how you are putting it right.
'I'm OK with my current supplier/ product.'	'You have not convinced me that it is worth the bother of changing. Make it worth my while, or I will do nothing.'	Ask what prompted the buyer to investigate offers from new suppliers. There must be a grain of discontent for them to go to the bother of seeking and receiving proposals.
'I'm not sure that we have got the timing right.'	'I'm not sure I want to go ahead with this – the change seems daunting.'	Ask what prompted the buyer to investigate offers from new suppliers. There must be a grain of discontent for them to go to the bother of seeking and receiving proposals. Reassure the customer about how well your company does risk management.
'The price is too high.'	'I'm going to play you off against your competitors. I need more benefit or a lower price to satisfy my professional role expectations.'	Reiterate value that the customer has already agreed in earlier stages of the sales process and try to move the conversation to the total cost of ownership or value surplus. Point out the risks of low-price deals. Trade rather than concede; for example, 'If you want us to do 10% less, you will have to pay us in 14 days rather than 45.' Walk away if necessary.

Empathy

You have to demonstrate that you appreciate where the customer is coming from, even if you think their negotiation stance is unreasonable. Consult the information in Chapter 21 about the importance of emotional intelligence, and recognise that negotiations are difficult for the customer, too. A consumer who may not negotiate very often may be apprehensive or defensive. A professional buyer's career is only ever as rosy as their last negotiation, so the pressure is on them. To be a good salesperson, you need to put yourself in the shoes of the other person ('boundary-spanning') and feel what they are feeling. You do not need to over-identify with their position; you just need to have their welfare in mind as well as your own.

Some sales textbooks include a technique called 'Feel, felt, found', which we can illustrate as: 'I understand why you feel that our price is too high. I, too, sometimes feel that it is difficult to justify a 10% premium over our competitors. But I have found that so many customers get much longer usage from our products that they are worth the asking price.' This demonstrates empathy to some degree, but since many professional purchasers are now aware of this technique it can come across as corny and false.

Rapport

Rapport is associated with trust, and you build trust by doing what you say you will, showing an interest in the customer and communicating well. You have probably already built up some rapport with your customer in the earlier stages of the sales process. How can you use that now? Can you break tense moments with a comment about a shared interest? Remind the customer of a laugh you shared earlier? Rapport building does not stop because you have moved from the 'nice' bits of the sales process into one which is more difficult. Stay human and remember that the other person still has the human values they had last time you met.

Influence

In all negotiations, explore your options. If both parties stuck to their opening stance, no progress would ever be made. 'What-if?' questions are handy: 'What if we delivered on Sundays rather than Mondays? There is an extra charge, but we can be more accurate about arrival time because the traffic is much less of an issue.' The behavioural change that salespeople want in business negotiations is for the customer to move the conversation from trade-offs to finalising contract details. They will only do this when they are satisfied that you have addressed all their concerns and they are getting a desirable value surplus from you as a supplier. You can suggest or prompt the move from trade-offs to closing the deal when you feel that negotiations are complete but be prepared to provide additional reassurance before the customer commits to moving on.

Tactics you may encounter

As we have seen from the sections in this chapter, purchasing professionals and some consumers may deploy pressurising negotiating tactics, particularly on price:

- **'Beyond our budget'** – A professional buyer may give you a target price on the basis that it is their budget for this purchase. Bear in mind that budgets are estimates, and it is good financial practice to have contingencies in budgets and allow for variances, especially where additional value can be realised.

- **'Take it or leave it'** – The buyer will lose out just as much as you will if negotiations fail. For example, if they force you to exit negotiations because their price demands are unreasonable, and next week their colleagues in operations need your brand on the shelves and it is not there, purchasing will get some flak. Don't be afraid to 'leave it'. If doing business with the customer would be bad business, let your competitor have the hassle.

- **'Let's split the difference'** – This can seem like a reasonable thing to accept within your ZOPA. However, you still need to know what it means in value terms. Make sure it is a splitting of value, not just an unconditional concession. Sometimes splitting the difference is a bad idea, resulting in both sides losing out or an absurd knock-on effect. For example, if you are negotiating with your son about wearing black shoes or brown shoes with a blue suit: if you split the difference, he walks out of the house wearing one of each.

- **Conditional threats** – 'If you do this or don't do this, we will have to go elsewhere.' Can you reverse the threat with a counter-tactic, such as, 'If we conclude the deal by Thursday, of course, I can make that happen for you'?

- **Risk reduction now for higher-value business later** – It is a fair point that when a customer switches supplier, they experience switching costs. This means that they might expect some financial compensation from the new supplier. However, are they really facing switching costs? You could ask what the costs are. How certain can you be that the higher-value business will follow? Can you ask for a longer-term contract with pre-agreed changes in price points?

- **Request for a gift or hospitality** – Explain your company's adherence to law and ethical codes. You want to help the individual you are dealing with by helping them to make a great deal.

Throughout this textbook, we have encouraged you to be an ethical salesperson. We also acknowledge that, however ethical you are, from time to time you will encounter prospects and customers who have questionable motives. Can you establish a climate of integrity in negotiations when you think someone is trying to manipulate you? Ask them to clarify their goals. Is their tactic consistent with what they say? Steer the negotiations back to their organisation or family's interests.

Summary

In this chapter, we have looked at the challenging process of win-win negotiations. Good negotiators are worth a great deal to organisations. We have looked at planning for success and best practice in negotiation. There is only so much that you can learn from a textbook, so we urge you to practise. Bear in mind that negotiation is going on around us all the time, in internal meetings and at home in family situations, as well as with customers. Negotiation skills will help you in all areas of life.

17

Closing The Sale

Introduction

The final stage in the sales process is usually called closing. This can be defined as the completion of a sales transaction (ie the customer signs an order or offers money in return for the product). In large B2B sales, the closing phase can involve a lot of complicated paperwork and project planning before any money is transferred. As Patricia Fripp (2020) says: 'Don't celebrate closing a sale; celebrate opening a relationship.'

The very expression 'closing the sale' can make buyers cringe. The corny phrase 'Always be closing!', popularised in the 1992 film *Glengarry Glen Ross* (Foley, 1992) – which did nothing for the reputation of the sales profession – should be treated with humour rather than as a serious approach to selling. The plot of the film focuses on four desperate salespeople in competition with each other to sell the most, each becoming more unethical in their actions to close the deal and save their jobs.

In *SPIN Selling*, Rackham (1988) defined closing as: 'A behaviour used by the seller which implies or invites a commitment, so that the buyer's next statement accepts or denies commitment'. Clumsy closing techniques can do harm, especially in large complex sales where you are negotiating with professional buyers. However, sales negotiations do have to be drawn to some kind of conclusion.

Not closing is equally problematic for you and the customer. If the customer has confirmed that you can meet their needs at a price they can afford, you have earned the right to ask for their business and/or suggest a way forward which requires their commitment. The conclusion could be a sale for the supplier, it may be a postponement while both parties draw breath, or it may be a 'thanks, but no thanks' from the customer.

The 'closing' phase of the sales cycle is fraught with risk. Techniques to persuade the customer to give you the business can reduce trust, which you need to secure repeat business (Hawes et al, 1996). A customer-oriented 'close' will focus on exchanging information, exploring 'what ifs' to minimise risk and problem-solving. At some stage, you have to ask the customer: 'Will you do business with us?' Let's consider how you might do that with integrity and confidence.

During the sale

The whole sales process should be focused on building a mutually respectful business relationship in which the customer would feel confident that, if they give a financial commitment to the supplier, they will get the benefits they need. A successful sales discussion will have involved discovering the customer's needs, making a value proposition that should be of interest to them, and ethical negotiation. Handling the early stages of a sales discussion professionally will improve the chances of a successful close.

Throughout the sales process, you can make incremental progress towards a conclusion. Listen for buying signals (see the next section) and make notes; both will help you when you prepare to close. Arguably, every time the customer agrees to advance the sales discussion to the next stage (eg from first meeting to a widening of contacts, or from needs exploration to the written proposal), you have achieved a mini-close. Nevertheless, several mini-closes do not clock up to a big close – that has its own dynamics.

Buying signals

Always remember that any customer has to endure a lot of emotional stress when buying something. They are facing change, and the comforts of the present situation are going to be disrupted. That will loom larger in their minds than the future benefits which they find difficult to imagine. They may find it difficult to understand the options that they have, and they will fear making a mistake. A professional buyer has professional pressure to make the right decision, and a consumer may have family expectation or social pressure. It is worth asking throughout the sales process: 'What are you happy with?' and 'What concerns you?'

There are several types of buying signals (adapted from Manning et al, 2011):

- Questions about the features and benefits of the product.

- Telling you about where they see your product fitting into their plans.

- Recognition (eg 'I am calling you because you have been recommended to me/ your company has a good reputation').

- Asking about specific requirements (eg 'We need deliveries every Friday').

- Movements and gestures (eg the customer looks more interested or is smiling and nodding).

- An objection which opens a possibility for an option (eg 'This will not work with our current capital budget. Can you offer us a finance plan?').

When could a customer ever be ready to buy, when buying entails such risk? It is when they are asking specific questions or looking particularly interested at a point in a discussion or demonstration that they are starting to imagine that the benefits of change will outweigh the risks. If they ask, 'Can you explain again how this software alerts us to machine failure before it happens?' or 'This model of bike – do you have any endorsements from a rider who can tell me how it performs on hills?' then you know that the probability of the customer buying is improving.

In business sectors, there are many buying decision-makers involved, and you have to track buying signals from all of them, as discussed in the Customer Engagement chapter. Even in consumer sectors, families as DMUs can be challenging. In the case of a car model, if the teenager says: 'Urgh, Mum! I don't want to be seen dead in that!' then you have to suggest an alternative model quickly. Pushing one decision-maker for a sale when others are unsure will sow the seeds of buyer's remorse later.

As mentioned earlier in this chapter, within long sales cycles you need ongoing commitment at each stage and sub-stage – it needs to be built up incrementally. Perhaps we can embrace a reinterpretation of 'always be closing'. It is necessary to check that progress has genuinely been made at each stage and sub-stage of a sale, so you should ask, 'Does this work for your engineers?' or 'Are we ready to move on to discuss X?' These questions enable you to determine whether the customer's commitment is consolidating. After a first meeting, is the decision-maker you have seen ready to introduce you to other members of the DMU? Are they prepared for a demo to technical staff? Are they even ready to longlist your organisation? At the end of each communication, note what little advances you have made.

Communications style

Throughout the sales process, but especially in the closing stage, you should listen more than you talk. You need to concentrate on the buyer's words, gestures and expressions, which will convey how comfortable they are concluding the deal.

If you remember what was said about communication in Chapter 13, you will realise how easy it can be for messages to be poorly delivered or misinterpreted on receipt. This is particularly risky in the closing of the sale. Throwaway lines can come back to haunt you. This will be especially true in a B2C sale where the customer might be perceived to have some vulnerability, such as a hearing impairment or difficulty seeing small print. If you summarise the small print for them rather than getting a magnifying glass, your sale will be subject to legal challenge. Be calm and be clear, and check that the customer has understood your meaning correctly.

Customers may wish to explain how they feel about the product/service or your company as the sales cycle concludes. In such cases, you may need to offer empathy and reassurance.

Try not to jump to fill a period of silence during a closing discussion. The customer may need time to think. After a while, you might ask if the extended silence means that the customer still has doubts. Be confident but be respectful. Think about yourself or your nearest and dearest in a buying situation and try to convey your empathy to the customer. In most European and North American business cultures, it is appropriate to maintain friendly eye contact when you ask for the order.

Preparation for a close

Focus on the main objective that the customer has said they want to achieve. Are you sure you have convinced them that the proposed product/service meets their expectations?

Review the objections that the customer has raised during the rest of the sales cycle and make sure that you have resolved them or can resolve them in this final stage. You should be prepared to raise them yourself; for example, 'I remember that you were concerned about the download speeds in your area. Can I check that the information we provided and the tests we did have reassured you?'

Check that all important clauses in the contract have been discussed. Do not introduce new terms at this stage, such as an installation charge or a fee for a guarantee. If you introduce any new material at this stage, the customer will be annoyed or worried about it. If you have made a mistake in negotiations that has to be put right, make sure you apologise and say, 'I have checked X and it is the case that Y applies rather than Z.' You may need to offer some compensation if it has a material effect on the customer's expectations.

Check your company's ethical guidelines before deciding on your final negotiation tactics. Review different methods of asking for the sale and practise them. Which suits this customer and this buying situation? Be aware that you might have to ask for the sale several times.

Offer the customer options. One of the most customer-oriented ways to close a sale is to let the customer choose what they want to buy from you. What choices can you offer which ensure that both the customer and your employer get a valuable deal?

Good practice in a close

Keep listening for buying signals, now more than ever. Is the customer hinting that they are ready to get on with the paperwork? If there is still hesitation, can you re-focus them on the main benefit they want from the change? The objections they raised in negotiations may be raised again, and you have to accept them. Show respect and empathy for the customer's concerns, then try to discuss how they can be overcome.

The following list offers a summary of good practice (adapted from Manning et al, 2011):

- Listen intently

- Focus the conversation on customer-perceived benefits

- Accept and respect objections.

- Do not introduce new contract terms or conditions

- Provide options

- Propose a mutual way forward

- Maintain respectful eye contact when you ask the customer to commit to the deal

If you are unsure about the customer's intentions during the concluding discussions, try a 'trial close'. A question such as, 'How close are we to concluding a deal?' might be a way of alerting the customer to the need for a decision.

You can then summarise the value being offered and ask directly if you have a deal. You may have to prepare some lists to show to the customer all the things you have discussed and the value the deal would bring to their organisation/household. Alternatively, you can offer the customer some options and ask which they prefer.

If you work in a large key account which has board-level sponsorship, it might be worth bringing the director who sponsors the key account relationship to the final meeting in a sales cycle. This emphasises the status that the customer has in your organisation and the board's commitment to making the business relationship work. You may also need help from a senior colleague if you are still in your training period. Otherwise, think twice about whether you need to involve a senior manager. If it looks like only they have the authority to close the deal, that could undermine your credibility.

What about my targets and deadlines?

Professional buyers are aware of their suppliers' reporting periods and will know that salespeople have monthly, quarterly and annual targets that they need to meet. Some consumers know this, as well. They may try to play on this in an effort to get a lower price or special service. You are urged not to use desperate tactics such as '10% extra discount if you sign by Friday' because it sends a message that the company is desperate for cash flow.

Senior directors have made promises to shareholders, though, and that will trickle down to your target and an expectation that you will get business by deadlines. That is important for your colleagues in operations, who have plans to make and deliver what you are expected to sell, and for your colleagues in finance who need to optimise the cash flow. Nevertheless, you have to get sales ethically and profitably. Do not be afraid of failure if the deal is not right for your employer. Bring forward your sales activity as much as you can so that you do not feel panicked on the last day of the quarter. Feel the panic on the first day of the quarter, and you have more chance of achieving your target ahead of your deadline.

Remember that customers also have a budget deadline; in most businesses, budgets are expected to be spent within specific timeframes. Many industry sectors experience a 'banana curve' of frenetic activity in the last quarter of a financial year ending 31 December because that is when many customers have to complete their spending. Most organisations in the UK public sector have a year-end of 31 March, so they order large projects in the January–March quarter. Although the restrictions on the timing of purchases have been much diluted by credit cards, consumer household budgets may also dictate when they buy. Consumer spending is also seasonal, with a peak in many sectors at Christmas. These are buying behaviours that your company will acknowledge in timing your targets. A savvy salesperson might seek out companies with different year-ends or consumers with varying attitudes to seasonal spending to even out peaks and troughs.

Avoiding negative closing techniques

As professional members of the Association of Professional Sales (APS), we suggest that you avoid using closing techniques which could later be interpreted in court as manipulative. Nevertheless, the following techniques appear on many websites and in many books, and there may be circumstances in which they are relevant.

The assumptive close

This is where you ask a question about some small detail which suggests that the customer has already decided to buy; for example, 'Would you like your gizmo in red or blue?' Professional buyers, who have been trained to spot sales techniques, might give you a hard time for trying this, but the assumptive close does seem to persist in consumer sales. Finding out a customer's colour preferences might keep the conversation going, but you are advised to rephrase your question as: 'If you were to buy this model, would you like it in red or blue?' This may help the customer to imagine ownership of the car in a more personal way, without a clumsy presumption that they have already decided to buy.

The special offer/time limitation/'fly-fish' close

Have you noticed how most furniture retailers always seem to be advertising a 'sale' with amazing reductions? All it says to savvy consumers is that the reductions are really the normal prices. Sometimes you will make special offers because you need to reduce the risk to the customer in trying something new or reward them for buying in bulk, and sometimes there really is a limited time in which to place an order for a product whose stock turnover is volatile. In most cases, though, professional buyers will play for even more concessions if you send this signal. And savvy consumers might take the offer and then use their fourteen-day cooling-off period to cancel the deal if they change their mind. Having a cancelled sale is more hassle than not having one in the first place. Legislators regard the time-limited close, in particular, as a 'pressure' technique, so if you did end up in court you would lose.

Try before you buy

Reducing the customer's risk with an opportunity to test or use a product before buying seems a reasonable thing to do. In B2B selling, customers may wish to try their current software on new hardware platforms or their ingredients in new factory equipment. They may or may not be more likely to buy, depending on the result – remember their interest in 'value-in-use'. However, letting consumers have things now which they have to pay for later can be dangerous territory. In the bad old days, some companies used to send products to people that they had not asked for 'free for one month' and then the company would demand money, even if they had made it very difficult for the consumer to send the product back. That is just extortion. In fact, consumers have the legal right to keep 'unsolicited goods', although they would generally prefer not to have things that they have not ordered. Currently, attempts to get consumers 'on the hook' with a free trial are regarded with suspicion.

The reverse close

If you ask, 'Is there any reason not to buy?' are you being manipulative or asking for information and feedback? If you truly need more information, you are extending the negotiation so that you can go over the prospect's concerns. Remember that communication is a subtle and nuanced experience for buyer and seller. 'Please could you explain what is causing you to hesitate at this point?' might be better phrasing in a UK business culture.

The leading close

This technique involves asking a lot of questions which should elicit a 'yes' answer and then asking for the sale. It would be irritating to professional buyers, and it would be seen as manipulative in consumer sectors.

The pressure close, or 'fear, uncertainty and doubt' (FUD)

Raising the spectre of what the customer would be missing, or what risks might ensue, if they do not buy, while waiving an order form and a pen at them, could be perceived as manipulation. However, you should have explored why the customer needs to change from their current practice in the needs discovery stage of the sales discussion. We know that 'do nothing' is a fearsome competitor, and plenty of sales are lost to 'do nothing'. You can save yourself a lot of time by exploring this scenario as early as possible in the sales cycle so that, if the customer is likely to take that option, you are prepared to spend your time pursuing better potential sales.

Outcomes of a close

'In using closing techniques, the sellers put pressure on customers to make a decision. Most people are less satisfied with decisions that they feel they have been pressurised to make than with those which they believe they've made entirely of their own free will.'
— Neil Rackham, author of *SPIN Selling* (1988)

What to do when it is a 'yes'

Enjoy the exhilaration of making a sale! Then get back down to earth quickly. Say thank you and follow up without delay to make sure the deal leads quickly to operational activity. Even if the sales process has been amicable, expect buyer's remorse, which is usually associated with consumers buying a product which involves a large financial and personal commitment, such as a car. Before the purchase, they can look forward to driving it. After the purchase, they have to get used to the new features of the car and accept that they are now stuck with any irritating features for several years and that they have depleted their finances so they're unable to buy other things that they might want. If the car fails in some way or faults are found soon after purchase, the remorse will be even worse.

Because of concerns about pressurised sales techniques and the social and psychological problems that can result from buyer's remorse, most major consumer purchases are subject to a 'cooling-off' period, during which time the customer can cancel the deal without penalty. During this period, if you disappear after a purchase and fail to check on feedback from the customer it may trigger resentment which could impact on their future purchases and lose you recommendations. You want the customer to say to friends, 'I went to X for my new car and salesperson Y was really helpful.' Buyer's remorse is less of a problem with smaller items, and if you are selling small items you will find that closing techniques are more successful because the customer perceives less risk.

In business selling, buyer's remorse still exists, and it is still essential to follow up and get involved in the operationalisation of the sale. It is more likely in a business sale that colleagues from operations and finance have been involved in the sales process, and you have a shared understanding of what has to happen at what times for the customer. Reassurance is still necessary. All installations and implementations have their teething problems, so make sure you know what is happening and how it is being resolved.

What to do when it is a 'no'

First, remember that it is not about you. The customer's refusal is not a judgement on you as a person or as a sales professional. Only they can judge when and if a new product/service is right for them or their organisation, and they have the right to decide that what you offered is not right for them. You may feel that they are making a terrible mistake. You could be right. Do not 'yes, but' the customer. No means no.

Thank the customer for considering your company. Ask for feedback, such as, 'What was it about the proposal that failed to meet your needs?' or 'How can we improve for next time?' Earn the right to keep talking to them. Perhaps the alternative that they plan to buy will not achieve the 'value-in-use' they expect. If you are still in contact, then you will be on call when they have that realisation and need to unravel their mistake. The 'nearly sales' of the past (and former customers) are a rich source of leads for tomorrow. The decision-makers know something about you and may be willing to give you a second chance after some time has elapsed.

What to do when it is a 'postpone'

What does it mean when a customer says, 'Not yet, but we might have budget next year', 'Not until you resolve X' or 'Not until I have spoken to Joe'? It means that you have not answered all their concerns. You need to unpick that by asking for feedback. Return with any extra information the customer says that they want as soon as possible. If they specify when they want a call-back, come back in the timeframe proposed by the customer (or a bit sooner). Sometimes a customer plays for time because they want to have another look at the competition or because they are sorely tempted by the easy prospect of 'doing nothing' rather than taking on change. You might be able to drop some hints about what they should look out for if they shop around or what the risks of waiting too long might be, but be friendly in accepting the postponement. Cautious customers usually reward polite persistence.

Summary

In this chapter, we have looked at the conclusion of sales discussions, how you can use best-practice techniques in 'closing', and how you can avoid potentially manipulative or unethical closing tactics.

PART 4

....

BEHAVIOURS OF A WORLD-CLASS SALES EXECUTIVE

18

Ethical Behaviour In Professional Sales

Introduction

In the minds of buyers (and we are all buyers in some contexts) giving trust to a sales representative is fraught with risk. Professional buying decision-makers have described integrity as the most important attribute they want from sales professionals (McDonald et al, 1997). Historically, selling was an unregulated function, and the sales job was precarious. Sales rogues were easy pickings for scriptwriters, which contributed to a negative stereotype of salespeople in popular culture (Hartman, 2006). This negative image might be summed up as someone who misrepresents products to get buyers to part with their hard-earned money for something that does not fulfil their needs. Unfortunately, mis-selling is still a worrying phenomenon in business, and court cases are reported across the globe. It is not always the fault of salespeople; in most cases, it is a corporate responsibility issue. But in the minds of customers, 'mis-selling' apportions the blame to the professionals at the customer interface, giving us a mountain to climb in the quest to gain trust. As Warren Buffett pointed out: 'It takes 20 years to build a reputation and five minutes to ruin it. If you think about that, you'll do things differently' (Anderson, 2016).

Despite negative images of selling and salespeople, the buying and selling that is necessary for the economy to grow has never ground to a halt. It has been going on since someone long ago wanted to exchange a stone axe for some decorative shells. In businesses and local communities, there have always been reliable and trustworthy salespeople who worked hard to achieve good reputations with customers.

In a complex and globalised economy, buyers need signposts, such as brands, to know which companies and individuals have worked hard to develop positive reputations. Membership in a professional association is a powerful way that a career salesperson can demonstrate their integrity to their contacts. This textbook is published by the Association of Professional Sales, which has been a driving force in developing vocational qualifications for sales.

Codes of conduct

There are many root causes of mis-selling and other corporate governance failures. Despite legislation and regulation, corporate scandals still occur. Most public limited companies (PLCs) have codes of conduct, which are designed to reassure stakeholders that the directors take ethical conduct seriously, and that they intend to avoid misconduct. A code of conduct cannot cover everything, and it cannot ensure an ethical climate in a company. Everything that happens every day in a company goes towards building the perception of an ethical climate or a climate where rule-breaking is tolerated. Nevertheless, a code of conduct is important, and it may be the first thing that you are asked to learn as a sales recruit. You may be asked to sign every year to confirm that you have read the code of conduct, that you have complied with it and that you will continue to comply with it. The code should help you to spot an ethical issue when one occurs and, if it does not make clear what you should do, it should make clear where you can go to for help.

There are many examples of codes of conduct which are published on company websites, and you may find it interesting to compare and contrast how top brands convey their ethical stance.

Typically, a code of conduct will include the following:

- A statement about core values, such as innovation and quality

- A statement about stakeholders, including shareholders, customers, employees, suppliers and the wider community

- A commitment to honesty and integrity

- Company policies

- Definitions of standards and behaviours

- Lists of what employees are expected to do

- Lists of behaviours which are expressly forbidden

- How stakeholders can raise concerns and report misconduct

A code of conduct is one element of the wider investments that companies can make to encourage an ethical climate, which is associated with salespeople taking pride in their organisation and developing better relationships with customers (Briggs et al, 2012). Students should refer to Appendix B, where the complete APS code of conduct is presented.

The importance of trust in trade

'In the long term, an honest and fair approach to doing business will always be the most profitable. And the business world holds such an approach in much higher esteem than is generally imagined.'
— Robert Bosch, industrialist and engineer (1921, quoted in Bosch, 2019)

We often talk about trust in business, but it can be challenging to get customers to pinpoint what trust means in an organisation that they buy from. Researchers Pirson and Malhotra (2007) defined trust as 'the willingness to be vulnerable to the actions of another party based on positive expectations regarding the motivation and behaviour of the other'. In other words, we part with money for their product or service because we believe in their good intention to give us something in return that will be of value to us. Customers build up that expectation based on their information about and experience of the integrity, benevolence and reliability of the person or company (Pirson and Malhotra, 2007). Information about the company's product quality, status as an employer, customer orientation, social and environmental responsibility, and financial stability are important indicators of the trustworthiness of a company (Matuleviciene and Stravinskiene, 2016).

Corporate reputation is difficult to establish and easy to lose. Companies invest large sums year after year into promoting a positive image of their brand to gain a premium place in the minds of customers. The brand becomes a shortcut for customers in making buying decisions and reduces the risk of the purchase. This is particularly true in consumer markets (see, eg Baek et al, 2010), but the value of being a trustworthy brand is also well-established in B2B markets (see, eg Kotler and Pfoertsch, 2007). As New Zealand's Most Trusted Brands survey recently identified:

'Trust is an emotion that fuels our decision whether we are conscious of it or not. It is that intangible quality that signals reliability and integrity. Whether it is a product or service, trust is what reassures us that we are making the right choice. Cost, quality and desirability are all important factors for consumers. Yet it's vital for a brand to stay true to its promises.'
(Reader's Digest, 2020)

Ulaga and Eggert (2006) examined trust by asking questions about the supplier's ability to keep promises, to demonstrate genuine concern to help the customer's business to succeed and to consider customer well-being as well as its own when making decisions. They found that 'Satisfaction with the supplier will only translate into commitment if the purchasing relationship is characterised by trust' (Ulaga and Eggert, 2006).

Buyers who interact with representatives from a company naturally infer that these individuals represent the company's brand. Therefore, buying decision-makers see individual salespeople as brand ambassadors. The way a company sells is a reliable indicator of its corporate values, and it has a significant impact on its reputation. Although how products are made, the way a company manages its administration and finance, and customer service are also relevant, individual trust of the salesperson is a necessary complement to the buyer's trust in the corporate brand. Individuals, therefore, have to be able to demonstrate integrity, benevolence and reliability as well.

What are ethics?

How can an organisation demonstrate integrity, benevolence and reliability? Integrity in business can be defined as (adapted from Zwilling, 2012):

- Meeting your commitments
- Being honest in communications
- Fulfilling the moral expectations of stakeholders
- Treating everyone with respect
- Building trust through being reliable

The term 'ethics' is widely used in connection with codes of behaviour in business. More broadly, it is associated with morality and is the branch of philosophy concerned with what is good for individuals and society. It encompasses intentions as well as actions, and the effort involved in trying to 'be ethical' can be demanding.

'In law, a man is guilty when he violates the rights of others. In ethics, he is guilty if he only thinks of doing so.'
— Emmanuel Kant, philosopher

In business, many companies have a code of conduct or business conduct guidelines explaining their approach to ethics – how the company sees right and wrong, and how the professionals working for it should approach ethical problems. We know that customers expect their suppliers to help salespeople to 'engage in positive moral judgement', and where they perceive that this occurs (and the company also demonstrates customer orientation) they associate it with better sales performance (Schwepker and Good, 2011).

An understanding of ethics can provide us all with principles to help us examine difficult issues objectively, while not underestimating the emotions that these problematic issues can generate. It can help us identify why ethical problems occur. It does not always provide a right answer; it can provide several or none which satisfy the parties to a dispute. Nevertheless, there has always been a human need for exploration of right and wrong.

Many of us learn particular moral codes from religion, culture or family expectations when we are very young, when we may only be able to absorb that a specific act is good or bad; for example, that stealing is bad and giving is good. As individuals, we develop a set of rules or duties which we try to follow to feel that we are doing the right things in our daily lives. However, there are challenges in applying absolute rules in life and at work. For example, followers of various religious, ethical and legal codes know that they must not steal and they must not kill. But they also know that in most legal codes, stealing is a lesser offence than murder, and even in the case of killing, killing in self-defence is regarded more leniently than pre-meditated murder, which is classified by degrees in many countries. So how do we know which of our duties matter most and what circumstances affect the severity of a breach?

An absolute in a business code of conduct might be: 'We do not accept gifts from suppliers.' This shows that giving is not always good; sometimes it is perceived as an attempt to get customer decision-makers to deal with you for personal gain – in other words, you are offering *a bribe*. That is associated with harmful effects. The harm might affect the customer (getting a lesser product than they would have got without the bribe), competitors (wasted time and money on a bid that was unsuccessful when perhaps they deserved to win) and broader society (people in a position to demand bribes getting richer than those who are not). In most countries, there is anti-bribery legislation, such as the Bribery Act, 2010 in the UK, which asserts that any 'distortion of trade' is illegal.

People generally support the idea that bribery is wrong until the 'what-if' questions start. How should a supplier behave to avoid being perceived to distort trade?

- What if the gift were a small token such as personalised golf balls, rather than a brown envelope stuffed with £1,000 notes?

- What if the supplier and customer staff working together on a project always went out for a pizza after they achieved a milestone and the supplier got paid?

- If a small gift or hospitality event is openly given and logged, is that better than something done secretly?

- If you are trading in a culture where gift-giving is normal and you do not give gifts, does that cause offence?

- Are you in a new situation not yet defined by laws and codes?

- Is the gift personal to a key decision-maker, given on the day of a contract being signed, or is it a 'beer and skittles' event for a whole team in an ongoing business relationship?

- Is some hospitality acceptable? If a customer turns up to a meeting at a supplier and is told to buy their own sandwiches, is that good because we have not offered a gift to the customer, or is it just plain rude?

The spectrum between the good of 'being hospitable' and the bad of 'distorting trade' is very broad (see Figure 18.1).

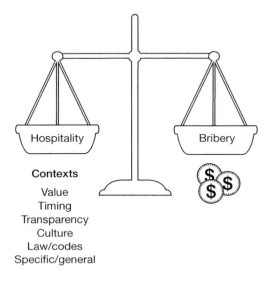

Figure 18.1: What constitutes a 'distortion of trade'?

We all need guidance in how to apply codes, as circumstances are rarely identical.

Since the dawn of civilization, philosophers have had different ideas about what is ethical or virtuous. The philosophical school of thought known as consequentialism could be interpreted as a view of ethics which judges good or bad based on the result of the act and not just the act itself.

Consequences are significant, but we cannot assume that good ends justify bad means, nor can we assume that because an outcome is OK for the majority of people we can ignore it causing misery to a minority. The understanding of ethics must go beyond a code to the analysis of contexts and consequences. In this respect, it is essential to explore scenarios and examples when developing exemplary behaviour (see Appendix A). Because codes alone do not help with interpretation, companies that are serious about their reputations need to go beyond the concept of a code and develop an ethical climate.

Ethical climate

We know from research studies (see McClaren, 2013) that a healthy ethical climate should be a dominant factor in a company's relationships with its employees, who can perceive that they will be treated fairly and can have pride in their work, and its customers, who like to know that they are dealing with a supplier who will treat them fairly. What might a robust ethical climate look like? It is evident in the culture of the whole organisation as well as the sales function, and it includes values, management style, codes and reward systems. It is evident in training which establishes specific work-related norms. Ethical evaluation is also used in recruitment and training.

Although many businesses now embrace a consultative leadership approach on most topics, in the case of ethics a directive leadership style is preferable as codes need to be consistently applied across the organisation, and they need to be seen to be enforced. There are specific challenges at the customer interface, so salespeople get specific coaching for dealing with ethical dilemmas, including those provoked by the customer (for example, customers asking for inducements to buy).

Besides the obvious advantages for the directors and vice-presidents of companies – ie they will not end up in jail if their company creates a positive ethical climate – there are specific advantages for salespeople. Salespeople who work for employers with strong ethical climates have less concern that the requirements of their job conflict with their personal values. They report higher job satisfaction, higher job performance and better commitment than salespeople working for firms where ethical standards are not clear (Jaramillo et al, 2006; Itani et al, 2017). There is also ample evidence that ethical behaviour plays a decisive role in customer relationships, leading to better customer satisfaction and better customer commitment to the supplier, which makes the sales job more enjoyable (Román and Ruiz, 2005).

Learning from ethical failings

When selling hits the headlines, it is almost always mis-selling:

> 'The next mis-selling scandal could be parked on your drive: PCP [personal contract plan] is a complicated and expensive product, pushed by silver-tongued salespeople.' (Barrett, 2017)

> 'Regulator moves to stop pensions mis-selling.' (Cumbo, 2017)

Some famous brands have been involved in sales scandals over recent years. These include:

- A well-known electronics manufacturer being accused of trying to bribe a prime minister

- The most expensive case in the history of the IT sector, when a customer sued over a system which it claimed had been sold dishonestly

- A major pharmaceutical company losing sales after a bribery investigation in a major economy

- A record fine in the USA for a global company after a long-running case involving alleged corruption

Many corporate scandals arise from external sources when the norms of doing business change without legislative guidance. For example, financial deregulation in the UK in the 1980s is often seen as the environment that created the mis-selling of the 1990s. Nevertheless, some companies were more cautious than others and avoided the trap of copying aggressive competitors on a path of reputational risk. It is worth noting that when challenged on poor practice, many decision-makers have said that they had to do what competitors did or lose market share. We may ask why no one thought to blow the whistle to the regulatory authorities, but it is fair to say that the market supervision at the time was lax compared to today's standards, so that might have been difficult to do.

After media attention about the fundraising practices of some UK charities in 2015, the Information Commissioner's Office carried out a two-year investigation. Thirteen charities were fined for breaching privacy laws (ICO, n.d.A).

In an ideal world, organisations would not be waiting for legislators to catch up with markets. There should be an appetite to take opportunities presented by a changing business environment, but short-term and long-term impact on all risks, including reputational risk, need to be examined through scenario planning.

Strategic failure in companies is another cause of ethical dysfunction. Without a focus on the customer, which identifies a needs-based type of segmentation (such as lifestyle), the customer may not be seen as a real person but as a 'target'. Although payment protection insurance (PPI) was a relevant product for a particular segment of bank customers – employees in insecure jobs – it was sold to everyone, often by stealth (customers did not know that it had been added to their loans). When such tactics become acceptable, there is no imperative to design products which suit customer needs, and compliance with what safeguards there are can be seen as a game of evasion. If employees and customers complain, companies resort to refuting the criticism and trying to deny any wrong-doing or need to pay compensation.

Some observers of mis-selling scandals note that management supervision of salespeople and agents is weak. Managers offered aggressive rewards for selling particular products, without direction about how the product is to be sold or to which customers. Most regulatory systems now insist that senior managers have a duty of care to ensure that reward systems do not drive inappropriate sales. It can be challenging to design reward systems, especially in the case of third-party sales agents, that are not highly associated with the volume of sales. However, it is possible to apply qualitative as well as quantitative measures.

Finally, poor processes are usually identified where mis-selling has occurred. Bureaucracy is always annoying to entrepreneurially minded people, but processes are necessary. It is a good idea for a company to employ quality control professionals who can design processes which are not a time-wasting burden to salespeople but help to make sure that the right thing happens for the customer. The importance of process in sales cannot be underestimated, as what happens at the customer interface must be traceable – back to the promises that senior managers make about good corporate governance to shareholders and government.

Integrity

A company's code of conduct will usually start by laying out some principles of doing business, and a word which is consistently used in this context is 'integrity'.

Definitions of 'integrity' focus on honesty and morality. Honesty is generally understood as telling the truth, but sometimes individuals perceive facts differently, especially when they are not aware of all the relevant ones, so whose truth is valid? When professionals are open and transparent about events, they can usually achieve a shared understanding of the truth, with a certain amount of forgiveness for admitted errors. Honouring your word is vital in business relationships, but it is not always easy. A colleague you relied on may fail to follow through, or circumstances may change between your making a promise to the customer and fulfilling it. It requires vigilance to complete every promise you make as a brand ambassador of your employer to the customer's satisfaction.

Morality is a difficult concept, and the world is awash with examples of people who claim it in public but lead double lives. Different cultures have different ideas about right and wrong, but a popular general principle is to respect who you are dealing with and treat them as you would like to be treated yourself if you were the buyer. There are a few individuals who set out to trick customers, and they make great material for television programmes, but most of us have a sense of right and wrong and empathy for our fellow human beings. We may not be perfect but demonstrating to the customer that we aspire to do the right thing will help to build trust.

Integrity is highly valued by professional buyers. No one wants to be the buyer who set up a deal with a supplier who does not deliver. It is humiliating personally, and it can be career-limiting, so, whether or not you think you are an honest person, the buyer will not necessarily find it easy to trust you. They have expectations, and when you do not meet them they expect communications to help them to accept the problem, as well as apologies and possibly compensation. For example, if you are the customer's main supplier of critical raw materials, and the customer's warehouse team are waiting for a delivery which you cannot make on time because of a traffic delay, you may expect that the delivery driver will let them know that they are stuck. If they do not, you may be the person who receives an angry call and must apologise and offer compensation for lost production time.

Project managers work according to Murphy's Law – the general principle that 'if it can go wrong, it will'. Keeping ahead of what is happening with customer orders and keeping the customer informed will help you to demonstrate that you take your duty of care to the customer seriously. Codes will also have a section explaining how to comply with laws which affect the business. There are several UK laws which are particularly relevant to sales situations, including the Bribery Act 2010 and the Misrepresentation Act, 1967.

Bribery, gifts and entertainment

In consumer sales situations, we may only get the chance to offer a customer a cup of coffee, but in business selling the opportunities to offer hospitality and gifts are endless. It might seem innocent to take a customer decision-maker out for a meal when meetings stretch into lunchtime or into the evening, and combining entertainment, sport and a seminar about a new product is a popular way to get time with customers. But you need to check the business culture of the country in which you are selling and the customer's policies about accepting hospitality as well as the attitude of individual decision-makers, especially the purchasing manager, who may be a member of the Chartered Institute of Purchasing and Supply (CIPS). The CIPS code of conduct requires members to 'enhance and protect the standards of the profession by… not accepting inducements or gifts (other than any declared gifts of nominal value which have been sanctioned by my employer) [and] not allowing offers of hospitality or those with vested interests to influence, or be perceived to influence, my business decisions' (CIPS, 2013).

Misrepresentation

One of the commonest allegations made against salespeople is that they misrepresent products and services to potential customers to make a sale. For example, if a salesperson sells a machine to a customer claiming that it will improve their productivity by 50% when, in fact, it is only possible to improve it by 25%, they have made a misrepresentation. When a customer buys something from a supplier, the sale is governed by the law of contract. A salesperson is a representative of their employer and is making contracts on their behalf; therefore, you need to understand the basic principles of contract law.

The notes below are drawn from English contract law, which has also influenced the laws of the US and Commonwealth countries.

A contract is a voluntary arrangement. One person (the seller) makes an offer (usually a product or service), and the other person (the buyer) accepts it by delivering the terms of the offer (usually the price). The law places considerable emphasis on ensuring that the buyer gave full, informed consent to the terms of the offer. That may be simple if the offer is a tin of baked beans, but in the case of a multimillion-pound construction project or a complex financial service it is not. Contract law has moved from placing emphasis on the duty of the buyer to understand what they are buying to placing responsibilities on the seller to test that the buyer truly understands what they are buying and how it is going to affect their life or their business. The terms of a contract may be written down (and must be within legal expectations of 'fair' terms), but buyers also rely on things that salespeople say or imply. It is explicit in the Consumer Rights Act 2015 that anything that is said or written by the seller is part of the contract if it affects the consumer's decision-making, not just during the sale but also after the sale.

The first Misrepresentation Act in the UK was passed in 1967, to enable consumers to exit from contracts and claim damages where false claims about products and services had been made. Misrepresentation by sellers can be fraudulent, negligent or innocent (see Table 18.1).

Table 18.1: Misrepresentation types

Type of misrepresentation	What it means	Buyer's redress
Fraudulent	The seller is aware that what they say is untrue	The contract can be cancelled, the buyer can claim damages, or both
Negligent	The seller does not take care to check that what they are saying is true	The contract can be cancelled, the buyer can claim damages, or both
Innocent	The seller does not know that what they are saying is untrue	The contract can be cancelled

Putting things right after a misrepresentation is costly. There are also indirect costs, especially when there has been a court case in the public domain or the misrepresentation was uncovered by a television programme. Reputational damage can last for a long time; consequently, most sales professionals do their utmost to explain their products and services openly and fairly.

Conflicts of interest

There can be many types of conflicts of interest in business. Companies ask their employees to avoid situations in which they might be perceived to get personal gain (for themselves or family members) from a business decision. For example, if you make a sale to a company run by your brother and the firm asks for special terms which you allow, are you allowing them because it is the right thing for your employer or the right thing for your brother? Although many cultures prefer buying and selling between people in family and tribal networks, in others it is regarded with suspicion. If your reward package includes shares, you must also be careful how you trade those shares to avoid insider trading, which means trading to your advantage based on inside information you have which is not available to other shareholders.

Working relationships

Companies often describe in their codes of conduct how they expect employees to behave to customers, colleagues and other stakeholders. They may outline legislative requirements, such as equal opportunities, or company principles, such as respect and diversity. They may also provide helpful guidance about discussing and comparing competitors' products and services fairly. The laws of libel and slander apply to organisations as well as individuals – you have to compare without disparaging. Also, although you may not expect to have to deal with journalists or councillors, there may be guidelines about press interviews or responding to enquiries from public representatives and officials.

Responsibilities online

A particular concern for many companies is employees' conduct on social media. We may all wish to let off steam about work with our nearest and dearest from time to time; however, we must do so privately. Employees with otherwise spotless records have been dismissed for derogatory comments about their employers on social media sites. Even comments not related to work, such as party photos, could be career-limiting. There may well be someone in your organisation who is watching you online, and it will have started as soon as you submitted your job application. You are expected to be professional in every aspect of life, not just in the day job.

Responsibilities in the wider world

Many companies these days like to state their contributions to local communities and society in general. Besides information about support for charities and efforts made to reduce waste, this can include making sure that the supply chain does not involve slave labour or pollution, although the Triple Bottom Line (TBL) that we discussed in Chapter 1 is a relatively new feature in company reports. Businesses use internal and external environmental, social and economic performance metrics to measure their impacts on people, profit and planet.

Company property and resources

A code of conduct will probably include a section about the use of company property ranging from cars and computers to fire extinguishers and paper guillotines. Salespeople need to pay particular attention to guidance about the use of data. The General Data Protection Regulation (GDPR) which came into force in the European Union in 2018 is not a riveting read, but you can read a summary of its terms so that you are aware of data privacy laws. The penalties for breaking GDPR laws are substantial (ICO, n.d.B). You will be handling customer information, and that information can only be gathered for legal purposes, primarily for the fulfilment of the contract. Anything extra, such as analysis for market research purposes, requires the express permission of the customer. The customer has the right to access data held about them and to have it removed.

How to raise a concern or ask a question

If a code of conduct is to be the foundation of an ethical climate, employees and other stakeholders must know how to ask questions about its interpretation. In a worst-case scenario, you need to know how to 'blow the whistle' if you think that a breach has occurred. Having a code of conduct is fine, but are employees actually encouraged to report things that go wrong?

In some countries, such as the USA and South Korea, public prosecutors can authorise rewards for whistle-blowers (Maslen, 2017). You may hear anecdotes about companies that reward employees who report bad practice, but you may hear more about companies who punish employees who express concern about poor practice. The risks of whistle-blowing are significant. Since these public celebrations of whistle-blowing are rare, most people are anxious that if they raise complaints they will be seen as a trouble-maker and have to leave their job while those breaching the code are protected. Your code's process for raising concerns should be obvious, and it should give assurances about its confidentiality and fairness.

Summary

In this chapter, we have looked at the professional standards relating to sales, the importance of trust in business relationships, what can go wrong, the nature of ethics and how a company can build a robust ethical code and positive ethical climate. Integrity is essential for people working in sales.

19

Proactive Selling

Introduction

The second behaviour necessary in a sales professional, as outlined in the L4 apprenticeship standard, is proactivity. If you need to dig a trench or climb a mountain, waiting for something to happen will not lead to success or make things easier. This is true in sales too: you need to act to make things move.

Proactivity is made up of two elements: a positive mindset and the development of effective habits which reinforce your resilience, creativity, and motivation.

A mindset is a set of beliefs and attitudes held by an individual or group (Dweck, 2008). In the case of a professional work environment, employers will expect your mindset to include planning and taking positive action to support the needs of the customer, the needs of the company and your own needs. You can develop and maintain a positive, proactive mindset through the ongoing development application of good habits.

Habits are actions that you take without focused mental debate, but it may take some effort to break bad habits or establish good habits. A bad habit is one that may give immediate satisfaction but have a long-term negative impact, such as smoking. A smoker may get immediate satisfaction from the act of smoking, and they continue to smoke even when they are aware of the long-term harm. Bad habits in a salesperson can include not following up, not taking action, not listening or interrupting.

A good habit acts as a trigger to take the right next step, both personally and professionally. Developing a habit of laying out your gym clothes before you go to bed will trigger you to avoid the temptation to stay in bed and encourage you to get up and exercise. Habits take a long time to become automatic, certainly longer than three to four weeks, but developing proactive habits as a salesperson and embedding them into your daily routines will lead to professional success. The Time Management chapter provides detailed advice about doing necessary tasks, but the following lists provide a quick example in the context of developing good habits.

Good daily habits:

- Completing visit reports in the CRM system

- Following up leads within one working day

- Reviewing follow-up actions and prioritising what needs to be done today

- Preparing for customer visits by reviewing customer history in the CRM system and conducting a Google search

- Keeping a reminder of your top ten prospects on your desk

Good weekly habits:

- Setting up appointments, ensuring the reason to connect with the customer and the objectives are clear

- Updating your pipeline report

- Reviewing your reflective journal

- Reviewing open actions and follow-up actions to prepare for the coming week

A sales professional demonstrates proactivity through a desire to create new customers and the drive to understand the steps necessary to do so. In this chapter, we will explore practical steps associated with generating new business.

There is also a motivational angle to proactiveness – you need managers and colleagues to see you as a 'go-getter' in a sales role. We will examine motivation in more depth in Chapter 20, but for present purposes ask yourself if you have a desire to get up in the morning to explore new things and develop personally and professionally. This desire is called intrinsic motivation. It is supposed to be a natural thing – animals will display an interest in things that do not offer an obvious reward. Most of us have an urge to get better at things we enjoy, such as making the next level in a sports league or a computer game. It helps to believe that you have the ability to work hard, practise and improve. We can all improve through dedication, but there is a difference between the musician who is only motivated to practise three hours a week and the musician who practises thirty hours a week.

Seeking out prospective customers

Transforming names on a list into customers is one of the hardest parts of the sales job, and employers see it as a reliable indicator of proactivity and resilience. If you can make sound judgements about the use of your time, engage prospective customers in conversations, and make sensible offers without being distracted by rejection, disinterest and tough negotiations, then you will probably have a successful start in sales. And if you remember that your long-term career is not just about making this sale but creating a customer who will come back to you and recommend you to others, you will build easier and quicker pathways to future success.

How marketing and sales find new customers

The 'doing' of phoning a stranger and making a connection is scary, but if it is preceded by sensible analysis and planning it can be less stressful. Many companies have large marketing departments who spend a lot of money on attracting new customers. They also have extensive CRM or ABM systems which capture, store and analyse information about target customers as well as existing customers. This does not mean that marketing or a software programme will magically provide you with quality sales leads, but the company will aim to ensure that the CRM/ABM system is populated with reliable information for you to use.

The American Marketing Association (AMA) defines 'marketing' as 'the activity, set of institutions, and processes for creating, communicating, delivering, and exchanging offerings that have value for customers, clients, partners, and society at large' (AMA, 2017).

Marketing involves tasks such as market research and generating marketing communications. Marketing institutions include specialist marketing agencies as well as the marketing departments in companies.

Sales and marketing share responsibility for sustainable business development (ie growing sales revenues profitably and maintaining positive relationships with customers). In many sectors, marketing takes the lead on identifying target market segments for the company and growing awareness of the brand in those segments. Marketing activity attracts incoming enquiries (lead generation), which should be subject to filtering to determine degrees of interest (lead qualification); where sales are most likely, a salesperson is asked to follow up. However, it can take a lot of knowledge and understanding of a customer to make a successful sales proposition, and the knowledge-gathering and analysis that marketing or a CRM system can perform is limited.

In the past, it was impossible for marketers to know customers. Market research could be done so that 'the market' could be broken down into groups of people or organisations with particular interests (segments). However, companies then had to spend large sums of money in the 'broadcast' media such as television, billboards and print publications. They placed advertisements during TV programmes that people in the target segments were likely to watch, on billboards they were likely to pass and in print publications they were likely to read. Although there was some approximate targeting, this has been called the 'spray and pray' approach to marketing communications. The challenge of marketing today is that it is all too easy to send many messages to someone who has browsed a website, which can come across as untargeted and intrusive.

Technology may have empowered business generation, but marketing systems must integrate a variety of information sources if they are going to help salespeople to get closer to customers. Before contacting a customer, it would be useful to know:

- The needs, opportunities and threats they might perceive in their lives or businesses

- Any circumstances which make them more likely to be interested in us rather than competitors

- How they prefer to buy

Even big and sophisticated companies do not have the type of marketing and CRM/ABM systems that would provide this information for every possible prospective customer, so what is the role of sales in lead generation and qualification?

Lead generation
Although a significant proportion of an established company's business may come from existing customers, it is still necessary to win new ones. There are some sectors where new customers are highly prized and offered considerable incentives; however, this risks encouraging a practice nicknamed 'tarting', where customers who have

the time and inclination swap suppliers again and again, while loyal customers get disillusioned by their lack of reward for their contribution to the company's success. In 2018, MoneySavingExpert reported that:

> 'The bank war has reignited this month with loads of bribes to tempt you to switch – so it's a great time to join the hidden bank-tarting movement sweeping the UK by switching again and again to make big money.' (Bannister, 2018)

Generally, marketing theory suggests that it is better to mend a leaky bucket by using strategies to keep existing customers before topping up the bucket with new ones. Studies indicate that it costs a company less to retain existing customers than to acquire new ones (eg Reichheld, 2001), but existing customers do still switch or lapse. Some causes of customer 'leakage' include:

- Customers with irregular buying patterns
- Customers who move home or company location and lose contact
- Other lifestyle changes (such as retirement or redundancy) affecting customer buying patterns
- Firms going out of business, merging or getting taken over
- Senior decision-makers in companies moving jobs or changing buying strategies
- A competitor making the customer a better offer

Given that leakage occurs, where do new customers come from?

- **Marketing** – All advertisements, web and media activity should encourage incoming sales enquiries; content marketing is becoming particularly important.
- **Trade fairs** – Although sometimes they are primarily a public relations exercise, exhibiting at trade shows connects you with potential new customers.

- **Footfall** – If you work in a retail outlet, the people who come into the store will be interested in your products.

- **'Lapsed bids'** – These are cases when you made a proposal to a prospect and they decided to do nothing ('do nothing' is your biggest competitor). After some time, they may be more likely to make a buying decision.

- **'Lapsed' customers** – These may also be revived. Maybe they haven't bought in your category for a while or they tried a competitor and are ready to switch back. Even customers who were angry with a supplier may try them again if they can see real change in the way the supplier operates.

- **Contacts from employees** – If employees are proud of where they work, they will bring in friends and family as customers.

- **Referrals from customers** – Surely the most welcome of leads, given that some trust has already been established.

- **Networking** – Both through a networking organisation such as a chamber of commerce and through professional social media such as LinkedIn, you should establish a profile which can encourage new contacts. Introduce yourself to people and listen to what they tell you about themselves, explain how your products/service can help them and give them your contact details.

- **Lists** – Some organisations sell contact lists but take care. Years ago, it may have been acceptable to stick a pin in a telephone directory and make a call. Now, there are harsh penalties for contacting a consumer or firm that has registered with the Telephone Preference Service (or equivalent in other countries) not to receive sales calls. Email contact also requires express permission. If you are given lists regularly, your colleagues who bought or compiled the list should have done all the necessary checking.

- **Self-generation** – You can self-generate leads and prospects through googling and keeping your eyes open.

The role of marketing in lead generation is critical, and in recent years there has been a shift towards consumers and business decision-makers seeking information about potential suppliers online. Suppliers have had to respond by providing lots of interesting and relevant online information. This is called content marketing. In consumer markets, it can involve short messages which may be location dependent and accompanied by a sales promotion, such as sending a message to someone's mobile when they are near a retail outlet suggesting a purchase and offering a discount. In B2B, where the sales cycle is usually much longer, it involves attending webcasts and downloading white papers or case studies that can indicate a prospect's level of interest in a product or service. Once marketing has established that a prospect has made a time commitment to content marketing, the salesperson can have reasonable confidence in the lead (see Wang et al, 2017).

As a sales professional, you may be asked to develop your own 'prospecting' plan. Prospecting (historically associated with digging for gold) is the process of identifying and approaching potential new customers. In addition to suggestions from marketing and the CRM system, you may want to make your own judgements about potential prospects. Be proactive but be focused. Opportunities that come from nowhere (known in the IT sector as 'bluebirds') may take up a lot of energy and go nowhere. You need a critical analysis of where you are most likely to progress a sale; in other words, you have to qualify leads.

Lead qualification

There are many things that you need to know before pursuing a lead. A lot of information might be available in the CRM system, or you might have to do some background research. In the latter case, your employer expects you to add it into the CRM system to save someone else time at a later date.

Some companies have CRM analytics which automate lead qualification to some degree. Some use 'web crawlers' based on algorithms which sort data from prospects' websites. As this data is provided by the prospects on their websites, its accuracy and quality are high, and it can save the salesperson time (D'Haen et al, 2016). However, algorithms are not a replacement for sound judgements, and it is wise to check out the websites of leads qualified by the system.

First of all, can you establish that this customer has a **need** for your product or service? In a retail setting, you can ask a prospective customer who is browsing what they are looking for. The answer will establish whether they are just idly browsing, whether they are looking at a particular category of product or whether they have an urgent need for a gizmo to solve a household issue. In a B2B scenario, you may have to deduce business needs from the prospect company's annual report or notices to shareholders and what the trade media say about it. What do they say the company is trying to achieve with their customers? Is it growing? Is it profitable? What are its values? Refer back to the Customer Needs Analysis chapter for a more in-depth discussion of customer needs. And be sure that your research helps you to decide how strong a lead you might have, as well as helping the prospect to believe that you are interested in them.

Is it clear that the person you intend to speak to has the **authority** to buy? Many people browse on behalf of their family or organisation but could only suggest to other decision-makers that a purchase might be a good idea. In companies, major buying decisions are almost always made by a DMU; increasingly, families make major purchases by consultation as well. If you do not yet have access to the decision-maker, how likely is it that you could persuade your contact to introduce you?

Even when all looks well for a prospect needing your product, they may not have the money to do so right now. You can ask how long the prospect has been planning this purchase and, in the case of a company, if there is a provision in this year's **budget** for it. The budget is the plan for what is going to be spent on operational goods/services and assets (such as computer equipment). Some consumers use the principles of budgeting to run their household, although consumers can buy on credit cards and businesses have overdraft facilities.

You have a responsibility to your employer to make sure that the purchase is properly funded. Even in consumer markets, bankruptcy can have an effect on the seller. In business markets, if a major customer runs out of funds and goes out of business, it can be disastrous, particularly for small businesses dealing with much larger customers. In such a case, work closely with your colleagues in credit control and ask them to check the customers' financing in detail. You sometimes need more than just a credit rating from an agency, which will be based on the company's past performance.

There is something else that you have to consider in lead qualification. Remember that your biggest competitor is 'do nothing'. Whatever you are selling – be it a new smartphone that requires the prospect to learn a new menu or a multimillion-pound power generation plant – you are selling change, and you are selling risk. What is the prospect's appetite for change? If their old phone is broken, they are ready to buy; if they are just curious about the latest features of new phones, they may not be. In the case of power generation, a reasonable alternative that will have been in the scenario plan is persuading customers to use less power or generate their own with solar or wind panels. Does the customer regard that as a viable alternative or a complementary strategy? You need to consider **appetite** for a new purchase, as well as need, authority and budget. Once you have qualified a lead, you need to open a dialogue with the prospect.

Constructive communication with prospects/customers

How communication works

Once you have decided that, on the basis of available information, this is the right prospect to approach, as a proactive salesperson you have to consider what you are going to say. Equally, you have to imagine what the customer might hear and say in response to you:

> 'The outcome of the sales call depends upon how well the salesman and the prospect have *communicated* with each other – how well they have achieved a common understanding that will enable both to fill their needs and achieve their goals.' (Webster, 1968)

Communications is never as easy as you might think. The Shannon and Weaver model (see Figure 19.1) has been widely used in marketing and sales since 1949 to design communications. It illustrates:

- **Information** – The salesperson decides what to say to the customer.

- **Transmission** – The salesperson decides how to say it.

- **Channel** – The means of conveying the message could be in person, by telephone or email. The channel can affect how well the customer hears the message. In person, they may concentrate on what you are saying, but they may well be multitasking with phone conversations and emails.

- **Reception** – The customer hears the salesperson's words but has to interpret them. There may be inherent problems here, such as if eg the customer is from another culture. This is not just a problem with national or regional cultures. If the message is technical and the customer has limited technical knowledge, they may misunderstand something you say. Remember that the customer has their own perspective on the context in which they are having the conversation, and they have expectations about what you are going to do and say.

- **Destination** – The customer has received and understood your communication about something which helps them make a buying decision.

- **Feedback** – The customer may ask questions to check their understanding. If they do not, you should ask questions to confirm their understanding as you cannot assume that they heard what you think that you said.

- **The return journey** – Encoding, noise and decoding all affect what the customer says to you, as well. Be sure to give feedback and check what you have heard.

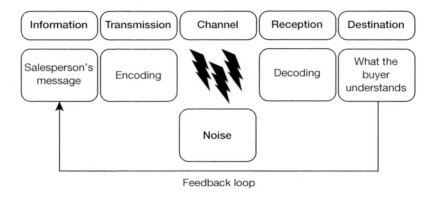

Figure 19.1: Communications model (adapted from Shannon and Weaver, 1949)

You cannot plan every sentence and model every response. What you can do and must always do in a sales conversation is to remember that it is an interaction involving another person. Much sales training in the past focused on the behaviour of the salesperson and assumed that the salesperson controlled the conversation. The buyer sees it differently. They are the customer, and they have seen a lot of branding messages about how companies value their customers. Even business buyers have personal and social needs as well as a commercial need. They need to look good in their organisation and to make a purchase that will enhance their career.

Planning communications with customers

We can use the acronym 'AIDA' to describe what happens in a sales meeting:

A – Get attention

I – Generate interest

D – Create desire

A – Stimulate action (preferably a buying decision)

If you are in a retail setting, you may be able to do all of these things in one conversation. In B2B, the sales cycle is longer, but in every conversation you should aim to progress from one stage to a more advanced one in the sales cycle.

Avoid launching straight into talking about how wonderful your product is. Many salespeople have learned about a product and are keen to share their knowledge but have no idea what to say when the customer asks a simple question about how it would work in their sitting room or factory floor. If you do not know how the product helps customers, you will have difficulty winning their confidence.

Table 19.1 shows a typical plan for an interaction with a prospect, which you can adapt to your own context.

Table 19.1: Prospect interaction plan

Call Plan: XYZ Widgets Limited	Type of lead: Employee referred Date and time of call: 11am 18-01-2020
Call objective	To establish need, authority and budget If positive response, make an advance to next stage To generate positive word of mouth from prospect
How do I establish the conversation?	Reminder of contact from colleague, explain who I am. Ask how they are and check if the call is convenient.
What am I going to ask?	Check circumstances of the company, referring to website info and comment from the colleague referring.
Listen for confirmation and then... NEED	Ask about particular needs which would be a good fit for the product. Explain advantages and benefits realised by other customers.
If customer interested...	Ask how you can help with the buying process – who needs to know about this product/service – when is the budget cycle, etc.
If customer not interested...	Seek feedback on their concerns and try to resolve them.
Possible advance	Aim for further discussion or personal meeting with other stakeholders; fall-back position to provide more information and call back; worst case – thank them for their time and get clear feedback about why the product/service is no longer of interest.

Should marketing and sales messages be consistent every time you interact with the prospect, or do you need to try different tactics? Recent research suggests that complementary messages are more successful than repeating the same message in every interaction. In other words, 'providing new kinds of arguments catches one's attention and has a higher likelihood of having an impact than utilising one specific influence tactic over different interactions' (Pöyry et al, 2017). You would look to your marketing department to help with a suite of complementary propositions, but you have to apply them to the prospect's specific situation, which requires planning.

Choosing channels of communications

As part of planning your interaction with the prospect, you have to decide how to open the dialogue. You have several options:

Asking for a meeting with the customer

A face-to-face meeting offers flexibility, and it is always interesting to meet someone in their own surroundings. It is also costly, and buyers may be suspicious about who ultimately pays for the journey and the time you spend on the meeting. In consumer markets, bear in mind that Trading Standards Officers advise consumers to avoid letting salespeople into their own homes and there have been many cases of pressure tactics being applied in the past. In B2B, the prospect will be a busy person under a lot of time pressure. They do not want to see you until they are sure there is something meaningful to discuss, so a face-to-face meeting is more likely to happen in the later stages of a sales cycle.

Telephone or VoIP

Assuming you have gained permission to call, this is usually the starting point for business interactions and many consumer sales. It is more difficult to get feedback from the other person over the phone, so a VoIP service such as Skype or Zoom is better when you have a good Internet connection. With only voice feedback, you also have to listen carefully for verbal cues and feedback. Is the other person getting bored or irritated? However, a telephone call is time-efficient, and most people spend a lot of time on the phone so have good telephonic communication skills. Never assume that a call is more casual than a face-to-face meeting. You may not have to wear a suit, but you do need to be polite and to speak to the prospect in a professional manner.

Email or social media

Buying decision-makers receive hundreds of sales emails each day. It is unlikely that they will open yours unless some prior activity (such as attending a webcast) indicates that the prospect has some interest in your product. You may have a better chance if you can get an introduction to a prospect via a mutual connection on a professional social media site such as LinkedIn – but be cautious. Professional social media sites are rigorous in blocking members who are reported for sending unwanted messages.

Is the art of letter-writing dead?

Junk mail preceded junk email and was dealt with ruthlessly. It went in the bin before a decision-maker even saw it. With the dominance of email, writing a letter has a new place in prospecting if it is personalised and includes a meaningful 'call to action' to the buyer, such as an invitation to a webcast that would interest them.

Starting conversations

As well as the information in the Customer Engagement chapter, it is important that you understand the basics of a sales conversation in a simple setting.

Talking to 'gatekeepers'

Any prospecting activity in B2B sectors will usually involve talking to call handlers and personal assistants before you get anywhere near anyone in a purchasing DMU. It is the job of a PA to make sure that the boss' time is never wasted. Because of the stereotype associated with sales, they will automatically assume that you are likely to waste the boss' time and therefore they must keep you out of the diary.

Think about the call-handler or PA as part of the DMU. You have to convince them that your product or service is worth them taking a risk on letting you speak to their boss. Be extremely polite, even if the PA is not polite to you. If you have been able to find out their name, use their title (eg Mr/Ms) and surname – *not* their first name. Acknowledge that their boss' time is precious and explain why your conversation will be worthwhile (saving money or time is a classically popular opening, but make sure you have simple and credible evidence to back up that claim). Be grateful for small mercies, such as a fifteen-minute telephone call at 8.15am, and make sure that you are punctual. If you asked to send some information by email, do it and follow up. Polite persistence usually has some eventual reward, even if it is the PA reporting back to you that their boss is not the right person to talk to but that Ms X would be interested, or that it is not the right time in the budget cycle.

In the case of calls to households (please see the Customer Needs Analysis chapter on the need for permission to call), you may also find yourself talking to someone other than your named contact. Similar principles apply. You may have to negotiate with the person who answers the phone to talk to another member of the family or to find out when they might be available to receive a follow-up call.

Opening selling conversations

Your first contact with the buying decision-maker may be a short telephone slot, and you may be feeling nervous. Practise beforehand until you get used to it. Use their name and title (eg Mr/Ms/Dr). Check you are speaking to the right person, wish them a good morning/afternoon, and check that it is still a good time for them to talk. Introduce yourself and your company briefly (eg 'I am Joe Bloggs from Smith & Jones Ltd; we are a new recruitment company in the Midlands'). In the North American and Northern European tradition, it is then expected that you will get straight to the point of the conversation. This would not be acceptable in many other cultures, and you should check with colleagues in particular countries about respectful protocol when/if you have to work there.

In retail, it is more likely that you have the luxury of approaching someone who is already in the shop and looking at products. You still need to remember polite forms of address (sir/madam), greeting and respecting their time. In many retail outlets, people have got used to sales assistants ignoring them so you may find that your proactivity is welcome. Nevertheless, allow the customer the space to do more browsing if they wish, but be ready with questions and suggestions.

Questioning tactics

Even though you are expected to get to the point, it is recommended that you start by reminding the decision-maker why they agreed to take the call and asking if you can check a few things. Here is your chance to show that you have done your homework, even if it has to be condensed; for example, 'I understand from your company report that you are growing very rapidly. How does this affect your recruitment plans?' Do wait for the answer before launching into the credentials of your wonderful candidates. From early in the conversation, you need to concentrate on any indication from the customer of their willingness to try you or buy from you.

Buying signals

If the customer engages easily in the conversation, that is comforting for you but does not necessarily mean anything. Some people are just curious about new sources of supply. Follow up any apparent interest (eg 'Who do you have on your books at the moment?') and check that the customer wants to progress the conversation to a proposal from you.

How to approach the customer's questions

Customers will put questions and 'yes, but's to you and interrupt your carefully written script. It is best to answer those questions openly as they come as the customer may perceive attempts to deflect questions and objections as manipulation. Do not assume that a lot of questions means that the customer is hostile. An informed customer may be one who is interested in switching supplier and is already working out how to minimise their risks.

Initial proposals

Some sales training formulae suggest holding off on a proposal until you are sure that the customer has acknowledged their need and the cost of the 'do nothing' scenario; however, in the course of a short phone call you probably do not have that luxury. A customer will be flattered by a few customer-centred questions but irritated by too many. Do not be afraid, if the customer asks, 'What are you selling?', to answer, 'Well-qualified engineers with experience in your sector who are immediately available'. The next question might be, 'If they are so well-qualified, why are they immediately available?', but you have now progressed the call.

Discussing options with customers

Most professional customers resist attempts by salespeople to get their commitment to any next step before they have had time to reflect, check and consult. Instead of a hard close on a particular 'advance' that you have planned, it makes sense to offer the customer choices; they can then tell you what next steps they are prepared to take. Summarise and check. Thank them for their time, close the call and then make sure you follow up in the way the customer requested.

Summary

In this chapter, we have looked at the salesperson's role in creating new customers. Professional salespeople are expected to have a proactive approach to the hardest of tasks. Engaging with complete strangers is difficult, especially when they know that you want them to part with their hard-earned cash or departmental budget. With planning and some common sense, you can grow to enjoy prospecting and make it enjoyable for the prospect. Do this well, and you will know that you can be successful in any aspect of selling.

20

Self-discipline, Resilience And Self-motivation

Introduction

The sales job involves complex communications and trying to balance the interests of customers, who are becoming ever more informed and demanding, and employers, who are always challenged by shareholders to deliver more profitable growth with fewer resources. There is a high level of turnover in sales jobs, but not just sales jobs. Emotional exhaustion is associated with all jobs which involve a high level of contact with other people (Salovey and Mayer, 1990). This is because dealing with people involves ambiguity, conflict and pressure.

The twenty-first-century workplace is an environment where change is constant and where emotional intelligence is said to be a better predictor of success than IQ (intelligence quotient) (Goleman, 2011). Can the qualities relating to the apprenticeship standard described in this chapter be learned, or are some people just lucky enough to be born with them and others not? These qualities are not 'on' or 'off' in a person; there is a whole spectrum of behaviours, many of which we have learned from early life experiences and role models (good and bad). We can move ourselves from a lower level to a higher level by engaging in learning activities. First of all, we have to be aware of what is being asked of us.

Self-discipline

Does this concept conjure up images of medieval mystics whipping themselves to atone for their sins? In reality, it is more about avoiding the sin in the first place! Self-discipline is key behaviour for a sales professional. It can be described as controlling our feelings and impulses, or at least recognising them and controlling the degree to which they are expressed to others. It also includes the ability to make ourselves do things that are needed, and which are our responsibility, even when they are unpleasant or we do not want to do them. As a salesperson, you need to do the work even when no one is watching you. Salespeople are the link between the company and its customers. If you do not have the self-discipline to do what needs to be done, the link is broken and the customer and the company both suffer. Self-discipline involves hard work and not waiting to be told to do something. It encompasses correcting, regulating and improving ourselves. It is also associated with doing the right thing rather than the easy thing, and at the right time, or within the deadline set. It requires recognition of our weaknesses and an ability to overcome them.

Resilience

Resilience as a physical phenomenon provides a useful analogy. Resilience is associated with elasticity – materials such as rubber which can ping back into shape after being put under pressure by pulling, pushing or stretching. The mental resilience of people is the ability to ping back into a good frame of mind quickly after experiencing difficulties. Those difficulties might be physical illness or personal disappointments from our own failings or adversity imposed by external factors, which can be anything from an economic crash to a grumpy boss. Indeed, it is 'other people' who are often quoted as the adversity which prompts the need for resilience.

Resilience is necessary when dealing with small irritations as well as major psychological stress. It helps us to adapt to change and learn from experiences. It is associated with a positive frame of mind, but it is important not to be unrealistically optimistic in difficult situations, each of which will require different tactics.

Resilience is often associated with courage. Courage is often defined as doing something anyway, despite the fear and uncertainty you may experience at the time (Brown, 2018). We often think of soldiers as courageous because of the physical dangers they face. There are few physical dangers in selling, but there are psychological challenges which many people would not contemplate facing. Salespeople are often called upon to demonstrate mental courage in order to continue to work in the face of frequent rejection.

Self-motivation

While self-discipline suggests an ability to get on with things that have to be done, self-motivation suggests making things happen. As a salesperson, the easiest way for you to take action is to want to do it. A sales professional can only be successful if they are self-motivated. Once again, we have to find this strength from within and not expect others to motivate us with money or status in return for our effort. The reward has to be internal (intrinsic): our satisfaction is doing something worthwhile. We find our own reasons and strength to do something, such as our own enthusiasm for a task, our interest in a topic, or our personal drive and commitment to improving something.

Building emotional intelligence

How do we improve our self-discipline, resilience and self-motivation? The ability to control and apply our own emotions, and those of others, to achieve positive outcomes has been summed up as 'emotional intelligence' (EI). Research on EI dates back to 1964, but it entered mainstream business thinking in the 1990s when it was popularised by Daniel Goleman's first book on the topic (1995). It has been criticised as unproven pop psychology (Locke, 2005), but that does not stop the research that we do have on this idea being helpful to those of us trying to succeed in life. As Salovey and Mayer's 1990 article on emotional intelligence has been cited by over 13,000 other academic papers, it is fair to say that there is plenty of objective analysis of EI.

The basic human emotions (Ekman, 1992) are:

- Happiness

- Sadness

- Surprise

- Anger

- Fear

- Disgust

To many Western philosophers, emotions are random interruptions of thought which can cause chaos. However, from an evolutionary point of view, most emotions are natural motivating forces – shortcuts to make us run faster when we are under threat or to be kind with our family members. In a complex work environment, the evolutionary function of emotions can be inappropriate and cause us to feel chaotic. When we have an awareness of how emotions are affecting us and others – and how we can understand, use and manage them – we may claim emotional intelligence as an ability. Our emotional intelligence comprises many aspects (adapted from Brackett and Salovey, 2006):

- **Perceiving emotions** – the ability to detect and decipher emotions in faces, pictures, voices and cultural artefacts, including the ability to identify one's own emotions.

Perceiving emotions represents a basic aspect of emotional intelligence as it makes all other processing of emotional information possible.

- **Understanding emotions** – the ability to comprehend emotional language and to appreciate complicated relationships among emotions. For example, understanding emotions encompasses the ability to be sensitive to slight variations between emotions and the ability to recognise and describe how emotions evolve over time.

- **Using emotions** – the ability to harness emotions to facilitate various cognitive activities, such as thinking and problem-solving. The emotionally intelligent person can capitalise fully upon their changing moods in order to best complete the task at hand.

- **Managing emotions** – the ability to regulate emotions both in ourselves and in others. The emotionally intelligent person can harness emotions, even negative ones, and manage them to achieve intended goals.

Perceiving emotions

There are two angles to the perception of emotion: recognising it in ourselves and recognising it in others.

Self-awareness has been described as the keystone on which EI is built, but it is extremely difficult to attain. There is a lot you can learn by reading about emotions, and it can be useful; but however much you read, it would never be specific to *your* emotions.

We live in our own worlds and often do not challenge our own perceptions. By seeking the opinions of others about what our emotions are doing at any particular time, we may take on that challenge. You should always expect feedback from your manager, coach or close colleagues (invited and uninvited) about how you react to situations at work. When you are practising dealing with feedback, it is sometimes easiest to start with close family members and friends. Be sure to convince them that you genuinely want to learn from their feedback. If this seems daunting as a starting point, there are online tests which can provide some computer-generated feedback but do make sure that they are from reputable sites. The use of 360-degree feedback tools which capture other people's perception of your skills, knowledge and behaviours can help you identify both your strengths and your areas for development.

Awareness

Feedback from tests and people close to us may surprise us and cause us to examine where it came from. We also have to reflect on the way we see things that we have done and what emotion drove us to do X rather than Y. Work-based learning almost always includes a 'learning log' where we can record our feelings about topics and what we learned. These reflections can also prompt us to notice our emotions and how they affect our lives and work. Perhaps we feel differently in our personal lives and our working lives, or perhaps we are consistent. Perhaps we get feedback from tutors or colleagues which prompts emotions we need to analyse. Warren Buffett, a legend in American business for his investment analysis, is alleged to write down the reasons why he makes a decision and revisit them when the effect of that decision is clear (Hagstrom, 2013). Another use for a learning log is to anticipate how you are going to feel about an assessment or the next topic and then see how accurate your prediction was (see Figure 20.1).

Self-awareness:

> 'lies at the root of strong character, giving us the ability to lead with a sense of purpose, authenticity, openness, and trust. It explains our successes and our failures. And by giving us a better understanding of who we are, self-awareness lets us better understand what we need most from other people, to complement our own deficiencies.' (Tian, 2015)

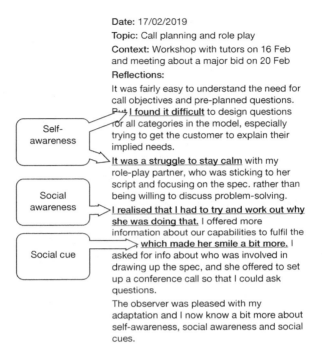

Date: 17/02/2019

Topic: Call planning and role play

Context: Workshop with tutors on 16 Feb and meeting about a major bid on 20 Feb

Reflections:

It was fairly easy to understand the need for call objectives and pre-planned questions. But I found it difficult to design questions for all categories in the model, especially trying to get the customer to explain their implied needs.

Self-awareness

It was a struggle to stay calm with my role-play partner, who was sticking to her script and focusing on the spec. rather than being willing to discuss problem-solving.

Social awareness

I realised that I had to try and work out why she was doing that. I offered more information about our capabilities to fulfil the which made her smile a bit more. I asked for info about who was involved in drawing up the spec, and she offered to set up a conference call so that I could ask questions.

Social cue

The observer was pleased with my adaptation and I now know a bit more about self-awareness, social awareness and social cues.

Figure 20.1: Learning log

It would be difficult to be successful in a sales role without social awareness as well. This involves awareness of situations and how people are reacting to them and adapting our behaviour to achieve the best outcomes from those situations. We can measure the degree to which we are aware of the emotions of other people by how accurately we identify emotions expressed by faces in photographs or feelings evoked by landscapes or other abstract images or sounds. In sales roles, success is often associated with empathy for the buyer or what is called 'boundary-spanning' – ie seeing the situation from their perspective.

Like all other behavioural skills, social awareness takes time to develop. Sales training often includes role-play exercises, and this gives you an ideal scenario for seeking feedback about how you read situations and people's reactions to them.

The communication considerations that we have discussed in other chapters give you some idea of the complexity of seeking meaning from other people. Things we say to each other may not be received the way they are intended. People in social situations are often not open about their reactions, and good salespeople have to look for hints about how they are feeling.

How we display emotions affects how other people react to us. To be a well-respected member of a particular society or culture, we have to conform to its expectations about emotional displays, and these can change over time. In the 1950s in the UK, the 'stiff upper lip' was expected, and any display of emotion might expose someone to disapproval or ridicule. After the social revolution of the 1960s, acknowledgement of emotions, positive and negative, became more acceptable. We can look for other people's emotions in 'social cues', but we also need to observe the interaction between our emotions and those of others. Our smiling might encourage others to smile; our nervousness might encourage others to be more dominant. There are a number of social cues you can easily identify:

- **Facial expression** – We like to look for smiles, but what do we do if the customer looks grumpy?

- **Body language** – If the person crosses their arms, looks away from the speaker or fidgets, it may indicate that you need to check for feedback on your message.

- **Gestures** – Some people talk with their hands.

- **Physical distance** – For example, some people lean forward towards a speaker when they are interested in their message.

- **Tone of voice** – Even on the phone, you need social awareness. Does the customer sound irritated or bored?

Please note that there are cultural variations in all social cues. You should study the culture of your customer carefully before making assumptions about their social cues.

Understanding emotions

There are, three means of effecting persuasion, as Aristotle identified: 'be able (1) to reason logically, (2) to understand human character and goodness in their various forms, and (3) to understand the emotions – that is, to name them and describe them, to know their causes and the way in which they are excited' (Aristotle, 2012).[27]

Awareness of emotions is the first step, but we would be very frustrated just to be aware of feelings and not be able to understand where they came from and what to do with them. In recent years, it has become evident that a technique used in treating depression, cognitive behavioural therapy (CBT), can be adapted to also help people without depression who want to improve their resilience and motivation in a variety of job roles, including sales (Neenan, 2017). Some people have found that the most critical stage in CBT is identifying the triggers of emotions because then you can move on to change how you respond to those triggers. In testing for understanding of emotion, a psychologist would look for a person's ability to discuss not only emotional triggers but also how particular emotions interact with each other (for example, anger and fear can be associated), how emotions change over time or when contexts change.

There are links between physical phenomena and emotions. For example, our bodies pump us with adrenalin, making our hearts beat faster, when we are fearful because our body associates fear with physical danger. However, the physical signs are not what is triggering the emotion. The bear chasing us is the trigger, even if it is not a real bear but an angry customer.

---

27 Aristotle's *Rhetoric* was originally written in the fourth century BCE. This quote is from a 2012 translation.

At first, we might be inclined to play a superficial 'blame game' and say things such as 'I am sad because it is raining' or 'I get angry easily because everyone in my family gets angry easily'. Perhaps these are genuine triggers, but we may need to dig a bit deeper to get a true analysis of where the emotion comes from. Why do we associate rain with sadness, when farmers might be glad of it? If we grew up among angry people, is our anger a defence mechanism which is not relevant in other contexts? There is good evidence that emotion can be contagious (Wild et al, 2001) – we feel happy among happy people and cry at funerals because others do. There is also good evidence that emotions are our own creation, and we can change instinctive thoughts about situations. Emotions are our way of responding to events. These events create triggers which elicit an emotional response.

Typical triggers of emotions

- Seeing a friend unexpectedly or receiving a gift could trigger happiness.

- Breaking up with your partner or losing £20 could trigger sadness.

- Winning the lottery could trigger surprise and happiness.

- Injustice or disrespect could trigger anger.

- Seeing a spider if you suffer from arachnophobia or thinking of asking someone on a date and believing you will be turned down could trigger fear.

- Seeing mouldy food or entering a dirty bathroom could trigger disgust.

Psychologist Albert Ellis (1973) provided an 'ABC' to understanding emotional triggers: A for Activity, B for Belief and C for Consequence. For example:

- **Activity** – The customer walked away from buying a washing machine they said they liked.

- **Belief** – I must have said or done something wrong.

- **Consequence** – I feel useless at selling (the emotion generated here is sadness that the customer's action has caused you to lose confidence).

In cases like this one, we need to move on to use and manage our emotions to get more positive outcomes without losing the curiosity to understand the other person. In the scenario above, it would have been vital to ask the customer directly why they had changed their mind as it would be more likely to be *their fear* (perhaps fear of changing brand or paying a lot of money when their paycheque is not due for three weeks).

Once we understand that most of the triggers for our emotions are illogical, they should become easier to manage. However, before we manage, let's spare some thought for using emotions.

Using emotions

As an abstract exercise, try to describe an emotion with nouns and adjectives which do not necessarily have an emotive role in language; for example, describing anger as a colour, flavour or temperature. Now, describe how a particular emotion, such as anger, could be a good or bad element in the performance of tasks (see Table 20.1).

Table 20.1: Good and bad uses for emotions in business scenarios

Emotion and sub-emotion	Characteristics	Good uses	Bad uses
Anger – Resentment	Red, bitter and hot, like a chilli pepper	'Righteous anger' when there has been an injustice. But this has to be controlled; otherwise, it might cause more conflict and retribution.	In a work situation, displaying anger may make colleagues fearful or upset. Then they will not want to work with me, and they may not tell me what I need to know.
Happiness – Pride	Purple, sweet and warm (mulled wine?)	It is good to have pride in a job well done and to encourage others to take pride in their work.	It can lead to complacency, and then to failure. If people see me as proud, they may flatter me to my face but ridicule me behind my back.

Until recently, it was often assumed that emotions, good or bad, should not be allowed into business activity. No matter how much we aspire to be rational and logical, emotions are part of the human condition, so more modern views encourage the use of emotions to improve discussions. This can be particularly true of sales situations, although a professional salesperson must not use emotions to manipulate a vulnerable customer. As Leary et al (2013) observe: 'Emotion plays a positive role in decision making, creativity, and relationship building—all key factors in reaching an agreement.'

Preparation for meetings and negotiations where emotions are likely to emerge makes sense. How is the customer likely to see things? How are they likely to react to you and your proposals? How can you channel your emotions to adapt? How do you emotionally prepare for this particular meeting or phone call? You do not want to be too tense or too carefree. In the first instance, most customers will want you to show them respect and friendliness (responding to their need for self-esteem). You need to find out what is important to them, so channel some confidence and curiosity. You will discuss problems and ideas, so you also need to be feeling creative. Using your emotions to improve the conduct of the meeting is as important as the information you prepare.

Can you use the emotions of the customer? You should certainly consider how you are going to use the customer's fear of change. Risk ought to be about the possibility of gain as well as loss, but test after test shows how humans consistently behave irrationally when there is the possibility of loss (Edwards, 1996). What reassurance can you provide?

Managing emotions

Ogilvie et al (2017) claim that 'it is critical to understand, and to self-regulate, in order to effectively navigate interpersonal interaction with customers or potential customers'. Preparation can help to manage the emotions that might emerge and how you respond to them. We have already established that emotions can be used. This is important because suppression of emotion is not the game; the game is to change from having emotions which are not useful to having ones which are useful. Training for managing emotions tends to focus on scenario planning – what if I felt this, or the customer felt that – how would the call go?

Some psychologists recommend mood music to help tap into the useful emotions you want. Other art forms are also useful. People who feel sad can alter their mood by watching a comedy. Exercise can also be an opportunity to change mood. These techniques may help in our leisure time, but we cannot tap into them during a long day at work. We can, however, practise cognitive reappraisal – seeing something in a different way which helps us to tap into a useful emotion. Some salespeople get frustrated when the customer keeps saying 'yes, but' in a meeting. Instead, they could think about changing their emotional lenses and feeling encouraged because the customer is exploring the proposal. In some ways, this links to creative thinking. Ask yourself to identify alternative explanations and reactions, and choose the useful one. This is not just about being positive – unrealistic optimism would not help you. It is about focusing on the task at hand and recognising the role that emotions are playing in its success or failure.

Can we manage the emotions of others?

One of the things we have to learn as we grow up is that the world does not revolve around us. Equally, we have to learn that we are not responsible for everything that other people feel.

Trying to make people feel how we want them to feel can backfire in unexpected ways. We may be accused of abuse of power or attempting to control and manipulate. However, that does not mean that we should not anticipate people's feelings and work with them. We would be poor sales professionals if we did not try to see things from the customer's point of view. A challenge salespeople face in trying to gain the trust of customers is an expectation that the salesperson will attempt to manipulate the customer so that they get the sale and the customer overpays for something they did not really want. This would not be an emotionally intelligent thing to do. There can be fine lines in using some behavioural techniques, and you can debate with colleagues and friends where they see differences between suggestion, persuasion and manipulation:

- **Suggestion** – something put forward for consideration and discussion
- **Persuasion** – a process of changing someone's attitude towards something
- **Manipulation** – influencing someone in an unfair way

If we have EI, the management of others' emotions is not a win-lose scenario. By perceiving and understanding the emotions of customers, we can suggest solutions for them, and we can give them choices. If they have an attitude towards a particular product based on incorrect or out-of-date information, we should seek to address it with evidence while understanding their misgivings. However, too much challenge to customer's perceptions can be counterproductive.

The growth mindset

The research of educational psychologist Carol Dweck is becoming influential. She has identified that as individuals, we have ideas about where ability comes from (Dweck, 2017). For example, some people argue that good salespeople are born, and some argue that good salespeople are made. We may have acquired these ideas from the way that others have treated us. In the past, parents and teachers were likely to praise children for things that came easily to them because society as a whole tended to endorse a focus on celebrating 'born' traits. The idea that abilities are innate indicates a 'fixed mindset'. We may all have observed what we perceive to be 'natural' skill – such as a gifted footballer or musician. However, the saying 'the harder I practise, the luckier I get' has been attributed to many gifted people.

If the highly gifted recognise the role of hard work in their success, are all abilities based on hard work, resilience, learning and practising? Dweck's (2017) research suggests that individuals with a 'growth mindset' who believe that they can improve their performance through learning, including learning from failure, are more successful. They may not be aware of their mindset, but they are aware of the importance of development. Dweck emphasises that a growth mindset is not just about hard work; it involves a willingness to try new things to achieve better performance and to get better over time. A person who has a growth mindset sees acquiring skills as a journey; they would say, 'I can't do this yet, but I am going to try X and see if that helps.' The value of a growth mindset is evident in reactions to success and failure, and the pathway from 'cannot' to 'can' is illustrated in Figure 20.2.

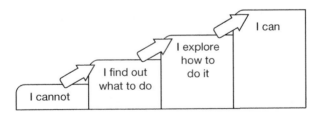

Figure 20.2: Pathway from 'cannot' to 'can'

Dealing with failure

We all know that failure happens, and we have all heard of famous people who had been written off as failures at some point in their lives and lots of movies are about failures who become heroes. But failure still feels horrible, so we try to avoid it. We do not want to be reckless, but a core feature of a growth mindset is being willing to keep trying different solutions to problems and to learn if something fails. People with fixed mindsets take failure as personal, undermining their belief in their abilities.

Failure is not personal. It is the method you tried that failed, not you as a person. If you analyse that method and adapt it and try again, the result may be more positive. Many famous inventors tried many times to meet a need before they found something that worked; Thomas Edison is alleged to have claimed that he failed 10,000 times on the way to inventing the light bulb (Merriman, 2017). He did not despair about every failure or care if other people thought he was crazy. He took the positive view that each failure showed a way not to do it so that he could continue to move forward.

We cannot carry the analogy of invention completely into sales; few employers or customers would tolerate 10,000 failed sales calls, but they do understand that there will be failures because you cannot please everybody all of the time. Make use of the role-plays and scenarios in your training and learn from when they go badly as well as when they go well. Always use the developmental feedback you get. Even great sportspeople have coaches and need to practise. The NBA all-star Michael Jordan has often been quoted about the failures he has experienced in losing games, missing more than 9,000 shots, and the success that has resulted as he has learned from these failures (Veronesi, 2010).

Dealing with success

Success would not be as lovely as it is without failure. They are related. When you have a run of success, it is easy to forget what failure feels like and become complacent. Some successful people forget to analyse what they are doing that causes success and then fail to notice when they stop doing it. When rejection follows, it comes as a surprise to them.

Of course, success should be celebrated. Spare a thought for all the people who helped you to succeed and thank them publicly. Then, remember that in sales your reputation is only as good as your last deal. You have completed a sale which hopefully made your customer and employer happy; now you have to work hard to do it all over again. If success starts to feel easy, should you take on new challenges?

Aiming for excellence

We will discuss your professional development in more detail in the Continuous Professional Development chapter, but for now here are a few points about how to use EI and the qualities of self-discipline, resilience and self-motivation in your day-to-day pursuit of excellence.

Monitoring your own performance

Set yourself a reasonable 'to do' list every day and consider how each task is going to help you to achieve your targets. How do you need to feel about some of the less attractive items on your list in order to make them happen? Try to get those positive emotions flowing. Check your progress at the end of each day. Certainly, some days you will be diverted from your good intentions and have to get back on track. Can you feel positive about the distraction? What have you learned from it?

Scale up your 'to do' list for your weeks, months and years in the job. All your experiential learning can now lead to higher qualifications and career achievement. Use your learning logs and feedback from people who can help you to get closer to your goals.

Reporting performance

You will be asked to give detailed statements measuring the success of particular activities within particular deadlines. For example, you must document each contact with a customer, possibly within minutes if it is an email or telephone call. You have to make a judgement about how effective the contact was.

Most of us have an aversion to reporting and administration. However, modern organisations are very complex, and the degree of accountability they have to legislators and customers is such that detailed reporting is part of any job. Even if the reporting system is old-fashioned and difficult to use, unfortunately, the best attitude to have is 'just do it'. Treat the reporting as an opportunity to reflect and something that keeps your manager happy.

Summary

In this chapter, we have looked at some of the qualities that a salesperson needs and how they can be learned and practised. The next chapter takes a look at the practical aspects of career development.

21

Continuous Professional Development

Introduction

When we learn about something, we struggle to absorb the new information and hold on to it. We do need to move on to higher levels of the mental process. Typically, at L4 in a work-based environment, you should be able to acquire knowledge, understand it and apply it, and be aspiring to analyse it and evaluate it:

- **Knowledge** – being able to recognise and remember information

- **Comprehension** – being able to understand meanings in information

- **Application** – being able to use information in different situations

- **Analysis** – being able to see constituent elements of knowledge, break it down and reassemble it

- **Evaluation** – being able to make judgements based on analysis of information

To acquire the breadth and depth of learning that you require, the apprenticeship requires you to use development plans.

Managing your learning journey

Designing a development plan

Starting out on a career in sales is exciting but may be also a bit daunting. You may feel that you do not have much knowledge about what development you need. You may think that the human resources department, your manager, or the training company or college running the apprenticeship will tell you all you need to know. As mentioned in the last chapter, in higher education (HE) and professional life you are expected to do some thinking for yourself. Indeed, your manager and coach will be asking you to manage your own learning journey, in partnership with them. Leverage all your contacts and resources to find out what your options are, but try and come up with your own ideas about what you want to learn and how.

Your manager will have determined some objectives for you. They must consider the goals of the business and what contribution you can make now versus what contribution you have the potential to make given the right development, so get their perspective on where you are and where you can go in a few weeks, a few months and a few years. Then you can ask about what types of training and development the company offers, and what is provided within the apprenticeship scheme.

In all apprenticeship schemes, there will be some classroom-based learning delivered by an education partner or a training company authorised by them. There will also be plenty of work-based learning, so your manager or coach should be lining up some projects for you. There will also be assessments that you have to pass. When you are doing work-based learning, it is easy to believe that experience is superior to other types of learning, but those who have studied the process of learning would disagree. It is important, but experiential learning is most powerful when combined with other types of learning:

'Truth is not manifest in experience; it must be inferred by a process of learning that questions preconceptions of direct experience, tempers the vividness and emotion of experience with critical reflection, and extracts the correct lessons from the consequences of action.' (Kolb, 2014)

To make this a bit clearer, in Figure 21.1 we have Kolb's (1984) learning cycle, which identifies four types of learning:

- **Experience** – learning from doing something

- **Reflection** – learning from thinking about what happened when you did something

- **Theory** – learning from models based on research which explain what ought to happen, or building your own model of cause and effect

- **Experimenting** – trying things to see what happens

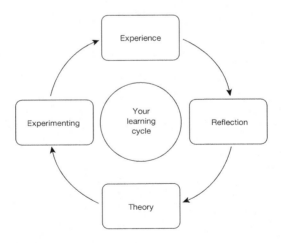

Figure 21.1: Your learning cycle (adapted from Kolb, 1984)

Kolb argues that if experience is driving our learning, we start from that and move round the circle; life is messy, though, so sometimes we start at different points. A full-time student might begin by examining theory, then undertaking a role-play or simulation, then reflecting. Experience may come much later. In the physical sciences, students typically learn a theory and then try it out in a test tube, which combines experimentation and starts to build up experience.

What does this mean for your development plan? Try to include developmental activity that can help you through all four types of learning. You may find one much more interesting than another but challenge yourself to use all four.

Kolb (1984, revised 2014) also identified four types of learners:

- **Activists** – who prefer to learn by doing and seeing what happens

- **Reflectors** – who prefer to learn by watching and thinking about what they watched
- **Theorists** – who prefer to learn by understanding the theory and concepts

- **Pragmatists** – who prefer to learn when there is a practical benefit

Your tutors will be familiar with Kolb's work, and your formal learning may include a learning journey which helps you to master all four learning types. You will be expected to undertake projects to experience a particular aspect of your job, and you will be expected to write reflective reports and logs. You will be introduced to the theory and expected to demonstrate that you understand it, and you will have the chance to experiment in role-plays and computer-assisted business simulations.

Meanwhile, in your development plan (see Table 21.1), remember that you must undertake this varied journey to reach a destination. Prioritise your learning goals and put them into a reasonable timeframe. Understand what you may find easy and difficult, and allow more time for difficult items. Think about what support you need to make progress. Refine your plan in consultation with your manager, coach, mentor and tutor. Then, start to implement it, measuring progress as you go.

Table 21.1: Sample development plan

Name: Liz Smith-Jones	PERSONAL DEVELOPMENT PLAN
Date: January 2017	Period: March 2017 – September 2017

Overall goal of this plan:	Readiness to take on 10 mid-tier accounts in 2018
Current target:	Increase account share in KA XYZ by 2% in 2017 (key account team target); my role is following up on satisfaction ratings after orders delivered, learning about the usage of products on the shop floor and feeding back to key account manager.
Strengths to build on:	Enthusiasm and curiosity. Ability to make connections with people easily.
Weaknesses to address:	The tendency to jump to the proposal before fully understanding customer needs. Difficulty in understanding the CRM system.
Possible disruptive factors:	The possible merger of key accounts XYZ and ABC, which will disrupt the key account teams (including me).

What do I need to learn?	What will I do to achieve this?	What resources or support will I need?	What do I need to ask for?	What will my success criteria be?	Target dates for review and completion
Questioning strategy in sales calls	2-day workshop with role-plays	Manager to authorise cover for 2 days out of office	Make sure I role-play with challenging peers; ask for detailed specifics in feedback.	Achieve at least 'very good' rating from tutors	End of April 2017
	Practise with coach	Book time with coach	Before and after (workshop) comparison; further feedback on improving my technique	Coach to note specific improvements after the workshop	End of May 2017

Cont.

Table 21.1 *cont.*

Name: Liz Smith-Jones   **PERSONAL DEVELOPMENT PLAN**

Date: January 2017   **Period: March 2017 – September 2017**

	Observe best-practice colleague	Ask JW if he would let me tag along	Customer's permission to sit in and take notes; ask JW questions on route to and from the call	New ideas to try	July 2017
	Ask customer X for feedback	Time to spend with contact at the customer	Within the XYZ key account team, ask customer contact if they are interested in discussing	Direct response from buying decision-maker about what they want in a sales call	September 2017
	Read articles on communication	Guidance from tutor	Specific readings which will help my thinking	New knowledge to use	March 2017
Analysing CRM data	2 days with marketing, plus 3 follow-up days	Manager to authorise cover; book time with marketing	How to use the system to understand trends; examples of good practice	Ability to scan CRM data and understand buying patterns	April 2017
	Work on some examples	Relevant colleague/ tutors to review	Feedback on the quality of my analysis	Positive feedback, but also points to improve	June 2017
	Discussions with mentor	Book time with mentor	Take some data and thoughts and discuss with him	Feedback on the accuracy of my conclusions	August 2017
	Read articles on 'analytics' and 'insight'	Guidance from tutor	Specific readings which will help my thinking	New knowledge to use	April 2017

Preparation for learning

Do you know people who roll up to a learning event in the nick of time, check emails on their phones all the way through, and are always late back from coffee breaks and the first to leave? Their attitude to learning is that they do not need it, and, like a self-fulfilling prophecy, they get nothing from it. A few people take their 'too cool for school' attitudes into workplace learning, and they do so at their own risk. Managers will ask tutors for feedback on individuals, and you want yours to be as positive as possible. Apart from wanting a career-enhancing report, what you put into a course will affect the learning event for everybody. Learning events can only ever be as good as the effort that participants put in. You cannot expect the tutors to spoon-feed you because they are trying to help you to think for yourself.

Your employer spends a lot of money on training and development, and it is in your career interests to make the most of what is on offer. To do that, you need to do the pre-reading that is expected so that you are ready to ask questions and make contributions in class discussions and exercises. If you are travelling by public transport, you can revise your reading on the way to the training event. Let your customers and colleagues know that while you are on the course, your responses to their queries may be delayed. Organise cover if you can and designate one person who can interrupt your learning if a matter is truly urgent.

Plan your journey with time to spare so that you can avoid stress. Use the travelling time to get in the right mood for learning on the way there and reflecting on the way back. Make sure that you have booked time with your coach or mentor to discuss the course/workshop when you get back.

Working with textbooks

Textbooks cannot be as exciting to read as thrillers and whodunnits, but we hope you find this one relatively easy to read and easy to use. It is a platform for exploring the content of your course, and you can dip in and out as you need to revise topics within chapters. You can use the index, or you can make your own with post-it notes on pages you find particularly useful. The content of a textbook can give you the basics you need to *pass*; you will not excel in an examination, essay or presentation at L4 and above by regurgitating textbook content. Learning at HE levels requires a more in-depth approach, which we will explore in the following sections.

Critical thinking

The short definition of critical thinking is that it is objective analysis and evaluation of a topic which leads to a reasoned opinion on that subject (Moon, 2007). This is the sort of process described in the section below on analysing the findings of others, in which we examine an article or a report to decide what we think about the topic presented.

Your tutors will often talk to you about 'critical thinking', and it is easy to assume that it is a reminder to be critical and wary of things, and not to take any information for granted. The Internet is full of fake news, so we should be careful, and a wary attitude is an excellent place to start. Things flash up on our screens which look interesting, but when we look a bit deeper they are complete rubbish. We do not want to be taken in by complete rubbish.

Nevertheless, we do need to make judgements and decisions in our working lives and beyond. We are busy, we have to take shortcuts, we have to work with what we have, and all these factors can result in a lack of critical thinking. We are human, and much of our thinking is flawed. It is hard to practise the best type of thinking every time we have to make a decision, and it does require self-discipline.

There are times when we can just go with our instinct, such as when we are in a rush at the supermarket and cannot be bothered to look at every food label in detail. We go for the brand of baked beans that tasted good last time. Equally at work, we do not want 'analysis paralysis' for matters of minimal importance. You have to make a judgement call on what matters require less thinking time.

Our progress at work is affected by the quality of our thinking. The more we practise critical thinking, the more respect we will get. Not every decision made will be a perfect one, regardless of how critically it was thought through, but at least if we make our mistakes with open eyes we have a better chance of learning what we can and cannot control in our lives and careers.

Critical thinking is about making good decisions, and it is also about continuously improving our thinking. From time to time, evaluate yourself against these criteria:

- Am I raising the right questions in meetings?

- Am I explaining myself clearly when I raise questions?

- Am I seeking out the right information?

- Am I using ideas, theories and models to explore issues?

- Am I able to reach rational conclusions?

- Am I able and willing to test my conclusions?

- Am I truly open-minded on every subject I have to deal with?

There is a link between our thoughts and our actions; poor thinking results in poor work which is costly in terms of our quality of life and rewards. 'Shoddy thinking is costly, both in money and in quality of life… Critical thinking is self-guided, self-disciplined thinking which attempts to reason at the highest level of quality in a fair-minded way' (Foundation for Critical Thinking, n.d.).

Analysing the findings of others

Throughout your working life, you will be asked to make decisions based on information, usually in the form of reports or presentations. When learning at an HE level it is important to be able to analyse data, information and opinions, usually set down in articles which have been published in academic journals. You will get plenty of practice during your apprenticeship.

You can also use the following list as a guide. When you read an article or report for the first time, take notes about:

- **The topic**

  - Does it arouse interest?

  - Is it worthwhile and important?

  - Is it clear what case the author is making and why?

  - Is the context for the report/article clear?

  - Could you easily summarise it?

- **The build-up of the argument for the proposal**

  In an article:

  - Is there some theoretical basis, or are theories being combined to form a new conclusion? If the latter, what are they? Does the combination make sense?

  - Does its review of prior research lead logically to a justification for the author's own research?

  In a report:

  - Is the background rationale for the proposal sourced from rational ideas?

  - Is it a restatement of old arguments, or is there a justification for something new?

  - Have the authors tested the status quo or are there underlying assumptions which may or may not be valid?

  - Have they stated any assumptions?

  - Is something missing?

- **Check any unfamiliar terms in a business dictionary**

  - If an author is frequently quoted, look up their original work.

  - If a report quotes a data source, check where it came from. If it is not quoted, ask for it.

- **The data**

  - Does the research strategy driving the collection of data seem logical?

  - What is the method?

  - Have large sample sizes been used to gather statistical data?

  - Is the data based on observation or surveys?

  - Has the data been rigorously analysed, or is it simple percentages?

  - Is the research based on several interviews (eg with customers who have given their opinions in depth)?

  - How rigorous is the evidence presented?

  - Do the authors point out any limitations in the evidence presented?

- **The appeal that the author is making**

  - It will usually be logical, and it may be grounded in the credibility of the data or the expertise of the contributors.

  - There is little place for emotion in academic articles, but sometimes authors use emotive language to make their points.

  - Business reports may need to convey a sense of urgency or to draw attention to a reputational risk in emotive terms. Does the report make you feel a particular way?

When you read the article for the second time, you can continue your analysis at a deeper level. Make notes about the credibility of:

- **The author**
  - Are they an expert in this field, or have they consulted experts?

- **Their evidence**
  - How much data is provided?
  - Is it analysed using a robust method?
  - Does it come from reputable sources?
  - Does it come from recent sources?

- **Their argument**
  - Is it logical or emotional?
  - Is it convincing?
  - Is it controversial?

- **The content**
  - Is it relevant and well-managed?
  - Is it substantial, comprehensive and meaningful?
  - Is it up to date?
  - Are pros and cons explored?
  - What is not there that you would like to see?

- **The style**
  - Is the report well-structured, well-presented and easy to read?
  - Does the document flow from paragraph to paragraph and section to section logically?

Look for positive things to say about the report as well as negative things. Imagine that you were a barrister defending the author in court – could you defend their work? If you were the prosecutor, how would you question it? This is particularly important if the topic of the report is controversial or emotive. For example, if you are being asked to make a decision about reorganising a department which involves people losing their jobs, you would want to make sure that you had all the relevant arguments for and against all options.

Finally, gather your thoughts and consider how to present them:

- State the argument presented by the authors.

- Explain the strengths and weaknesses of their arguments as you perceive them.

- State your conclusion and justify it.

Evaluating ideas

Many great inventors tried a lot of things that did not work before making their great discoveries. The quantity of ideas precedes the quality of ideas. When you have dozens of ideas, you have to sort out which ones you are going to prioritise for their usefulness, so you need evaluation criteria and a scoring system (see Table 21.2).

Table 21.2: Sample idea evaluation

Evaluation criteria	Fits with company mission?	Improves our market opportunity?	Fits our operational capabilities?	Ethical?	Acceptable level of risk?	Total
Idea 1	5	7	8	9	4	33
Idea 2	7	3	5	7	9	31
Idea 3	2	8	8	9	7	34

'Multi-criteria decision-making' systems underpin many aspects of business analysis, as we discussed in Chapter 3.

Evaluating experience

You should adopt critical thinking when you evaluate life experiences and work experiences as well; few experiences are a total waste of time. You have noted learning goals in your development plan, and you can plan what you hope to gain from experience at work.

If there is a specific planned experience, such as a project, that you are asked to take on, there may be a learning contract that you complete with your manager and tutor. It will probably be mapped to specific behaviours, knowledge and skills in the apprenticeship standard. Typically, a learning contract will describe the project, the stakeholders, the objectives, deadlines, what resources you are going to use (including formal learning) and how you are going to get feedback at the end of the project. It may also determine how you are going to document your activities for the assessors.

There are other unplanned and coincidental experiences which are informal but just as important in your learning journey. You can learn a lot about a company's culture from being in it, and you can learn skills from doing tasks allocated to you which may not have a strategic purpose or being hauled in to help when there is a crisis. What you hoped to achieve and what you actually achieve after a period working in a company may be entirely different. You should still set down your objectives and try to move towards them, but welcome what else comes along. Your criteria for judging the value of experiences can include:

- What was I asked to do?/What did I volunteer to do?

- Did I make a decent contribution?

- Did I learn anything that I can use next week or even next year?

- Did I acquire a skill (even if it is just how to operate the photocopier)?

- Did I communicate well with my colleagues and/or the customer?

- Did I meet anyone interesting or useful?

- Did I get any feedback, and can I use it in different contexts?

- Do I understand what happened as a result of what I did?

- Was this a good or bad experience in terms of outcome? (eg Did we win the business/lose the business?) Could I have done anything to make it better?

- Do I feel good or bad about this experience? Could I have done anything to feel better?

- Is there any information I need to gather to consolidate my learning about this experience?

- Would I like to do this sort of task again? Why, or why not?

- How did this experience affect how I feel about my employer and my job?

- Did I learn anything about myself in this experience?

If the experience was a disappointment, discuss it with your manager, coach or mentor. Should you re-set your goals? Can you try something similar in terms of acquiring the right skills, but different in terms of its contexts and what you can contribute? Also, talk to other apprentices in the company or on your course. They may have had some wobbles with their work experience too. A problem shared is a problem halved.

Reflection

We have already discussed the importance of keeping learning logs (see Figure 20.1). There are other ways of reflecting, and they do not have to be lonely.

Talking something through with colleagues, your coach and your mentor is a form of reflection. You might also spend some time on 'work shadowing', where you visit customers with a senior salesperson, or have observation days in marketing or even purchasing. By observing the work of others, you can reflect on what they do and why it is successful (or not). Work shadowing involves observing a professional in another or more senior role, to gain an understanding of their work.

Reflective writing is a step beyond the notes in your learning log; it is worth some specific discussion as, in work-based learning, many assessments may require you to write a reflective report on a project. Reflection suggests holding something up to a mirror; we look in it to focus on something, and we may need to magnify it to see it clearly. Reflecting on an experience is not just about describing it but also about trying to bring more insight into what happened. Similarly, a reflective report requires you to look back at an event from different perspectives and think about what it means and what you are going to do as a result of experiencing this event (see Table 21.3).

Table 21.3: A typical narrative for a reflective report

What is the topic?	What project, event or idea has stimulated your reflection?
What were your feelings at the time?	What was good and bad about doing this task?
How did your feelings change as the task evolved?	Does this indicate how you were learning?
Analysis	What sense do you make out of what happened? What is it like, and what is it not like? How does it relate to what theory you know? Are there parallels with experiences from other jobs, hobbies, life experiences or 'war stories' you have heard from colleagues?
Conclusions	What general conclusions do you draw from a work perspective? What conclusion do you draw for your own learning journey?
Reflecting forward	As a result of this reflection, what do you intend to read, try out or do differently?
Appendices	

Learning from theories, concepts and models

Most early learning relies on using models which may have been discovered a long time ago and applying them to problems set in class. Where would we be without the models of Pythagoras, who worked out thousands of years ago how to calculate the area of a circle? The formulae of Newton and Einstein are still used to help us understand the universe; similarly, academics and consultants who study how businesses work have created models to demonstrate general rules. The problem with studying businesses is that they are not a collection of molecules constructed consistently. They involve people, and people behave in very complex ways, so the study of business cannot be as exact as physical science. Nevertheless, many models used in business analysis do stand the test of time in that they have some predictive qualities. The Boston Matrix discussed in Part 1, for example, which maps the relationship between market growth and market share and its effect on product profitability, is widely used in businesses in North America and Europe.

Most models have passionate supporters and some critics. A typical complaint about 2x2 boxes (a widely used analysis format in business studies) is that they are a snapshot at a point in time, with no indication of tipping points between the categories identified. They suggest that soft boundaries between 'types' are hard, and they are not granular enough to guide budget allocation. They may be OK for setting high-level strategy, but they do not explain how to operationalise it.

Nevertheless, they help decision-makers do the thinking they have to do. It is worthwhile and interesting to discuss what research studies have revealed about the way businesses work and to consider whether the emerging models have any relevance to your organisation. Yes, there will be variations on the theme, but there will also be guiding lights to better practice.

A more worrying question when it comes to learning from theory is that decades of business research have been invested in models which are clearly proven as helpful, yet they are not used in many companies. When there is a lot of research resulting in tested models and theories that can help companies to improve performance, why not take a shortcut and learn from it? When you see a model that strikes you as useful, ask yourself, 'Why would a company not use it?' That is a challenging question.

Idea generation

Using other people's thoughts is a handy way of getting to knowledge, but it should be complemented by your own original thinking. Do use your learning log to jot down thoughts that occur to you as you are learning.

Your work activity and learning may involve creativity sessions. Each facilitator will have their own techniques to help you to form ideas. Productive ideas may include:

Asking 'why?'

Have you ever been annoyed by the airport announcement, 'The flight is late due to the late arrival of the incoming aircraft'? Did it just make you wonder why the incoming flight was late? If a problem seems to lack a solution, try and break it down by asking why (or why not) again and again until the constituent parts of the problem are clear. If it cannot be solved in full, perhaps it can be reduced by fixing some of the parts.

Reversal

Sometimes the value of something is made obvious when you look at its opposite. For example, management by walking about has to be better than management by hiding away. Job enrichment has to be better than job impoverishment. You can do the same with problems. If the challenge is that we want to make more customers pay on time, let's ask ourselves what we would do if we wanted them to pay later, take those answers and reverse them. It sounds absurd, but it gets the mind working.

SCAMPER

SCAMPER (Eberle and Weber, 1990) is a prompt used in idea generation workshops, particularly for exploring product and service improvement. It stands for:

- Substitute
- Combine
- Adapt
- Modify
- Put to another use
- Eliminate
- Reverse

It is possible to combine SCAMPER elements – for example, take two lists of random product features, mix them up and try to combine the resulting pairs into a new product.

Murder boarding

If you want the opposite of the positive thinking usually present in idea generation meetings, try blurting out the negatives about the topic. For example: Why do so many hand dryers not dry hands? What are all the wrong things about them that we could put right?

Classroom scenarios

A great deal of training for salespeople has always relied on enabling trainees to practise sales techniques in the low-risk environment of the training room. You will probably do dozens of role-playing exercises. You are not learning acting skills, but you may be asked to take on the character and behaviour of someone different from you. This will help you with boundary-spanning (ie understanding the perspectives of other people that you are likely to work with). You will learn as much from role-playing a buying decision-maker as you will when you are in the more comfortable shoes of the sales professional in a particular situation.

Role-plays are typically short (up to 30 minutes) one-on-one interactions between a seller and a buyer. You will be given the scenario, such as what stage in the negotiations you are at, what has happened in previous meetings and a few details about the characters involved. Usually, your role is to advance the sale to the next stage in the cycle, but you may be asked to be a grumpy buyer who has just learned that the model of car the salesperson has proposed to them got a bad review from a consumer organisation. There may also be larger role-plays, including ones where you're in the task force in a crisis, such as a large customer going out of business.

Computer-based scenarios

Computer-based business scenarios are widely used in work-based learning and in universities and colleges. Typically, several teams compete against each other. You make decisions in a limited timeframe and then the algorithms in the simulator show how those decisions would have played out as business results, given the other actions taken by competitors. There are many benefits in this type of experimentation, not least of which is learning that competitors will try to block you, and if all players in a market follow the easy pickings they all jeopardise their profits.

CASE STUDY: SIMULATION AT A GLOBAL ENGINEERING COMPANY[28]

A global engineering company used a key account planning simulation (SAM2Win) in a two-day workshop to develop the

---

28 Extract from a contribution by Ed Bradford in *Malcolm McDonald on Key Account Management* (McDonald and Rogers, 2017). Used with his kind permission.

account planning skills of its global account management staff. Five decision rounds were undertaken with great intensity and speed. There was also a specific session on using the procurement aspects of the simulation to learn how to align the supplier's selling strategy with the account's procurement strategy.

The workshop not only rapidly enhanced the participants' competencies in developing an account plan, but it also provided a common language and understanding of what good account management looks like. At the end of the workshop, participants developed a personal action plan to apply their learning to their own accounts. One participant was pleased to say that she had already started segmenting her account on the back of an envelope before she left the room!

Eventually, you have to experiment in real-life situations. If a customer is grumpy, you must think, 'What can I try to make this person feel better?' Your learning from role-playing will give you a variety of options, and you will find techniques that are successful in particular situations.

Succeeding in academic assessments

Every apprentice has to take assessments. Indeed, assessments are a fact of corporate life. We are assessed in so many things that we do. Surprisingly, many work-based students find the assessments set by academics to be particularly stressful, but this need not be the case. You may always want to excel, but the assessments are not designed to be easy. They are designed so that the 'norm' is a pass. If you want a high mark, you must put in a lot of effort, and you have to balance that with everything else you have to do at work and in your personal life. Usually, your assessment will be aligned with work activity, which reduces some pressure.

Read the assessment brief very carefully. If you do not understand it, ask for help. It should tell you what you are being asked to do and in what timeframe. It should also explain how marks will be allocated. Tutors may provide examples of past work and explain how it was marked, and give you extra handouts with details such as how 'reflection' should be demonstrated. Table 21.4 shows a sample marking scheme.

Table 21.4: Sample marking scheme

Criteria	Weighting	Mark out of 10	Weighted mark	Comments
Use of models	20	7	140	
Customer focus	20	8	160	
Quality of evidence	30	5	150	
Logical flow	20	6	120	
Presentation, including grammar and spelling	10	3	30	
Total			600/1,000	

Marks are usually expressed as a percentage; in this example, the student would be awarded 60%.

The type of assessment and the marking criteria should fit in with the bigger picture of the course objectives and achievement of the apprenticeship standard, although this is not always evident to a student during the assessment. It can be sometime later when they email their tutors to comment that they have just successfully used a particular learning challenge (which seemed pointless at the time) in practice.

Learning at work

Formal and informal development opportunities

As an apprentice, you will have the richest variety of learning and development opportunities. Formal learning generally refers to your learning at college or in formal training events organised by your employer. It is often classroom-based, but it can be delivered by virtual learning environments to your personal computer or mobile phone. Informal learning is more likely to be driven by you, by events or by colleagues. Work shadowing, for example, is informal learning. You will discover that there are things you want to know which are not currently in your plan, or things you learn that you did not expect to learn, because of a work situation. Both types of learning are valid. Look out for learning wherever you can get it.

Working with your manager

The role of leaders in any context is to help their team members to succeed. When we join the workforce, it is difficult to know what to expect from a manager. Perhaps you have had a part-time job in a shop and are used to the manager or duty manager giving direct instructions about tasks which need to be completed so that the shop can operate legally and customers can buy what they need. As a junior executive, you should expect your manager to be more remote, in the sense that you may not see them every day and they may only be able to meet with you once a week or even once a month. Your discussion topics should include your target and your objectives, and how to achieve them, but there should also be some discussion about the 'bigger picture'. In any sales management role, there is a degree of transformational leadership (inspiring the team to new levels of success) and transactional management (making sure that things that need to be done get done).

A manager should explain what the company is about, what it is trying to achieve and how it is planning to achieve it. They will explain your role in that and what success will mean for you personally in terms of recognition and reward. They will ask about your performance, and you can check for their feedback on it. A good manager will appreciate your effort as well as your results, and you may discuss ideas about new tactics to try. Ultimately, the sales manager is under significant time pressure and pressure to deliver the sales forecast. They do not want to manage you in detail, but they do expect you to give them all the relevant information they need in a timely fashion so that when you do meet, you focus on the relevant matters.

You have probably noted that in the sporting world, managers of teams are now usually called head coaches. Coaching is considered to be different from managing. Managing has the connotation of short-term performance and productivity-oriented administration. In some companies, managers have dual roles as managers and coaches, but that always creates a time conflict. You may have a separate coach who is a field sales team leader or even an external consultant.

Being coached

Coaching is sometimes regarded as a luxury in business and a necessity in sport. No one would expect a top footballer to perform to their best without a coach, while in business there is not much time available for coaching or being coached. Things are changing, though, and as an apprentice you should look forward to learning from your coach.

Expect a coach to anticipate a long-term relationship in which they will agree objectives with you, define what you have to do and outline what they will do to help. They will help with your current work scenarios and be interested in your longer-term learning needs. They should help you to reflect on your learning and create new ideas for future activities. A coach may also assess some of your work-based learning assignments. Expect them to challenge your thinking and encourage you to be more ambitious. Coaches should be good listeners and able to suspend judgement. They do want to drive your performance, so they are not just there to be sympathetic. They will set goals for you and hold you accountable for achieving them.

Being mentored

A mentor is an experienced person within the company or external to it who is focused on your long-term career development rather than your operational and tactical success. Even if they are within the company, they should be willing to advise you about career development beyond your current employment and they should be supportive. They should be in a senior position, which means that they will often have much more experience than you. If they have had rapid career success, that may be interesting to you. They should be able to offer sound, constructive advice. A mentor is also expected to help you network within your company and within the sector.

Many individuals have found that their early career mentor has been the biggest influence on their career. It is an interesting combination of 'who you know' and 'what you can learn from who you know'. Always prepare questions for meetings with your mentor, be willing to go with the flow if the conversation diverges from what you expect, take reflective notes afterwards and always follow up on their suggestions.

Changes at work

Career pathways

Your employer has probably recruited you to a formal position on an internal career pathway. A career pathway maps out your route to the top from your current role; they are often drawn as ladders or stairs. The HR department will have designed career pathways for internal development of all junior staff to higher levels in the organisation, across all functions. Not everyone makes it all the way up the ladder; nevertheless, this is your guide to greatness. It will explain what achievements you need to step up the ladder. It should be an essential appendix to your development plan, as it will keep you focused on progression.

Proactive career change

When an employer is investing in you, there is every reason to be loyal. Nevertheless, not every employer can help every employee realise their maximum potential, the status of an employer may change over time, and we as individuals change over time and need to do different things.

The following list includes typical triggers for thoughts about a job change. Usually, people do not change jobs unless more than one of them is in place.

- You lack passion for what you are doing. If you do not get up in the morning keen to find out what the day at work will bring, are you starting to lose your drive? If this feeling is sustained over days and weeks, explore it with your mentor before doing anything drastic. Do try to avoid getting into a situation where you feel over-stressed at work and dread it.

- You feel that you have hit your ceiling with this company; for example, if all top roles have recently gone to people recruited externally, are the possibilities for internal promotion curtailed?

- You feel that you have lost confidence in the people you work with or work for. It happens. Sometimes a company gets into a downward spiral, and in such cases, you need to get out if you can.

- Your circumstances change – you need to take on caring responsibilities, or your health means that you cannot do your job anymore. Many employers can help you into a role which accommodates your new circumstances, such as moving from field sales to part-time telesales from home, though it is not always possible.

Your first option, if you are doing well in your current job, should be to look around your organisation for upward or sideways moves that would inspire you. If you feel that you would benefit from a change, take charge of your external job hunt. Head-hunters and agencies can be helpful, but remember that it is their clients who pay their fees.

If you want to maximise your opportunities, do your own research and tell trusted members of your network that you are 'in the market' for a job change.

Dealing with an unexpected career change

Employers often talk about the employability of young people, but what we all need in the twenty-first century is 'employagility' (Fletcher-Brown et al, 2015). Over the course of your career, you will change jobs, you may have career breaks, and you may want to take your work skills into self-employment, voluntary work or personal development. Generally, in education environments, we like to talk about your proactive career changes, but some will be forced on you. Many people in their fifties have been made redundant two or three times. Sometimes, they volunteer for redundancy when their employer re-organises, but sometimes the redundancy is forced and comes as a shock. Many companies that have been prosperous suddenly hit the headlines, and their employees are worried about whether they will even get paid for work done.

Do not be disheartened when redundancy happens. It happens to everybody, and most people turn it into an opportunity. Even when they have loved their job, they find a new and better job. Employers who are phasing redundancies will offer support from career advisors, but if you cannot access this luxury there are helpful resources online. Do use employment agencies; they may be able to get you temporary jobs to help pay the bills, and they will be able to advise on curriculum vitaes (CVs, also known as resumes), applications and interviews.

You will also have to do your own research about vacancies; you should particularly check job opportunities on professional social media such as LinkedIn. Be realistic about the likely success of applications, and be ready for hard work, because applying for jobs is just as demanding as having a job. You need to broaden your horizons and be flexible so that you can increase the number of jobs you consider. Your network will be important. Fellow professionals can be very supportive, and they may know of companies who are hiring.

Creating and maintaining a CV

Even if you are not planning to leave your wonderful employer who has invested in your apprenticeship, it is still a good idea to have a CV in your learning portfolio. You should update it whenever you have completed part of your learning or a project.

It is sometimes argued that a CV is a leaflet marketing you as a potential employee. Employers are now wary of glowing CVs, and even if you are applying for an internal promotion you will often be asked for an additional statement matching your skills to the job specification. Anticipating this, in addition to your CV, which should be relatively short (two sides of A4), you could keep some notes about specific achievements in case you need to map your career to a specification.

A CV serves the purpose of a quick review of key aspects of your career:

- Your work experience to date. Most people list job roles and dates, with a short explanation of each role.

- Your education, qualifications and professional recognition (such as membership of the APS). This may seem important when you are fresh out of education, but you do not need to list every GCSE. Focus on your most recent qualification.

- Skills – sales skills, but also computer programs such as Excel.

- Career achievements – measurable success from projects you have led.

- Personal interests (eg voluntary work, sports).

- Any career objectives or personal qualities you wish to add.

Make it easy to read and edit your CV to highlight the qualifications and experience mentioned in the job advertisement. The selection panel will have dozens of CVs to read, and yours needs to tick all their boxes to get past the first sift.

There is no correct or incorrect way to list the key details that the employer wants from a CV, but make sure that it is clear and logical. You only have two pages, so you have to be concise. Also, make sure that spelling and grammar are correct.

Interviews

As a sales professional, you may feel confident about talking to an interview panel. Nevertheless, you should prepare carefully for this encounter. Research who is on the panel and what their interests are. Expect to be asked why you applied for this job and why you left your last job. The panel will also ask how you are going to drive this company to the next level. Practise your answers. Expect to be asked if you have questions for the panel, and make sure that you have challenging questions for them.

Summary

In this chapter, we have looked at your career development plan and some of the activities and issues you will need to address. Remember to keep up to date with career development activities; this is a life-long skill that you will need.

Conclusion

'Every new beginning comes from some other beginning's end.'
— Seneca the Younger, Roman philosopher

In every end, there are new beginnings, and the ending of a textbook is no different. This textbook has been designed to help you to master the knowledge, skills and behaviours needed to become a world-class sales executive. We hope you have enjoyed your learning journey. We hope that it will stay with you during your career in sales – not just as a souvenir, but as a reminder of some essential principles when the day job seems to have overwhelmed your best intentions. We expect that the chapter on time management will need to be revisited more than any other!

Besides reading this book, you will have been working on in-company projects and college assessments. You will also have been experiencing the day-to-day activities and the ups and downs of the sales role. All learning is a combination of conceptualising from knowledge, experimentation, experience and reflection. It is also a cycle. Once progress has been made, you need to reach out for the next step. Whether you are young, and this is the first step in your sales career, or whether you are transitioning into sales from another career, you need to keep on learning. In sales, change is constant. There are new customers to win, new products to introduce, and new technological and social trends to master.

This book will have been your guide to achievement of a diploma in sales. Congratulations! Whenever you achieve a major milestone, and you need time to enjoy success, reflect on it, and then consider what to do next. There are many exciting career paths within the sales profession. Besides developing new business, you could become a key account manager, inside sales manager, channel manager or sales director. You might take on a role encompassing marketing, such as chief customer officer. You might aspire to run your own company providing outsourced sales or a new product or service. Always seek out new learning to help you succeed in new roles. Your future learning journey with the Association for Professional Sales may include a higher-level diploma in sales, which will involve learning more about strategy and leadership, or you may wish to learn about specific topics in more depth. Whatever your next career step, we wish you well.

Thank you for choosing this book. It is intended to be a 'living document', frequently updated with new trends and examples, so please provide feedback to us directly and/or via the APS. We would also be very grateful if you would contribute your own experiences (anonymously is fine!) as examples to help the next cohort of learners to benefit from up-to-date material.

Dr Beth Rogers, FaPS, PFHEA
Dr Jeremy Noad, FaPS, FRSA

Appendix A: Ethical scenarios

The following scenarios are fictional but are typical of situations salespeople and sales managers face regularly.

1. You are at a trade conference and meet up with a customer who asks to be taken to a particular club. It turns out to be a lap-dancing club. The customer orders lots of drinks and leaves you to pick up the bill. The only card you have on you is your corporate credit card, so this transaction will be picked up. What do you do?

2. You fly out to a customer's branch in a troubled part of the world. When you try to board a plane from the customer's city back to the capital city, an armed airport official demands a bribe. This is a country where you might 'disappear' if you question the authorities, so you pay £100 and get home. What do you do when you get back to work?

3. Someone in your account team is a great enthusiast for a new software product, which she claims can achieve exceptional technical feats. One customer decides to take her up on a particular claim in a 'try before you buy' pilot. You know that the pilot is likely to fail because the customer's system is not an ideal context for the product. How do you recover the situation?

4. A customer keeps sending orders over and above the annual plan. She is also inviting you to meetings which seem pointless. You start to wonder if there is some personal motive. What do you do?

5. You hear 'on the grapevine' that confidential information supplied to a customer has been shown to a competitor. The person who told you does not want to get his source of information into trouble. What do you do?

Discussion points for ethical scenarios

1. You will have to explain what happened, and do not expect any sympathy for being naïve. You are likely to face disciplinary action. Could you have escaped if you paid with your own credit card? Possibly, but the gossip from the conference might get back to your boss. The customer has misbehaved, too, and might be playing the same game with other suppliers. It may be a rogue individual, or it may be how that company does business. Either way, consider whether you have a duty to report the incident to a trade or professional body.

2. Your safety was at stake, and you have a good case for being reimbursed for the money. Your company may want to review with its travel insurance company whether visits to that country can be justified.

3. You have to step in to avoid a case of misrepresentation. Deal with your colleague first. Hopefully, they will see the error of their ways; if not, you may have to escalate it to their line manager. Then, negotiate with the customer for a rethink about what the pilot can realistically achieve.

4. It sounds like there can only be a personal motive. This woman is putting her own career on the line, and you need to issue a discreet wake-up call but take advice from your manager and a human resources colleague first.

5. There is little you can do with a rumour. Continue with the bid but be cautious and aware. If hints about the competitors are being fed to you, you can be sure that they are getting some information about your bid as well. If there is an NDA in place, you may wish to check it and subtly mention any key terms in negotiation meetings.

Appendix B:
The APS Code of Conduct

All members of the APS are committed to working in an honest, ethical and responsible manner.

This is our Sales Code of Conduct. We agree to:

1. Maintain the highest standards of integrity in all business relationships

2. Provide our customers with a buying experience in which we 'do the right thing and thereby get the right results'

3. Promote and protect good sales practices

4. Always act in line with my organisation's codes and within the law

Sales professionals who uphold and promote the APS Sales Code of Conduct are making a pledge to judiciously balance their responsibilities to their customers, to their employer organisation and to their profession. The principles listed above and described in more detail below, assist sales professionals in complying with the ethical requirements of this Code and in meeting their responsibility to act in the public interest. APS members must commit to the Code as long as they are members of APS.

APS fundamental principles of sales professionalism

The APS Sales Code of Conduct is made up of four fundamental principles. APS members are encouraged to consider the spirit of these principles as their 'moral compass'. They should also review the Standards of Sales Practice documentation and education materials on the APS website. In particularly difficult circumstances, members may also wish to contact member services for specific support. The four APS principles are:

1. Maintain the highest standard of integrity in all business relationships, by:

   – Rejecting any business practice which might reasonably be deemed improper

   – Operating with honesty and accountability in all aspects of my duties, my products, my company and my industry

   – Never using my authority or position for my own improper financial gain

   – Declaring to the responsible person(s) in my organisation any personal interest that might affect, or be seen by others to affect, my impartiality in decision making

   – Ensuring that the information I give in the course of my work is accurate and not misleading; avoiding being misleading by omission of materially important information

   – Never breaching the confidentiality of the information I receive in a professional capacity.

   – Being truthful about my skills, experience and qualifications

 — Never engaging in conduct, either professional or personal, which would bring the profession or the Association of Professional Sales into disrepute

2. Provide our customers with a buying experience in which we 'do the right thing and thereby get the right results', by:

 — Striving at all times to provide an excellent and honest experience for my customers, including the accuracy of disclosures and taking responsibility for the veracity of all claims made about the product or service supplied

 — Using plain language wherever possible to provide clear and concise descriptions of the product, solution or service being offered

 — Taking responsibility for the appropriateness of products and solutions offered to the best of my knowledge

 — Ensuring fairness and transparency of pricing terms and conditions in commercial relationships

3. Promote and protect good sales practices by:

 — Continuously developing my personal, professional knowledge, skills, competence and ability to exercise judgement to 'do the right thing and thereby get the right results'

 — Fostering the highest standards of professional competence amongst those for whom I am responsible

 — Ensuring that my actions with customers improve my customer's life, improve their colleagues' lives and positively impact those around us, ultimately helping to improve the broader economy

 — Responsibly managing any business relationships where unethical practices may come to light, disclosing improprieties and taking appropriate action to report and remedy them

- Not providing inducements or gifts that would cause customers or employees of my organisation to be in breach of employers' code of ethics, business principles, inter alia

- Continually developing my knowledge of human rights, fraud and corruption issues, and applying this in my professional life

- Optimising the responsible use of resources which I have influence over for the benefit of my organisation

- Following APS guidance on professional practice

4. Always act in line with my organisation's codes and within the law, by:

- Adhering to the laws of the countries in which I practise, and in countries where there is no relevant law in place, I will apply the standards inherent in this Code

- Applying my best efforts to ensure agreed contractual obligations are fulfilled

(Reproduced with the kind permission of the APS.)

For further information

The APS is a not-for-profit organisation that advances and promotes excellence in the sales profession. Since the APS was founded in November 2014, it has established itself as the leading global professional body for sales, providing development, standards and leadership. Find out more at www.the-aps.com.

References

Chapter 1

Abrams, JJ (2009) *Star Trek* [film] (CBS Paramount)

Ansoff, I (1957) 'Strategies for Diversification', *Harvard Business Review*, 35(5), pp 113–112

Beverland, M (2009) *Building Brand Authenticity: 7 habits of iconic brands*. New York: Springer

Bungay, S (2010) *The Art of Action: How leaders close the gaps between plans, actions and results*. New York: Nicholas Brealey

Coca-Cola (n.d.) 'Mission, Vision and Values', www.coca-cola.com.sg/our-company/mission-vision-values [accessed 14 July 2020]

Drucker, PF (1955) '"Management science" and the manager', *Management Science*, 1(2), pp115–126

Geneen, H and Moscow, A (1984) *Managing*. New York: Doubleday Books

Keller, KL and Kotler, P (2016) *Marketing Management*. New York: Pearson

Kennedy, JF (1962) 'Moon Speech – Rice Stadium'. Speech presented at Address at Rice University on the Nation's Space Effort in Rice University, Houston (12 September 1962). Available at: https://er.jsc.nasa.gov/seh/ricetalk.htm [accessed 14 July 2020]

King, ML (1999) 'I Have a Dream'. Address delivered at the March on Washington for Jobs and Freedom, Washington, DC (28 August 1963). Available at: https://kinginstitute.stanford.edu/king-papers/documents/i-have-dream-address-delivered-march-washington-jobs-and-freedom [accessed 14 July 2020]

McDonald, M and Rogers, B (1998) *Key Account Management: Learning from supplier and customer perspectives.* Oxford: Butterworth-Heinemann

McDonald, M and Rogers, B (2017) *Malcolm McDonald on Key Account Management.* London: Kogan Page

Microsoft (2018) 'About Microsoft' [online]. Available at: www.microsoft.com/en-us/about [accessed 14 July 2020]

Piercy, NF and Lane, N (2005) 'Strategic imperatives for transformation in the conventional sales organization'. *Journal of Change Management,* 5(3), pp249–266

Porter, ME (1984) *Competitive Strategy.* New York: Free Press

Ries, A and Trout, J (1981) *Positioning: The battle for your mind.* New York: McGraw-Hill

Waterman, RH, Jr (1987) *The Renewal Factor: How the best get and keep the competitive edge.* New York: Bantam Books

Wernerfelt, B (1984) 'A resource based view of the firm'. *Strategic Management Journal,* 5(2), pp171–180

Chapter 2

Allen, K and Butler, S (2016) 'The way we shop now: The revolution in British spending habits'. *The Guardian* [online] (6 May 2016) Available at: www.theguardian.com/business/2016/may/06/the-way-we-shop-now-the-revolution-in-british-spending-habits [accessed 14 July 2020]

Berry, LL, Zeithaml, VA and Parasuraman, A (1990) 'Five imperatives for improving service quality'. *MIT Sloan Management Review,* 31(4), p29

Clarke, J (2015) 'The UK's worst call centres named and shamed'. *The Telegraph* (21 May) [online]. Available at: www.telegraph.co.uk/finance/personalfinance/11620116/The-UKs-worst-call-centres-named-and-shamed.html [accessed 14 July 2020]

Cooper, T (2004) 'Inadequate life? Evidence of consumer attitudes to product obsolescence'. *Journal of Consumer Policy,* 27(4), pp421–449

Davidson, L (2016) 'The companies with the best customer service in the UK'. *The Telegraph* (20 January) [online].

Available at: www.telegraph.co.uk/finance/newsbysector/
retailandconsumer/12109854/The-companies-with-the-best-
customer-service-in-the-UK.html [accessed 14 July 2020]

Gartner (n.d.) 'Gartner Hype Cycle' [online]. Available at: www.
gartner.com/technology/research/methodologies/hype-cycle.jsp
[accessed 14 July 2020]

Garvin, DA (1984) 'Product quality: An important strategic
weapon'. *Business Horizons*, 27(3), pp40–43

GHI (2018) 'The power of a GHI endorsement' [online]. Available
at: www.goodhousekeeping.com/uk/the-institute/a23506525/the-
power-of-a-ghi-endorsement [accessed 14 July 2020]

Grant, J and Rogers, B (2010) Auditing a strategic account
management pilot: a case study in the marine manufacturing
sector. *Journal of Selling and Major Account Management*, 10(3),
pp8–28

Henderson, B (1970) 'The product portfolio' [online]. Available at:
www.bcg.com/publications/1970/strategy-the-product-portfolio.
aspx [accessed 14 July 2020]

Hibberd, A (2018) 'Experience marketing's marvellous
medicine'. *Campaign* [online] (31 January). Available at: www.
campaignlive.co.uk/article/experience-marketings-marvellous-
medicine/1455978#rEpMwH1Sz7ExMTg5.99 [accessed 14 July
2020]

Holt, R (2013) 'Sinclair C5 voted biggest innovation disaster'. *The
Telegraph* [online] (25 March). Available at: www.telegraph.co.uk/
technology/news/9951876/Sinclair-C5-voted-biggest-innovation-
disaster.html [accessed July 2020]

Kotler, P (2019) *Marketing Management*. London: Pearson UK

Levitt, T (1965) 'Exploit the product life cycle'. *Harvard Business
Review*, 43 (November), pp81–94

Maechler, N, Sahni, S and Van Oostrum, M (2016) 'Improving
the business-to-business customer experience'. McKinsey &
Company [online] (3 March). Available at: www.mckinsey.com/
business-functions/marketing-and-sales/our-insights/improving-
the-business-to-business-customer-experience [accessed 14 July
2020]

McDonald, M and Rogers, B (2017) *Malcolm McDonald on Key
Account Management*. London: Kogan Page

Moore, GA (1991) *Crossing the Chasm*. New York: Harper Business

Moore, GA (2014) *Crossing the Chasm* (3rd edition). New York: Harper Collins

Oxford Economics (2017) *Sizing Worldwide Tourism Spending (or 'GTP') and TripAdvisor's Economic Impact.* TripAdvisor Strategic Insights [online]. Available at: www.tripadvisor.com/TripAdvisorInsights/w2841 [accessed 14 July 2020]

Porter, M (1979) 'How competitive forces shape strategy'. *Harvard Business Review,* 57(2), pp137–145

Rogers, B (1996) *Creating Product Strategies.* London: International Thomson Business Press.

Rogers, E (1962) *Diffusion of Innovations.* New York: Free Press

Rogers, E (2003) *Diffusion of Innovations* (5th edition). New York: Free Press

Turk, V (2020) 'Zoom took over the world: This is what will happen next'. *WIRED UK* [online] (6 August). Available at: www.wired.co.uk/article/future-of-zoom [accessed 10 August 2020]

Yamamoto, M and Lambert, DR (1994) 'The impact of product aesthetics on the evaluation of industrial products'. *Journal of Product Innovation Management,* 11(4), pp309–324

Chapter 3

Cozens, C (2001) 'It's A Skoda campaign – honest'. *The Guardian* [online] (13 December). Available at: www.theguardian.com/media/2001/dec/13/advertising3 [accessed 15 July 2020]

Godin, S (1999) *Permission Marketing: Turning strangers into friends and friends into customers.* New York: Simon and Schuster

Ketchen, DJ (2013) 'We try harder: Some reflections on configurational theory and methods'. In PC Fiss, B Cambre and A Marx (Eds) *Configurational Theory and Methods in Organizational Research.* Bingley: Emerald Group

Ofcom (2017) *Communications Market Report* [online]. Available at: www.ofcom.org.uk/__data/assets/pdf_file/0017/105074/cmr-2017-uk.pdf [accessed 15 July 2020]

Rackham, A (2017) 'Burberry: How Christopher Bailey reinvented the brand with the chequered past'. BBC News [online]

(24 November). Available at: www.bbc.co.uk/news/entertainment-arts-41818169 [accessed July 2020]

Ries, A and Trout, J (1981) *Positioning: The battle for your mind.* New York: McGraw-Hill

Rodionova, Z (2016) 'Aldi and Lidl are now beating their competitors on non-budget items'. *Independent* [online] (5 April). Available at: www.independent.co.uk/news/business/news/aldi-and-lidl-are-now-beating-their-competitors-on-non-budget-items-a6969461.html [accessed July 2020]

Trout, J (1969) '"Positioning" is a game people play in today's me-too marketplace', *Industrial Marketing*, 54(6), pp51–55

Victor, P (1998) 'Yardley, no longer smelling of roses, goes into receivership'. *Independent* [online] (27 August). Available at: www.independent.co.uk/news/yardley-no-longer-smelling-of-roses-goes-into-receivership-1174316.html [Accessed 15 July 2020]

Chapter 4

Armstrong, G, Kotler, P, Harker, M and Brennan, R (2015) *Marketing: An Introduction.* Harlow: Pearson Education

Auto Trader Group Plc (2016) *Annual Report and Financial Statements 2016* [online]. Available at: https://plc.autotrader.co.uk/ar2016 [accessed July 2020]

Experian (2016) *The Art of Customer Profiling* (White Paper) [online]. Available at: www.experian.co.uk/assets/marketing-services/white-papers/wp-the-art-of-customer-profiling.pdf [accessed July 2020]

Fiocca, R (1982) 'Account portfolio analysis for strategy development'. *Industrial Marketing Management*, 11(1), pp53–62

Friend, SB, Curasi, CF, Boles, JS and Bellenger, DN (2014) 'Why are you really losing sales opportunities? A buyers' perspective on the determinants of key account sales failures'. *Industrial Marketing Management*, 43(7), pp1124–1135

Hesping, FH and Schiele, H (2015) 'Purchasing strategy development: A multi-level review'. *Journal of Purchasing and Supply Management*, 21(2), pp138–150

Kearney, AT (2014) *Assessment of Excellence in Procurement Study, 2014: Procurement-powered business performance* [online]. Available

at: www.kearney.com/documents/20152/4992784/Assessment+
of+Excellence+in+Procurement+Study.pdf/ac352efe-3520-1715-
5bf7-4a1e1c17e02e?t=1503501790245 [accessed 15 July 2020]

Kraljic, P (1983) 'Purchasing must become supply management'.
Harvard Business Review, 61(5), pp109–117

McDonald, M and Rogers, B (1998) *Key Account Management:
Learning from supplier and customer perspectives*. Oxford:
Butterworth-Heinemann

McDonald, M and Rogers, B (2017) *Malcolm McDonald on Key
Account Management*. London: Kogan Page

Nelson, T-N (2017) 'Obsess over your customers, not your rivals'.
Harvard Business Review [online] (11 May). Available at: https://
hbr.org/2017/05/obsess-over-your-customers-not-your-rivals
[accessed 31 May 2020]

Robinson, P, Faris, Y and Wind, CW (1967) *Industrial Buying and
Creative Marketing*. Boston, MA: Allyn & Bacon

Rogers, B (2007) *Rethinking Sales Management*. Chichester: Wiley &
Sons

Weihrich, H (1982) 'The TOWS matrix: A tool for situational
analysis'. *Long Range Planning*, 15(2), pp54–66

Chapter 5

Andersen, A (2000) 'Best practices: Developing budgets'. *Inc.* [online]
(12 January). Available at: www.inc.com/articles/2000/01/16379.
html [accessed July 2020]

Ebb, F (1966) 'Money' [song]. *Cabaret*.

Kennedy, T and Affleck-Graves, J (2001) 'The impact of activity-
based costing techniques on firm performance'. *Journal of
Management Accounting Research*, 13(1), pp19–45

Markey, R and Reichheld, F (2011) 'Introducing: The Net Promoter
System'. Bain [online]. Available at: www.bain.com/insights/
introducing-the-net-promoter-system-loyalty-insights [accessed 15
July 2020]

Reichheld, FF (2003) 'The one number you need to grow'. *Harvard
Business Review*, 81(12), pp46–55

Robert Half (2019) 'The Robert Half FTSE 100 CEO Tracker' [online]. Available at: www.roberthalf.co.uk/reports-guides/ftse-100-ceo-tracker [accessed 2 June 2020]

Weston, J (2016) 'Why are so many CEO's from a finance background?' All About Finance Careers [online] (28 April). Available at: www.allaboutfinancecareers.co.uk/finance-news/why-are-so-many-ceo-s-from-a-finance-background [accessed 15 July 2020]

Chapter 6

Angevine, C, Plotkin, C and Stanley, J (2018) 'The secret to making it in the digital sales world: The human touch'. McKinsey & Company [online] (25 May). Available at: www.mckinsey.com/business-functions/marketing-and-sales/our-insights/the-secret-to-making-it-in-the-digital-sales-world [accessed 8 June 2020]

Baldwin, C (2014) 'M&S uses social media to make customers happy and drive sales'. Computer Weekly [online] (28 March). Available at: www.computerweekly.com/news/2240217064/MS-uses-social-media-to-make-customers-happy-and-drive-sales [accessed 8 June 2020]

Barker, C (2015) 'The cloud for clouds: IBM and The Weather Company work on big data weather forecasts'. ZDnet [online] (31 March) Available at: www.zdnet.com/article/the-cloud-for-clouds-ibm-and-the-weather-company-work-on-big-data-weather-forecasts [accessed 18 July 2020]

Burgess, B (2016) *Account-based Marketing (Re)defined*. Lexington, MA: ITSMA

CSO Insights (2018) *The Growing Buyer-Seller Gap: Results of the 2018 Buyer Preferences Study*. Miller Heiman Group [online]. Available at: www.csoinsights.com/wp-content/uploads/sites/5/2018/06/2018-Buyer-Preferences-Study.pdf [accessed 18 July 2020]

Davis, FD (1989) 'Perceived usefulness, perceived ease of use, and user acceptance of information technology'. *MIS Quarterly*, 13(3), pp319–340

Gartner (n.d.) 'Gartner IT Glossary: "Customer Experience"' [online]. Available at: www.gartner.com/en/information-technology/glossary/customer-experience [accessed 15 July 2020]

IHS (2017) *The Internet of Things: A movement, not a market*. IHS Markit [online]. Available at: https://cdn.ihs.com/www/pdf/IoT_ebook.pdf [accessed 8 June 2020]

Information Technology Marketing Association (ITSMA) (n.d.) 'Account-based marketing' [online]. Available at: www.itsma.com/account-based-marketing-hot-topic/ [accessed 15 July 2020]

McGinnis, D (2019) 'How the future of AI will impact business'. Salesforce [online] (1 April). Available at: www.salesforce.com/blog/2019/04/future-of-ai-artificial-intelligence-businessimpact.html [accessed 18 July 2020]

Office for National Statistics (ONS) (2018) 'Dataset: EMP04: Employment by occupation' [online] (11 September). Available at: www.ons.gov.uk/employmentandlabourmarket/peopleinwork/employmentandemployeetypes/datasets/employmentbyoccupationemp04 [accessed 18 July 2020]

Rogers, B (2003) 'What gets measured gets better'. *Journal of Targeting*, Measurement and Analysis for Marketing, 12(1), pp20–26

Rogers, B (2015) 'Can the internet of things create a new wave of value?' *International Journal of Sales Transformation*, 1(3), pp20–23

RS Components (2016) 'RS Components wins Best B2B eCommerce category at eCommerce Awards for Excellence' [online] (7 October). Available at: https://hken.rs-online.com/web/generalDisplay.html?id=footer1/release/161007_ecommerce_award_uk_hken [accessed July 2020]

SAS Institute (n.d.) 'Internet of Things (IoT): What it is and why it matters' [online]. Available at: www.sas.com/en_us/insights/big-data/internet-of-things.html [accessed 19 July 2020]

Savas, LP (2018) 'NuORDER'S Online Trade Show marketplace enables brands and retailers to connect year-round'. Trade Show News Network [online] (26 April). Available at: www.tsnn.com/news/nuorder's-online-trade-show-marketplace-enables-brands-and-retailers-connect-yearround [accessed 8 June 2020]

Schultz, RJ, Schwepker, CH and Good, DJ (2012) 'An exploratory study of social media in business-to-business selling: Salesperson characteristics, activities and performance'. *The Marketing Management Journal*, 22(2), pp76–89

Smith, J (2014) 'How to use social media to make sales'. *Forbes* [online] (10 January). Available at: www.forbes.com/sites/jacquelynsmith/2014/01/10/how-to-use-social-media-to-make-sales-2014/#9e339267a5d9 [accessed 8 June 2020]

Sun, NY (2015) 'BASF launches online store on Alibaba'. *Plastics News* [online] (2 July). Available at: www.plasticsnews.com/article/20150702/NEWS/150709967/basf-launches-online-store-on-alibaba [accessed 18 July 2020]

Travis, T and Hansen, I (2019) 'Rationalize your CRM Sales Investments Using Gartner's Sales Technology Stack Model'. Gartner Research [online] (23 August). Available at: www.gartner.com/en/documents/3956588/rationalize-your-crm-sales-investments-using-gartner-s-s [accessed 7 August 2020]

Tybjerg, K (2003) 'Wonder-making and philosophical wonder in Hero of Alexandria'. *Studies in History and Philosophy of Science Part A*, 34(3), pp443–466

Wang, Z and Kim, HG (2017) 'Can social media marketing improve customer relationship capabilities and firm performance? Dynamic capability perspective'. *Journal of Interactive Marketing*, 39, pp15–26

Ward, J and Daniel, E (2012) *Benefits Management: How to increase the business value of your IT projects*. Chichester: John Wiley & Sons

Chapter 7

Davies, IA and Ryals, LJ (2014) 'The effectiveness of key account management practices'. *Industrial Marketing Management*, 43(7), pp1182–1194

McDonald, M and Rogers, B (1998) *Key Account Management: Learning from supplier and customer perspectives*. Oxford: Butterworth-Heinemann

McDonald, M and Rogers, B (2017) *Malcolm McDonald on Key Account Management*. London: Kogan Page

McEvoy, SP, Stevenson, MR, McCartt, AT, Woodward, M, Haworth, C, Palamara, P and Cercarelli, R (2005) 'Role of mobile phones in motor vehicle crashes resulting in hospital attendance: A case-crossover study'. *BMJ*, 331(7514), p428

Roxburgh, C (2009) 'The use and abuse of scenarios'. McKinsey & Company [online] (1 November). Available at: www.mckinsey. com/business-functions/strategy-and-corporate-finance/our-insights/the-use-and-abuse-of-scenarios [accessed 15 July 2020]

Ward, J and Peppard, J (2002) 'The evolving role of information systems and technology in organizations: A strategic perspective'. In: J Ward and J Peppard, *Strategic Planning for Information Systems.* Chichester: John Wiley & Sons, pp1–59

Weihrich, H (1982) 'The TOWS matrix: A tool for situational analysis'. *Long Range Planning*, 15(2), pp54–66

Chapter 8

IDC (2015) *Selling to the Information-driven Business: An International Data Corporation InfoBrief sponsored by Salesforce* [online] (May) Available at: www.pardot.com/whitepapers/selling-information-driven-business [accessed 11 June 2020]

Office of National Statistics (n.d.) 'About us' [online]. Available at: www.ons.gov.uk/aboutus [accessed 15 July 2020]

Sakuma, A and Saliba, E (2016) 'Five tips on how to spot fake news online. NBC News [online] (22 November). Available at: www.nbcnews.com/news/us-news/five-tips-how-spot-fake-news-online-n687226 [accessed 15 July 2020]

Society of Motor Manufacturers and Traders (SMMT) (n.d.) 'About SMMT' [online]. Available at: www.smmt.co.uk/about [accessed 15 July 2020]

Chapter 9

Aeon, B and Aguinis, H (2017) 'It's about time: New perspectives and insights on time management'. *The Academy of Management Perspectives*, 31(4), pp309–330

Drucker, PF (2017) *What Makes an Effective Executive* (Harvard Business Review Classics edition). Boston, MA: Harvard Business Review

Kipling, R (2016) *Rewards and Fairies*. London: Macmillan Children's Books

Logan, DC (2009) 'Known knowns, known unknowns, unknown unknowns, and the propagation of scientific enquiry'. *Journal of Experimental Botany*, 60(3), pp712–714

McKeown, G (2012) 'If you don't prioritize your life, someone else will'. *Harvard Business review* [online] (28 June). Available at: https://hbr.org/2012/06/how-to-say-no-to-a-controlling?utm_source=feedburner&utm_medium=feed&utm_campaign=Feed%3A+harvardbusiness+(HBR.org) [accessed 11 June 2020]

NHS (2018) 'Easy time management tips' [online] (9 November). Available at: www.nhs.uk/conditions/stress-anxiety-depression/time-management-tips [accessed July 2020]

Chapter 10

Auh, S, Spyropoulou, S, Menguc, B and Uslu, A (2014) 'When and how does sales team conflict affect sales team performance?' *Journal of the Academy of Marketing Science*, 42(6), pp658–679

Belbin, M (1993) *Team Roles at Work*. Oxford: Butterworth Heinemann

Branson, R (2017) 'My top 10 quotes on collaboration'. Virgin [online] (20 July). Available at: www.virgin.com/richard-branson/my-top-10-quotes-collaboration [accessed July 2020]

Burns, T and Stalker, GM (1961) *The Management of Innovation*. Oxford: Oxford University Press

Cespedes, FV, Doyle, SX and Freedman, RJ (1989) 'Teamwork for today's selling'. *Harvard Business Review*, 67(2), p44

Deeter-Schmelz, DR and Ramsey, R (1995) 'A conceptualization of the functions and roles of formalized selling and buying teams'. *Journal of Personal Selling and Sales Management*, 15(2), pp47–60

Guenzi, P and Troilo, G (2007) 'The joint contribution of marketing and sales to the creation of superior customer value'. *Journal of Business Research*, 60(2), pp98–107

Hoegl, M (2005) 'Smaller teams—better teamwork: How to keep project teams small'. *Business Horizons*, 48(3), pp209–214

Hoegl, M and Gemuenden, HG (2001) 'Teamwork quality and the success of innovative projects: A theoretical concept and empirical evidence'. *Organization Science*, 12(4), pp435–449

Hughes, DE, Le Bon, J and Malshe, A (2012) 'The marketing-sales interface at the interface: Creating market-based capabilities through organizational synergy'. *Journal of Personal Selling and Sales Management*, 32(1), pp57–72

Ishikawa, K (1968) *Guide to Quality Control*. Tokyo: JUSE Press

Jackson, SE and Joshi, A (2004) 'Diversity in social context: A multi-attribute, multilevel analysis of team diversity and sales performance'. *Journal of Organizational Behavior*, 25(6), pp675–702

Janis, IL (1971) 'Groupthink'. *Psychology Today*, 5(6), pp43–46

Jordan, WG (1905) 'Self-control: Its kingship and majesty'. In *The Revelation of Reserve Power*. London: Fleming H Revell Company

Kotler, P, Rackham, N and Krishnaswamy, S (2006) 'Ending the war between sales and marketing'. *Harvard Business Review*, 84(7/8), p68

Peltokorpi, V and Hasu, M (2014) 'How participative safety matters more in team innovation as team size increases'. *Journal of Business and Psychology*, 29(1), pp37–45

Rogers, B (1996) *Creating Product Strategies*. London: International Thomson Business Press

Salojärvi, H and Saarenketo, S (2013) 'The effect of teams on customer knowledge processing, esprit de corps and account performance in international key account management'. *European Journal of Marketing*, 47(5/6), pp987–1005

Senge, PM (1990) *The Fifth Discipline: Mastering the five practices of the learning organisation*. New York: Transworld

Senge, PM (1995) *Learning Organizations*. Cambridge: Gilmour Drummond Publishing

Tagliere, DA (1993) *How to Meet, Think, and Work to Consensus*. Amsterdam: Pfeiffer & Company

Tuckman, BW (1965) 'Developmental sequence in small groups'. *Psychological Bulletin*, 65(6), pp384–399

Tuckman, BW and Jensen, MAC (1977) 'Stages of small-group development revisited'. *Group and Organization Studies*, 2(4), pp419–427

Chapter 11

Bell, L, McCloy, R, Butler, L and Vogt, J (2020) 'Motivational and affective factors underlying consumer dropout and Transactional Success in eCommerce: An Overview'. *Frontiers in Psychology*, 11, p1546.

Berry, LL, Carbone, LP and Haeckel, SH (2002) 'Managing the total customer experience'. *MIT Sloan Management Review*, 43(3), pp85–89

Gentile, C, Spiller, N and Noci, G (2007) 'How to sustain the customer experience: An overview of experience components that co-create value with the customer'. *European Management Journal*, 25(5), pp395–410

Gustafsson, A, Johnson, MD and Roos, I (2005) 'The effects of customer satisfaction, relationship commitment dimensions, and triggers on customer retention'. *Journal of Marketing*, 69(4), pp210–218

Homburg, C, Müller, M and Klarmann, M (2011) 'When should the customer really be king? On the optimum level of salesperson customer orientation in sales encounters'. *Journal of Marketing*, 75(2), pp55–74

Mansfield, P and Warwick, J (2002) 'The impact of post-complaint satisfaction with the salesperson, retailer, and manufacturer on relationship commitment'. *Marketing Management Journal*, 12(2), pp10–22

Meyer, C and Schwager, A (2007) 'Understanding customer experience'. *Harvard Business Review*, 85(2), pp116–126

Reichheld, FF (1996) 'Learning from customer defections'. *Harvard Business Review*, 74(2), pp56–67 [online]. Available at: https://hbr.org/1996/03/learning-from-customer-defections [accessed 12 June 2020]

Ulaga, W and Kohli, AK (2018) 'The role of a solutions salesperson: Reducing uncertainty and fostering adaptiveness'. *Industrial Marketing Management*, 69, pp161–168

Womack, JP and Jones, DT (2003) *Lean Thinking: Banish waste and create wealth in your corporation*. New York: Simon & Schuster

Chapter 12

MIT Management (2014) 'MIT Sloan Executive Education Blog: The digital business transformation imperative' [online] (12 June). Available at: https://executive.mit.edu/blog/the-digital-business-transformation-imperative [accessed 13 June 2020]

Powell, A (2015) 'Sales prospecting tip: Use Google Alerts to work hot leads'. HubSpot [online] (20 January, updated 30 October 2019). Available at: https://blog.hubspot.com/sales/sales-prospecting-tip-use-google-alerts-work-hot-leads [accessed July 2020]

Westerman, G, Bonnet, D and McAfee, A (2014) *Leading Digital: Turning technology into business transformation*. Boston, MA: Harvard Business Press

Chapter 13

Harich, KR and LaBahn, DW (1998) 'Enhancing international business relationships: A focus on customer perceptions of salesperson role performance, including cultural sensitivity'. *Journal of Business Research*, 42(1), pp87–101

Kaski, T, Niemi, J and Pullins, E (2018) 'Rapport building in authentic B2B sales interaction'. *Industrial Marketing Management*, 69, pp235–252

McDonald, M and Rogers, B (2017) *Malcolm McDonald on Key Account Management*. London: Kogan Page

Merritt, A (2013) 'International body language: A language with no words', *Daily Telegraph* [online] (14 May). Available at: www.telegraph.co.uk/education/educationadvice/10055769/International-body-language-a-language-with-no-words.html [accessed 14 June 2020]

Sturges, JE and Hanrahan, KJ (2004) 'Comparing telephone and face-to-face qualitative interviewing: A research note'. *Qualitative Research*, 4(1), pp107–118

Chapter 14

CACI (n.d.) 'What can ACORN do for me?' [online]. Available at: https://acorn.caci.co.uk/what-can-acorn [accessed 14 June 2020]

Gallup, G (1947) 'The quintamensional plan of question design'. *The Public Opinion Quarterly*, 11(3), pp385–393

GOV.UK (1974) 'Consumer Credit Act 1974' [online]. Available at: www.legislation.gov.uk/ukpga/1974/39/part/V/crossheading/cancellation-of-certain-agreements-within-coolingoff-period [accessed 24 July 2020]

Goulston, M (2018) '5 tips to help you sell even if you hate selling'. The Business Journals [online] (31 January). Available at: www.bizjournals.com/bizjournals/how-to/marketing/2018/01/5-tips-to-help-you-sell-even-if-you-hate-selling.html [accessed 15 July 2020]

Hancock, MQ, John, RH and Wojcik, PJ (2005) 'Better B2B Selling'. *The McKinsey Quarterly* [online] (23 June). Available at: http://web.qx.net/nrice/docs/Better_B2B_Selling_McKinsey.pdf [accessed 13 June 2020]

Hotson, J (2017) 'How to build a pitch deck that focuses on the customer, not your product features'. *Forbes* [online] (13 December). Available at: www.forbes.com/sites/forbesbusinessdevelopmentcouncil/2017/12/13/how-to-build-a-pitch-deck-that-focuses-on-the-customer-not-your-product-features/#7443c6a42a75 [accessed 13 June 2020]

Kaski, TA, Hautamaki, P, Pullins, EB and Kock, H (2017) 'Buyer versus salesperson expectations for an initial B2B sales meeting'. *Journal of Business and Industrial Marketing*, 32(1), pp46–56

Kestenbaum, R (2017) 'This is how millennials shop'. *Forbes* [online] (14 June). Available at: www.forbes.com/sites/richardkestenbaum/2017/06/14/this-is-how-millennials-shop/#529103f3244c [accessed 14 June 2020]

Lewis, C (2018) 'Rich people's habits today will be the mainstream trends of tomorrow'. *Marketing Week* [online] (19 January).

Available at: www.marketingweek.com/colin-lewis-rich-people-trends [accessed 6 June 2018]

Marshall, GW, Goebel, DJ and Moncrief, WC (2003) 'Hiring for success at the buyer-seller interface'. *Journal of Business Research*, 56(4), pp247–255

ONS (2016) 'The National Statistics Socio-economic classification (NS-SEC)' [online] (19 January). Available at: www.ons.gov.uk/methodology/classificationsandstandards/otherclassifications/thenationalstatisticssocioeconomicclassificationnssecrebasedonsoc2010#history-and-origins [accessed 14 June 2020]

PAMCo (2020) 'PAMCo Data' [online]. Available at: www.pamco.co.uk/pamco-data/latest-results/ [accessed 15 July 2020]

Rackham, N (1988) *SPIN Selling*. New York: McGraw-Hill

Singh, S, Marinova, D, Singh, J and Evans, KR, (2018) 'Customer query handling in sales interactions'. *Journal of the Academy of Marketing Science*, 46(5), pp837–856

Spiro, RL and Weitz, BA (1990) 'Adaptive selling: Conceptualization, measurement, and nomological validity'. *Journal of Marketing Research*, 27(1), pp61–69

Tegeltija, S (2016) 'Window salesman refused to leave a distraught woman's home... and has landed the company he works for a £10,000 fine'. Wales Online [online] (22 February). Available at: www.walesonline.co.uk/news/local-news/bay-window-salesman-refused-leave-12144253 [accessed 14 June 2020]

Zaleznik, A (1970) 'Power and politics in organisational life'. *Harvard Business Review*, 48 (3), pp47–60 [online]. Available at: https://hbr.org/1970/05/power-and-politics-in-organizational-life [accessed 14 June 2018]

Chapter 15

Agarwal, AJ (2016) '5 tips to give a top online sales presentation'. *Forbes* [online] (23 May). Available at: www.forbes.com/sites/salesforce/2016/05/23/5-tips-to-give-a-top-online-sales-presentation/#75f947532eb3 [accessed 15 July 2020]

Davies, M (2017) *Infinite Value: Accelerating profitable growth through value-based selling*. London: Bloomsbury

Dwyer, KK and Davidson, MM (2012) 'Is public speaking really more feared than death?' *Communication Research Reports*, 29(2), pp99–107 [online]. Available at: www.researchgate.net/publication/271993200_Is_Public_Speaking_Really_More_Feared_Than_Death [accessed 15 June 2020]

Friend, SB, Curasi, CF, Boles, JS and Bellenger, DN (2014) 'Why are you really losing sales opportunities? A buyers' perspective on the determinants of key account sales failures'. *Industrial Marketing Management*, 43(7), pp1124–1135

Hinterhuber, A and Snelgrove, TC (eds) (2016) *Value First then Price: Quantifying value in business-to-business markets from the perspective of both buyers and sellers*. Abingdon: Routledge

Kleiner, G (2016) 'Salesforce competence and proficiency: The chief cornerstone of effective customer value management'. In A Hinterhuber and TC Snelgrove (eds) *Value First then Price: Quantifying value in business to business markets from the perspective of both buyers and sellers*. Abingdon: Routledge

Raynor, ME and Ahmed, M (2013) 'Three rules for making a company truly great'. *Harvard Business Review*, 91(4), pp108–117

Rosenthal, B (2013) 'The only way to prepare to give a presentation'. *Forbes* [online] (19 June). Available at: www.forbes.com/sites/forbesleadershipforum/2013/06/19/the-only-way-to-prepare-to-give-a-presentation/#2211cfe6b84e [accessed 18 July 2020]

Sant, T (2018) *Persuasive Business Proposals: Writing to win more customers, clients, and contracts* (3rd edition). New York: AMACOM Division American Management Association

Searcy, T and DeVries, H (2013) 'The 7 best practices of the Big Sale Presentation'. *Forbes* [online] (16 January). Available at: www.forbes.com/sites/dealmakers/2013/01/16/the-7-best-practices-of-the-big-sale-presentation [accessed 18 July 2020]

Vitasek, K (2016) 'Using best value to get the best bottom line. In A Hinterhuber and TC Snelgrove (eds) *Value First then Price: Quantifying value in business to business markets from the perspective of both buyers and sellers*. Abingdon: Routledge

Chapter 16

Barker, E (2014) '6 hostage negotiation techniques that will get you what you want'. *Time Magazine* [online] (26 March). Available at: http://time.com/38796/6-hostage-negotiation-techniques-that-will-get-you-what-you-want [accessed 18 July 2020]

Dietmeyer, B (2018) 'I can get the same thing cheaper!' *Think! Inc. B2B Street Fighting Blog* [online] (8 February). Available at: https://web.e-thinkinc.com/blog-b2b-street-fighting/i-can-get-the-same-thing-cheaper [accessed 18 July 2020]

Harvard Law School (2012) *BATNA Basics: Boost your power at the bargaining table.* Negotiation Management Report #10 [online]. Available at: www.pon.harvard.edu/freemium/batna-basics-boost-your-power-at-the-bargaining-table [accessed 18 July 2020].

Philippart, M (2016) 'The procurement dilemma: Short-term savings or long-term shareholder value?' *Journal of Business Strategy*, 37(6), pp10–17

Snelgrove, T (2017) 'Future view: Evolving the measurement of best customer value from using a total cost of ownership to total profit added methodology'. *Journal of Creating Value*, 3(2), pp210–216

Chapter 17

Foley, J (1992) *Glengarry Glen Ross* [film]. Zupnik Enterprises

Fripp, P (2005) *Inside Secrets of Superstar Sales Presentations.* Seattle: Made for Success Publishing

Hawes, JM, Strong, JT and Winick, BS (1996) 'Do closing techniques diminish prospect trust?' *Industrial Marketing Management*, 25(5), pp349–360

Manning, GL, Reece, BL and Ahearne, M (2011) *Selling Today.* Upper Saddle River, NJ: Pearson Education

Rackham, N (1988) *SPIN Selling.* New York: McGraw-Hill

Chapter 18

Anderson, G (2016) 'How well are you managing your company's reputation risk?' *Governance Directions*, 68(5), p290

Baek, TH, Kim, J and Yu, JH (2010) 'The differential roles of brand credibility and brand prestige in consumer brand choice'. *Psychology and Marketing*, 27(7), pp662–678

Barrett, C (2017) 'The next mis-selling scandal could be parked on your drive'. *Financial Times* [online] (6 July). Available at: www.ft.com/content/785fe8e6-5fe2-11e7-91a7-502f7ee26895 [accessed 18 July 2020]

Bosch (2019) *Code of Business Conduct* [online]. Available at: https://assets.bosch.com/media/en/global/sustainability/strategy/vision_and_goals/bosch-code-of-business-conduct.pdf [accessed 18 July 2020]

Briggs, E, Jaramillo, F and Weeks, WA (2012) 'The influences of ethical climate and organization identity comparisons on salespeople and their job performance'. *Journal of Personal Selling and Sales Management*, 32(4), pp421–436

Chartered Institute of Procurement and Supply (CIPS) (2013) *CIPS Code of Conduct* [online] (10 September). Available at: www.cips.org/Documents/About%20CIPS/CIPS_Code_of_conductv2_10_9_2013.pdf [accessed 18 July 2020]

Cumbo, J (2017) 'Regulator moves to stop pensions mis-selling'. *Financial Times* [online] (21 July). Available at: www.ft.com/content/f46c4d46-568a-11e7-80b6-9bfa4c1f83d2 [accessed 17 July 2020]

Hartman, KB (2006) 'Television and movie representations of salespeople: Beyond Willy Loman'. *Journal of Personal Selling and Sales Management*, 26(3), pp283–292

ICO (n.d.A) 'Charity fundraising practices'. Information Commissioner's Office [online]. Available at: https://ico.org.uk/your-data-matters/charity-fundraising-practices [accessed 17 July 2020]

ICO (n.d.B) 'Penalties'. Information Commissioner's Office [online]. Available at: https://ico.org.uk/for-organisations/guide-to-data-protection/guide-to-law-enforcement-processing/penalties [accessed 17 July 2020]

Itani, OS, Jaramillo, F and Chonko, L (2017) 'Achieving top performance while building collegiality in sales: It all starts with ethics'. *Journal of Business Ethics*, 156(2), pp417–438

Jaramillo, F, Mulki, JP and Solomon, P (2006) 'The role of ethical climate on salesperson's role stress, job attitudes, turnover intention, and job performance'. *Journal of Personal Selling and Sales Management*, 26(3), pp271–282

Kotler, P and Pfoertsch, W (2007) 'Being known or being one of many: The need for brand management for business-to-business (B2B) companies'. *Journal of Business and Industrial Marketing*, 22(6), pp.357–362

Maslen, C (2017) 'Anti-corruption Helpdesk: Whistle-blower reward schemes'. Transparency International [online]. Available at: www. transparency.org/files/content/corruptionqas/Reward_for_whistle-blowing_2017.pdf [accessed 17 July 2020]

Matuleviciene, M and Stravinskiene, J (2016) 'How to develop key stakeholders trust in terms of corporate reputation'. *Engineering Economics*, 27(4), pp472–478

Maunder, S (2020) 'Competition watchdog to take action over mis-selling of leasehold houses'. *Which?* [online] (28 February). Available at: www.which.co.uk/news/2020/02/competition-watchdog-to-take-action-over-mis-selling-of-leasehold-houses [accessed 17 July 2020]

McClaren, N (2013) 'The personal selling and sales management ethics research: Managerial implications and research directions from a comprehensive review of the empirical literature'. *Journal of Business Ethics*, 112(1), pp101–125

McDonald, M, Millman, T and Rogers, B (1997) 'Key account management: Theory, practice and challenges. *Journal of Marketing Management*, 13(8), pp737–757

Newton, P (2013) Mis-selling shames the whole sector. Utility Week. [online] (3 April). Available at: https://utilityweek.co.uk/mis-selling-shames-the-whole-sector [accessed 18 July 2020]

Pirson, M and Malhotra, D (2007) *What Matters to Whom: Managing trust across multiple stakeholder groups.* Cambridge, MA: Hauser Center for Non-profit Organizations, John F. Kennedy School of Government, Harvard University

Reader's Digest (2020) 'Most trusted'. Trusted Brands New Zealand 2020 [online]. Available at: www.trustedbrands.co.nz/default. asp#mostTrusted [accessed 18 July 2020]

Román, S and Ruiz, S (2005) 'Relationship outcomes of perceived ethical sales behavior: the customer's perspective'. *Journal of Business Research*, 58(4), pp439–445

Schwepker, CH, Jr and Good, DJ (2011) 'Moral judgment and its impact on business-to-business sales performance and customer relationships'. *Journal of Business Ethics*, 98(4), pp609–625

Ulaga, W and Eggert, A (2006) 'Relationship value and relationship quality: Broadening the nomological network of business-to-business relationships'. *European Journal of Marketing*, 40(3/4), pp311–327

Zwilling, M (2012) '5 ways to see if your business integrity is showing'. *Forbes* [online] (30 March). Available at: www.forbes.com/sites/martinzwilling/2012/03/30/5-ways-to-see-if-your-business-integrity-is-showing/#1d17a1992421 [accessed 18 July 2020]

Chapter 19

American Marketing Association (AMA) (2017) 'Definitions of marketing' [online]. Available at: www.ama.org/AboutAMA/Pages/Definition-of-Marketing.aspx [accessed 18 July 2020]

Bannister, R (2018) 'How to play the bank bribe bonanza game and earn £1,000+'. MoneySavingExpert [online] (23 January). Available at: www.moneysavingexpert.com/news/banking/2018/01/how-to-play-the-bank-bribe-bonanza-game-and-earn-1000 [accessed 18 July 2020]

BBC News (2018) 'Carillion: Support for small firms ends in 48 hours' [online] (16 January). Available at: www.bbc.co.uk/news/business-42695661 [accessed 18 July 2020]

D'Haen, J, Van den Poel, D, Thorleuchter, D and Benoit, DF (2016) 'Integrating expert knowledge and multilingual web crawling data in a lead qualification system'. *Decision Support Systems*, 82, pp69–78

Dweck, CS (2008) *Mindset: The new psychology of success.* New York: Random House

Pöyry, E, Parvinen, P and McFarland, RG (2017) 'Generating leads with sequential persuasion: Should sales influence tactics be consistent or complementary?' *Journal of Personal Selling and Sales Management*, 37(2), pp89–99

Reichheld, F (2001) *Loyalty Rules! How today's leaders build lasting relationships.* Boston, MA: Harvard Business Publishing

Shannon, CE and Weaver, W (1949) *A Mathematical Model of Communication.* Urbana, IL: University of Illinois Press

Wang, WL, Malthouse, EC, Calder, B and Uzunoglu, E (2017) 'B2B content marketing for professional services: In-person versus digital contacts'. *Industrial Marketing Management*, 81, pp160–168

Webster, FE, Jr (1968) 'Interpersonal communication and salesman effectiveness'. *The Journal of Marketing*, 32(3), pp7–13

Chapter 20

Aristotle (2012) *The Art of Rhetoric.* London: HarperCollins

Brackett, MA and Salovey, P (2006) 'Measuring emotional intelligence with the Mayer-Salovey-Caruso emotional intelligence test (MSCEIT)'. *Psicothema*, 18, pp34–41

Brown, B (2018) *Dare to Lead: Brave work. Tough conversations. Whole hearts.* London: Vermillion

Dweck, C (2017) *Mindset: Changing the way you think to fulfil your potential.* New York: Hachette

Edwards, KD (1996) 'Prospect theory: A literature review'. *International Review of Financial Analysis*, 5(1), pp19–38

Ekman, P (1992) 'An argument for basic emotions'. *Cognition and Emotion*, 6(3–4), pp169–200

Ellis, A (1973) *Humanistic Psychotherapy: The rational-emotive approach.* Saint James, MO: Three Rivers Press

Goleman, DP (1995) *Emotional intelligence: Why it can matter more than IQ for character, health and lifelong achievement.* New York: Bantam

Goleman, D (2011) *Leadership: The power of emotional intelligence.* Northampton, MA: More than Sound

Hagstrom, RG (2013) *The Warren Buffett Way*. Hoboken, NJ: John Wiley & Sons

Leary, K, Pillemer, J and Wheeler, M (2013) 'Negotiating with emotion'. *Harvard Business Review*, 91(1–2), pp96–103

Locke, EA (2005) 'Why emotional intelligence is an invalid concept'. *Journal of Organizational Behavior*, 26(4), pp425–431

Merriman, KK (2017) 'Leadership and perseverance'. In J Marques and S Dhiman (eds) *Leadership Today: Practices for personal and professional performance*. Cham, Switzerland: Springer

Neenan, M (2017) *Developing Resilience: A cognitive-behavioural approach*. Abingdon: Routledge

Ogilvie, J, Rapp, A, Agnihotri, R and Bachrach, DG (2017) 'Translating sales effort into service performance: It's an emotional ride'. *Journal of Personal Selling and Sales Management*, 37(2), pp100–112

Salovey, P and Mayer, JD (1990) 'Emotional intelligence'. *Imagination, Cognition and Personality*, 9(3), pp185–211

Tian, A (2015) '5 ways to become more self-aware'. *Harvard Business Review* [online] (11 February). Available at: https://hbr.org/2015/02/5-ways-to-become-more-self-aware [accessed 16 July 2020]

Veronesi, JF (2010) 'Failing to succeed'. *Home Health Care Management and Practice*, 22(2), pp151–153

Wild, B, Erb, M and Bartels, M (2001) 'Are emotions contagious? Evoked emotions while viewing emotionally expressive faces: quality, quantity, time course and gender differences'. *Psychiatry Research*, 102(2), pp109–124

Chapter 21

The Foundation for Critical Thinking (n.d.) 'Our conception of critical thinking' [online]. Available at: www.criticalthinking.org/pages/our-conception-of-critical-thinking/411 [accessed 18 July 2020]

Eberle, R and Weber, J (1990) *Scamper*. Buffalo, NY: D.O.K. Publishers

Fletcher-Brown, J, Knibbs, K and Middleton, K (2015) 'Developing "Employagility": The 3Es case for live-client learning'. *Higher Education, Skills and Work-based Learning*, 5(2) pp181–195

Kolb, DA (1984) *Experiential Learning: Experience as the source of learning and development*. Englewood Cliffs, NJ: Prentice Hall

Kolb, DA (2014) *Experiential Learning: Experience as the source of learning and development* (2nd edition). Upper Saddle River, NJ: Pearson FT Press

McDonald, M and Rogers, B (2017) *Malcolm McDonald on Key Account Management*. London: Kogan Page

Moon, J (2007) *Critical thinking: An exploration of theory and practice*. Abingdon: Routledge

Acknowledgements

This book would not be possible without the help and support of many people. We have done our best to cite our sources and give credit where credit is due. This book has been influenced by our experiences working with great and interesting people, and through our learning from publications and our own research.

This book would not have happened without the Association of Professional Sales' desire to light the pathway to professionalism for all those involved in sales. Thank you to Andrew Hough, Ben Turner and the APS team, who have been supportive all the way.

We are also grateful for our publishing team at Rethink Press, including Kathleen Steeden, Maya Berger, Anke Ueberberg, Lucy McCarraher and Joe Gregory. This is our first book together, and we couldn't be happier with this partnership.

We want to thank the following for allowing us to integrate their thoughts, quotes and models in writing this book: AJ Agrawal, Founder of Verma Group; Darren Bayley, Sales Director, Straumann UK; Edmund Bradford, co-author of *Marketing Navigation* and Managing Director of Market2Win Ltd, www.market2win.com; Mark Davies, Managing Director of Segment Pulse, segmentpulse.com; Nick De Cent, *International Journal of Sales Transformation*, www.journalofsalestransformation.com; Dr Emma Donaldson-Fielder, Director of Affinity Coaching and Supervision www.affinitycands.com; The Fred Ebb Foundation; Patricia Fripp of Fripp.com; Ed Thompson, Distinguished VP Analyst, and Lexy DeLaurentis, Communications Compliance Specialist, Gartner Inc, www.Gartner.com; Seth Godin, author, sethgodin.com; Dr Mark Goulston, author, WhatMadeYouSmileToday, www.wmyst.org and www.markgoulston.com; Bev Burgess, Senior VP ITSMA, www.itsma.com; Professor Malcolm McDonald, Chairman of Malcolm McDonald International and Emeritus Professor at Cranfield University School of Management; Anne Merritt of Annemerritt.com; Professor Neil Rackham of Sheffield University and author of *Spin Selling*; Readers Digest New Zealand; Dr George Westerman of MIT Sloan School of Management; Dr Mellissa Zimdars of Merrimack College, MA.

We especially thank our families and friends for being so understanding while we wrote this book. Finally, we would like to thank each other for getting this far together.

Index

Page numbers in italics indicate tables or figures.

The Authors

 **Dr Beth Rogers, FaPS, PFHEA** is best known for pioneering sales education in higher education in the UK. She is a Principal Fellow of the Higher Education Academy, recognised not just for her reputation in the field of sales education but also for her achievements in innovative learning and teaching methods and her leadership of academic teams. She is a Visiting Fellow at Cranfield University School of Management and formerly Head of Marketing and Sales subject group at the University of Portsmouth School of Business and Law, as well as an examiner and lecturer in sales topics at three other universities in Europe.

Her doctoral dissertation was on resource decision-making in the sales function. She has authored and co-authored articles for academic journals and practitioner magazines and four business books, including the popular *Rethinking Sales Management.*

Before her academic career, Beth worked in business development roles in the information technology sector and spent nine years as a consultant working with global companies across four continents and in a variety of business sectors. She is currently a non-executive director of a medium-sized enterprise and mentor to a start-up sales services company.

in www.linkedin.com/in/bethrogerssales

Dr Jeremy Noad, FaPS, FRSA is an award-winning sales and marketing professional with over twenty-five years' experience. In the last ten years, he has worked with businesses in over fifty countries to grow revenue, increase profits, and improve productivity and effectiveness. He has worked with blue-chip organisations, both in the UK and internationally, as well as holding board member roles in SMEs.

Jeremy gained his doctorate at the University of Portsmouth, researching sales performance. He has been the research editor at the *International Journal of Sales Transformation* since it launched in 2015.

In addition to his professional role, Jeremy is an advisory board member to three SME organisations, focusing on supporting their growth and ongoing success. As a speaker, his topics include leadership, coaching and transformation. He is an advocate for improving the professional status of sales and supporting individuals and organisations who want to improve their sales success.

🐦 @jeremynoad

About The Association Of Professional Sales

The Association of Professional Sales (APS), is the government-backed professional body representing salespeople. They are a not-for-profit organisation, founded to build professional standards, trust and education across the sales industry, and have led the development of sales apprenticeships in the UK.

We recognise the need for the sales profession to have a body that has credibility amongst senior practitioners to represent the profession to governments, business, and consumer groups, which leads the way on ethics, standards, qualifications and career development. We also promote a wider understanding of the importance of good selling and sales as a professional career option.

We have worked with employers, training providers, academics and the Institute for Apprenticeships to win government approval for Level 4 and Level 6, B2B sales apprenticeships.

We are delighted to be working with Beth and Jeremy to deliver a professional pathway for those who work in sales.

The APS is on the register of end-point assessment organisations. We have completed the virtuous circle of creating the apprenticeship standards, getting them agreed by the government, then satisfying their criteria to oversee the assessment of new apprentices.

We stand for:

- Providing overall thought leadership and driving research on issues identified by the body

- Providing guidance on best practices, professional development

- Working with academia to raise the number of professional qualifications options in the UK

- Striving for recognition in the award of Chartered status to the body

- Contributing to and raising the standards and status of the sales profession

- Making a career in selling aspirational by demonstrating what senior-level selling is all about   .

- Providing a platform to share of insights, ideals, experiences, and leading-edge thinking

- Championing a commitment to best practice and ethical professional sales standards

- Providing a robust continuing professional development (CPD) programme

- Supporting sales professionals to play a constructive and strategic role in their organisation

To find out more visit https://the-aps.com.

Printed in Great Britain
by Amazon

85363913R00275